Doodle Dogs

by Miriam Fields-Babineau

Doodle Dogs For Dummies®

Published by: **John Wiley & Sons, Inc.,** 111 River Street, Hoboken, NJ 07030-5774, www.wiley.com

Copyright © 2022 by John Wiley & Sons, Inc., Hoboken, New Jersey

Published simultaneously in Canada

For general information on our other products and services, please contact our Customer Care Department within the U.S. at 877-762-2974, outside the U.S. at 317-572-3993, or fax 317-572-4002. For technical support, please visit https://hub.wiley.com/community/support/dummies.

Wiley publishes in a variety of print and electronic formats and by print-on-demand. Some material included with standard print versions of this book may not be included in e-books or in print-on-demand. If this book refers to media such as a CD or DVD that is not included in the version you purchased, you may download this material at http://booksupport.wiley.com. For more information about Wiley products, visit www.wiley.com.

Library of Congress Control Number: 2021945451

ISBN 978-1-119-82225-7 (pbk); ISBN 978-1-119-82226-4 (ebk); ISBN 978-1-119-82227-1 (ebk)

SKY10029768_091221

Contents at a Glance

Table of Contents

Introduction

A Doodle is the result of the intentional breeding of a Poodle with another purebred dog or, sometimes, a Doodle with a Doodle, or a Poodle with a Doodle (say that ten times fast!). Doodles are popular canine companions, and it's easy to see why: They're cute, sweet, athletic, and excellent family dogs.

Poodles are the perfect parent breed to create Doodles because they're intelligent, versatile, and social. In fact, Poodles were parent breeds for many of today's current purebred dogs, such as the highly popular Labrador Retriever, who in an earlier version of its evolution was a Curly-Coated Retriever. When looking at a Curley-Coated Retriever, you can easily recognize the Poodle genes: It has a lanky, athletic body; long legs; narrow head; and, of course, a tight, curly coat.

Doodle Dogs For Dummies explores the reasons for the popularity of Doodles, from their origins to living with them, and it helps you decide whether a Doodle is right for you and your family (and if so, which one).

To narrow the choices, I explain which purebred dogs, mixed with a Poodle, might best fit in with your lifestyle. Awareness of the characteristics of each purebred parent will enhance your understanding of the possible appearance and behavior of their offspring.

When you've made a choice and brought your new Doodle puppy home, you'll need to ensure they quickly adjust to their new environment. I fill you in on everything from feeding and grooming to housetraining and health considerations.

Keeping your Doodle healthy is only part of what it means to own a Doodle. These designer breeds require clear communication and consistency, which you can get through obedience training. Doodles are highly intelligent and active, so you need to know how to guide them in the right direction and stimulate their brains (in order to keep them on the straight and narrow). Socialization is also important — Doodles are very sensitive and aware of their environments.

In this book, I explain how to address behavior problems before they occur and how to handle them if they become bad habits.

When you have a well-behaved Doodle companion, you may want to continue to spice up your lives with fun dog sports and activities. Doodles love action! The more you train your Doodle for activities such as agility, dock diving, or retrieving games, the happier and better adjusted they'll become. Engaging in these activities with your Doodle will enhance your relationship in so many ways.

In this book, I've gathered all the information you need to find, obtain, raise, care for, and train your Doodle. I also help you understand the needs of your senior Doodle and how to integrate a second dog into your family.

Doodles are unique and fun! When you understand them inside and out, you'll have years of great experiences ahead of you.

About This Book

Although you'll find all kinds of useful information in each chapter of this book, you don't have to read it from cover to cover to benefit from it. Each chapter contains all the tools you need to accomplish specific goals. I know you're busy, so in this book, I tell you only what you need to know and nothing you don't.

If you're short on time, you can safely skip the sidebars (text in gray boxes) — the information they contain is interesting but not critical. You can also skip any paragraphs marked by the Technical Stuff icon (see "Icons Used in This Book, later in this Introduction, for more information).

Within this book, you may note that some web addresses break across two lines of text. If you're reading this book in print and you want to visit one of these web pages, simply key in the web address exactly as it's noted in the text, pretending as though the line break doesn't exist. If you're reading this as an e-book, you've got it easy — just click the web address to be taken directly to the web page.

Foolish Assumptions

Because you've picked up this book I assume you're not a dummy. You're either thinking of getting a Doodle or you already own one. Plus, the fact that you want to find out more about your dog makes you exceptionally intelligent. I make some other assumptions about you:

>> You have, or are about to get, a Doodle because you wanted a unique individual to love and live with.

>> You want just the facts; you need to make sure you accomplish your goals. You don't want all the scientific jargon and terminology explaining the background of each topic.

>> You have a big heart to take on a dog and give them a happy home.

Icons Used in This Book

Icons are those little eye-catching pictures in the margin of this book. These icons are eye-catching for a reason: They flag important information. Here's what they mean:

TIP

The Tip icon helps you solve problems faster or explains an easier way to approach an issue.

WARNING

The Warning icon prevents you from doing something dangerous to your dog, yourself, or others. Heed this icon!

TECHNICAL STUFF

The Technical Stuff icon marks information that's interesting, though not vital to your Doodle's well-being. Although you really don't need to read the information marked by this icon, you won't lose much time doing so, and it may help you understand your dog better.

REMEMBER

The Remember icon flags anything you should commit to memory.

Beyond the Book

In addition to the book you have in your hands, you can access some extra content online. Check out the free Cheat Sheet for questions to ask when adopting a dog, tips on temperament testing, and a checklist of supplies to have on hand. Just go to www.dummies.com and type **Doodle Dogs For Dummies** in the Search box.

Where to Go from Here

Because this book is written in a modular manner — with each chapter a stand-alone unit — you don't have to read everything in order. In fact, if you already have a Doodle, you won't need to read the chapters on where to find a dog, nor will you need the information on making sure a Doodle is right for you. If you get a Doodle, you might want to find out more about how to train them than solve problems that they likely haven't developed. Or, if you've had a Doodle for many years and you're curious about the changes they'll be going through as they age, you may want to skip to the chapter about senior dogs. Use the Table of Contents and Index to find the chapters that appeal to you now, and come back to this book as your needs and interests change.

Regardless of where you begin reading, you're sure to discover new things that inspire you to spend time with your Doodle and enhance both of your lives.

Yours is a partnership for life. Have fun together!

1

From Poodle
to Doodle

IN THIS PART . . .

Discover the history of Doodles.

See why Poodles make such great parents.

Find out about the different varieties of Doodles.

» **Exploring common Doodle personality traits**

» **Considering Doodles' health**

» **Training a Doodle at any age**

Chapter **1**

Meet the Doodle

The first known Doodle was created in 1955, when a Poodle was crossed with a Cocker Spaniel to create the Cockapoo. Cockapoos became very popular, because they're generally sweet, intelligent, and great family dogs. In 1969, the great-granddaughter of Charles Dickens, Monica Dickens, bred the first Goldendoodle, by crossing a Golden Retriever with a Standard-size Poodle. She was looking for a sweet, athletic dog who didn't shed all over her house like the typical Golden Retriever does. It took decades, however, for the Doodle to become highly desirable. And, though still not highly sought after by the dog-adoring public, there were dog enthusiasts who continued to cross their purebred dogs with Poodles to enhance specific characteristics, such as better swimmers for retrieving or faster runners to aid in hunting.

In this chapter, I fill you in on the different Doodle sizes and personality traits, as well as their health traits and how to train them at any age.

Doodle Sizes

Doodles come in almost every size imaginable — from the tiniest Yorkidoodle to the largest Pyredoodle. The one that's right for you may depend on your lifestyle. For example, if you live in a big city and don't have a fenced-in yard, you may want to consider a Toy-size dog, one who will get plenty of exercise just running around your home. If you live in a rural area and want a dog who can run beside you as you gallop on horseback through the woods, a larger dog may be a better choice.

The following sections explore the Doodle sizes to help you decide which size is right for you.

THE ORIGINS OF THE DOODLE

The start of the Doodle craze is credited to an Australian breeder, Wally Conron, the breeding manager for the Royal Guide Dog Association of Australia. He bred Labrador Retrievers to aid those who were physically challenged. He was tasked with obtaining or breeding a dog who didn't shed or distress someone who had an allergy to canine dander. While Conron tried to teach numerous Poodles to work as service dogs, he wasn't successful until he bred a Standard-size Poodle to one of his Labrador Retrievers. A few of the offspring of the pair turned out to be good service dogs, plus low shedding. But although Conron eventually fulfilled the request for that one client, his crossbred puppies didn't sell well because most people preferred purebred dogs.

Conron marketed his new designer dogs as Labradoodles, a term used for a mix between Labrador Retriever and Poodle, in Donald Campbell's 1955 book, *Into The Water Barrier*. Through the brilliant publicity of proclaiming Labradoodles dogs who don't shed, and because they could be a multitude of colors, Labradoodles' popularity took off. There was a bit of deception in their marketing ploy, however, because while *some* Labradoodles are low shed, many shed almost as much as purebred Labrador Retrievers do! But the marketing ploy worked nevertheless.

It wasn't long before other purebred dogs were crossbred with Poodles of all varieties. One of the major reasons for doing so was to create non-shedding dogs, but it has turned out that very few of them actually are non-shedding. Plus, much like their Poodle parent, they require professional grooming.

One of the reasons that Conron required so much time to create a Labradoodle who worked well as a service dog was that not all the Labradoodles he produced were of the appropriate character to perform the job of an assistance dog. There were a large variety of personalities in one litter, from super-hyper and unable to focus to outright fearful. A service dog must have confidence, intelligence, and the desire to work hard. Those traits are rare and require working with many dogs from puppy to adult to ensure that one can make the cut. That's why you'll come to know more dogs who have failed assistance dog training than those who have succeeded.

The current reasons for creating Doodles are their popularity, adorable appearance, and ability to fit well into most families. And although some (such as Goldendoodles, Labradoodles, and Bernedoodles) can be trained to be assistance dogs, most are able to be emotional support companions, which is basically why we have dogs in our lives anyway. There are still some Doodles, however, who can be outright fearful or reactive, usually due to lack of early training and socialization.

Overall, Poodle dogs of all varieties — Standard, Miniature, and Toy — tend to enjoy longer life spans than most other dog breeds. The smaller the Poodle, the longer they tend to live. It's not unheard of for a small Poodle to live beyond 17 years, whereas there are few other purebred dogs who can achieve such longevity.

Having a Poodle parent improves Doodles' possibility of living a long life, provided those great Poodle dog genes have been inherited. Unfortunately, because Doodles are a mix, you never know which genes will be prominent and in which capacities. For example, a Doodle can have a curly Poodle coat, instead of the straighter coat of the other parent dog, and have behavioral characteristics more like the non-Poodle parent, instead of the Poodle parent.

Toy-size Doodles

Toy-size Doodles weigh less than 30 pounds and are typically created by crossing a Toy Poodle with a Toy purebred dog. Examples of a Toy-size Doodle are Peka-poos (Pekingese x Toy Poodle), Maltipoos (Maltese x Toy Poodle), Shipoos (Shih Tzu x Toy Poodle), and Yorkipoos (Yorkshire Terrier x Toy Poodle).

Some of these Toy purebreds have straight coats, *brachycephalic* (broad and short) skulls, or bulging eyes, but mixing them with Toy Poodles creates offspring with curlier, lower-shedding coats; longer noses for easier respiration; and healthier eye placement. It can also serve to reduce the dog's overall tendencies for behavioral reactivity. An example can be the Pekingese or Maltese breed's tendency to *resource-guard* (using assertive behavior to guard an object or person). Toy Poodles rarely have the resource-guarding tendency, and they can pass this trait on to their Doodle offspring.

TIP

Regardless of the size of your dog, be sure to go through training. A little dog may not be able to do a lot of damage, but a bite is a bite, and the barking of little dogs can be even more annoying than the excessive barking of big dogs.

Toy-size Doodles make greats lap dogs, happy to play fetch in your home and relax with you on the couch. They enjoy outdoor play, too, but they don't require as much activity as larger dogs do. A Toy-size Doodle is more likely to tire of activity within 30 minutes, whereas a larger dog typically requires several hours of activity every day.

Toy-size Doodles are great in homes with very young children, elderly residents, or family members who aren't highly mobile. Because they're small, teaching them to do their business on a pad may be more convenient than if the dog were a larger size. This makes them ideal in urban areas, where going outside to potty isn't always possible.

If you live in a suburban area, a Toy-size Doodle can still be easier to care for than a larger dog, especially if you're very busy. A smaller Doodle may be easier to take with you to work. If you work from home, a Toy-size Doodle can warm your lap as you type or attend Zoom meetings.

Toy-size Doodles also make great therapy dogs. They can easily sit on laps, beds, or chairs and soothe the soul just by being there. And traveling with a small dog can be easier than it is with a larger one. Toy-size Doodles fit under the seat on airplanes or in over-the-shoulder carrying cases. For those in urban areas who use public transportation where dogs must be held, small dogs make this a breeze — they're lightweight and fit into a backpack, happy to look over your shoulder and watch the world go by!

Miniature-size Doodles

Miniature-size Doodles can weigh anywhere from 30 to 50 pounds and are typically created by crossing a Miniature Poodle with a Toy purebred dog.

REMEMBER

Because the Doodle pups are a mix of two purebreds, it's tough to know exactly how big they'll grow to be. A lot depends on the other parent. For example, if the Doodle pup is the offspring of a Bernese Mountain Dog and a Miniature Poodle, the puppy can mature to anywhere from 40 to 60 pounds, depending on which size genes are dominant. But if the Doodle is a mix between a Beagle and a Miniature Poodle, it may be closer to 30 pounds at full maturity. Size can vary greatly within the litter, too. Most breeders have a fairly good idea of the ultimate size of the Doodle pups they've bred, but there are always outliers and no breeder can *guarantee* the size of their puppies upon maturity.

Miniature-size Doodles aren't small enough to be lap dogs, but they often want to be! They're just so adorable that it's tough to not hold them on your lap when they're young puppies. Beware of setting a precedent, however — your Doodle pup is learning the rules the moment they enter your life.

TIP

From the day you bring home your puppy, set the rules that you'll want them to adhere to when they're fully mature. This way, you'll reduce misunderstandings and build a more harmonious relationship with your new best friend.

Miniature-size Doodles require time outside to exercise, but they're still easily manageable in an urban or suburban environment — you'll just need to be willing to take them for walks five or six times per day. If you have a safely fenced yard for relief and exercise, all the better. Miniature dogs don't tend to be as athletically inclined as the larger varieties, but they still need to run, and they thrive on having a job, whether it's chasing off squirrels or meeting postal carriers and delivery people.

Standard-size Doodles

Standard-size Doodles typically weigh 50 to 100 pounds and are typically created by crossing a Standard Poodle with another large breed. This variety of Poodle is often very tall, with long legs and an athletic body. They're highly energetic and intelligent and acutely aware of everything around them. Standard Poodles have been a hunter's working companion for centuries because of their ability to work tirelessly all day and because they enjoy water (they were created to retrieve downed waterfowl from waterways). You can be most certain that your Standard-size Doodle will enjoy swimming — some are totally obsessed with it!

TECHNICAL STUFF

The classic Poodle coif of keeping the hair long on the chest, joints, and head aided in buoyancy and maintaining warmth when they were used as waterfowl retrievers. Their close-cut hind ends allowed them unrestricted movement while working.

Regardless of which purebred dog is paired with a Standard Poodle, it will be tall and quite possibly very solid. They can weigh up to 100 pounds, even if one of their parents is only 70 or 80 pounds (such as a Golden Retriever). If the parent dog is of a giant dog breed (like a Great Pyrenees or Saint Bernard), you can bet on your Standard-size Doodle maturing to be even larger.

Because of their high energy level and environmental awareness (which can translate to becoming reactive to certain stimuli), Standard-size Doodles are best-suited for suburban or rural areas. They need to run and require a securely fenced area to do so. Running a couple times a week isn't enough — they require daily, high-quality exercise.

Standard-size Doodles also need consistent training, using a positive approach. They may be large, but their personalities tend to be very sensitive. Standard Poodles aren't hard-headed canines — they're easily taught and directed, which is part of what makes them such high-quality working dogs. You can depend on their offspring, even when mixed with another type of purebred dog, to also be sensitive.

REMEMBER

Positive training techniques, along with consistency and clear communication, enhances and speeds up the training process. Dogs trained in this manner are highly motivated to perform. With the forward-thinking Doodle, you'll have a willing partner and close companion.

Doodle Personalities

Both purebred and mixed-breed dogs (like Doodles) can have a huge range of behavior traits, from super-assertive to overly submissive. Some easily accept and remain calm in any situation, while others become highly reactive at the slightest movement. And, although early training and socialization can prevent any dog from becoming an excessive barker or jumper, all Doodles tend to have some typical behavior traits across the board. They can be super-sensitive, very intuitive, and, in the case of the Standard-size Doodles, hyperactive. Understanding your Doodle's personality will help you take the right approach in every interaction.

Super-sensitive

Most Poodles are very sensitive, so you can count on your Doodle also having a sensitive personality. This means that they don't handle aggressive actions or loud, harsh voices very well. It can also make them shy around strangers and other dogs they've never met.

Standard Poodles also tend to be very reserved. Taking the time to allow your Doodle to make the first overtures will help prevent a fearful reaction, such as backing away or urinating. And, because Doodles are generally very friendly, you can count on their reaching out at some point. Just be patient.

A sensitive dog requires a special approach to training and overall rule setting. Clearly explain your desires through a positive, consistent approach. Your Doodle will probably be quick to learn a new concept, but you may need to break it down into smaller parts and gradually add criteria to attain the ultimate goal. Repetition and clarity are key features of this approach.

REMEMBER

Teaching your Doodle should involve capturing and shaping, not correcting. (You can find more about training in Chapter 10.) Overcorrecting your Doodle will cause the dog to be shy and shut down — you may see your dog lying down in a corner, facing the wall. Yes, Doodles are *that* sensitive!

Being sensitive also means you shouldn't flood your dog with a situation in which he's insecure. *Flooding* means pushing your dog into something that's frightening to him in order to teach him it's no longer frightening. For example, your Doodle may be afraid of other dogs they don't know. Flooding them would be to put them in a room with a bunch of other dogs and let them work it out to the point where they're playing with all the dogs instead of cowering in a corner. With Doodles, that's the wrong approach. They'll be so overwhelmed that they *will* cower in a corner and then be afraid of that situation moving forward. Instead, meeting one dog at a time, in a relaxed environment, will give your Doodle time to adjust in their own way.

Regardless of which TV dog trainer you've watched, keep in mind that success doesn't happen in 30 to 60 minutes. When the TV dog trainer puts a new dog in with a group of dogs and claims that's the best way for them to learn manners, don't believe it. That's flooding, and it can backfire big time, resulting in a dog being injured and/or traumatized. Training takes time and patience, as well as understanding the dog well enough to read their signals. There are no overnight cures for inappropriate behavior.

Sometimes a sensitive Doodle can be mistaken as fearful or having been abused. Lack of confidence can often appear similar to a dog who has had these emotions or experiences, but it doesn't actually mean they're accurate. It merely takes more time for an adult Doodle to warm up to a new environment, people, or other animals — especially if the individuals are outgoing and come at the Doodle, which can be intimidating.

Sensitivity can often make the training process challenging. It may take a while to figure out how to motivate a Doodle when they would rather just watch the world go by and try to remain unnoticed. But every dog is motivated by something. And when you've discovered this key — the one thing that they'll do anything to get — even a sensitive Doodle will gradually come out of their shell and discover a whole world of wonder, learning how to better understand their people and home. As this process progresses, your sensitive Doodle will become more confident and accepting of new situations.

Because Doodles have a tendency to be super-sensitive, Doodle breeders should expose developing puppies to an array of sounds and experiences. Early socialization is *very* important. Exposure to people of all genders, ages, and attitudes will prevent the maturing Doodle pup from becoming intimidated later in life.

And, as your Doodle passes through several important behavior development periods, you should continue to offer them varied experiences and exposure to people of all races, genders, and ages. A confident Doodle is much easier to live with than one who is easily intimidated or overly sensitive.

Between 2 to 4 months of age is an important family bonding time. This is when your Doodle will develop a sense of belonging to your family. But while this occurs, be sure to socialize them as much as possible. Let them meet other people and dogs in your community. Take them in your car to places that they'll enjoy, such as a park, doggy daycare, or the house of a friend who also has a dog. This is especially important if you rarely have visitors or go anywhere. Try to become more social, at least for the next couple months as your puppy's behavior patterns are forming.

Very intuitive

Doodles are highly intelligent. You can thank their Poodle parent for much of this. But many Doodle combinations with purebred dogs can enhance this attribute even more — examples include Goldendoodles and Bernedoodles. In these instances, *both* parents are already highly intelligent. Mixing them can bring two different types of intelligence together, creating a highly intuitive dog. Some Doodles, such as the Sheepadoodle or Pekapoo, may not be as quick to understand new concepts, but they're certainly an improvement over their non-Poodle parent's intellect.

An intuitive dog figures things out very quickly. Often, you just need as few as two repetitions to achieve understanding of a concept. This can occur either purposefully, such as during a training session, or inadvertently, in everyday routine. Here are a few examples:

> » Learning which door to go to when going outside to potty
> » Learning the feeding schedule
> » Learning what time of day one of the family members returns home from work or school
> » Learning who will allow him to jump on them
> » Learning who takes them for walks

Because Doodles are so intuitive, obedience training can be very enjoyable, because you may not have to break down exercises into as many small increments as you might with many purebred dogs. They naturally follow your body language and quickly understand your vocal tones and words. Because they're also highly sensitive, they can read your emotions, too, which is part of their being so intuitive.

Because of their intuitiveness, owners of Doodles sometimes believe they don't need to do anything to educate their dogs — the dogs seem to quickly pick up on the daily routines, housetraining rules, and which couch is theirs. But all dogs need an education — there's more to life than lounging around the house. And Doodles are rarely couch potatoes — at least not until they're seniors.

As a professional trainer, I find that many Doodles have the right temperament, intelligence, and intuition to be excellent performance dogs. These three traits are required to remain motivated to perform under somewhat stressful and distraction-filled situations. Their intuition helps them remain one step ahead, because they know the pattern, the subliminal communication signals of their human teammates, and how to keep everybody entertained. Doodles spread joy everywhere they go!

Hyperactive

If you've got a Doodle, you're sure to experience their high energy levels. This is especially true if you've got a *Double Doodle* (the offspring of a Doodle and a Poodle, or the offspring of two Doodles). The Poodle genes are very strong, and a curlier coat isn't the only trait you'll experience. A Standard-size Doodle will have super-high energy levels, be more reactive to their environment, and be more mischievous. All the more reason to keep them occupied!

The Doodle tendency to be hyperactive also makes some common behavior problems — such as jumping up on people or other dogs — more challenging to stop. No doubt about it, Doodles love to jump. Jumping up is one of the more difficult issues that you'll face when you have a Doodle. So, as intelligent, intuitive, and motivated as Doodles are to learn, you may need to be very consistent and persistent to teach your Doodle not to jump on you. Do *not* offer any means of reward for the behavior (see Chapter 12).

Young Doodles have tons of energy. You need to commit to ensuring that your dog has plenty of exercise and brain stimulation. Training daily is helpful, but it's not enough. Your Doodle needs to run and play. Only other young dogs will fulfill this need. Or, if you're a runner and you're willing to gradually build up your Doodle's stamina to your level, you've got a great running partner!

Doodle Health

Because Doodles are actually mixed breeds (though intentionally mixed), many are healthier and have a longer life span. But you never know where the genes will fall, so there are no guarantees.

There are two ways to have an idea of what lies ahead: Rely on your dog breeder's experience with their litters, or contact the owners of other Doodles who were purchased from the same breeder. One or two pups may have different health experiences from the majority, but an average assumption can be made over time (see Chapter 4).

Life span

Poodles enjoy a longer than average life span. Standard Poodles typically live 12 to 14 years, some as long as 16 years. Miniature Poodles and Toy Poodles typically live 13 to 18 years. Compare this to the average life span of most large dogs, who typically live 8 to 12 years, and most medium dogs, who typically live 12 to 14 years. Few Toy breeds live longer than 10 to 14 years. Add these longer-lived

Poodle breeds to the mix, and you've got a good chance of getting a few more great years with your Doodle.

Although the Doodle's life span may be similar to that of a parent Poodle, it ultimately depends on great nutrition, healthy environment, and appropriate exercise.

Potential health issues

Doodles are a mix of two different breeds, so there's always a chance of your dog being affected by any of the numerous illnesses or other afflictions common in the parent breeds. Because one parent is consistent in all Doodles — the Poodle — you can only assume that the following list of breed-specific issues are ones to be aware of (more on specific purebred dog health concerns in Chapter 3).

>> **Standard Poodle health issues:** The Standard Poodle has a few more health problems than the other varieties of Poodle. These include

- *Idiopathic epilepsy:* A condition in which a dog is prone to seizures without a known cause

- *Addison's disease:* A condition in which the adrenal glands don't produce hormones necessary for physical function

- *Cushing disease:* A condition in which the adrenal glands produce abnormally high levels of cortisol

- *Sebaceous adenitis:* A destructive inflammatory disease in the sebaceous glands, which are located around hair follicles on the skin

>> **Miniature Poodle and Toy Poodle health issues:** These Poodle variations may experience the same health issues as the Standard Poodle, they're less likely to do so. They do, however, have some leg bone abnormalities not common in larger dogs, such as

- *Luxating patella:* A condition in which the dog's kneecap moves out of position, causing lameness

- *Legg-Calve-Perthes disease:* Degeneration of the *femoral head* (the ball portion of the hip joint)

Do some research on the other parent breed so you're aware of other possible health problems.

To minimize the chances of your having to deal with these issues with your Doodle, buy only from a reputable breeder who has done appropriate health clearances on their parent dogs. These include checking for orthopedic problems, as well as heart and eye problems (see Chapter 4). You may luck out with a healthy dog from other sources, but chances are, you'll end up spending a lot of money for veterinary care and professional training.

TIP

If you're adopting a Doodle from a rescue organization or animal shelter, do a little research on breed health concerns so you can potentially recognize any structural, coat, or eating disorders and know how to address them (see Chapter 7).

Doodle Training

Every dog needs training. And, due to the high energy level and intelligence of your Doodle, education will be the key to a great relationship. Doodles need direction, consistency, and patience. They may be easy to train, but without training, your Doodle will drive you crazy.

Puppies: Up to 4 months old

Training begins the moment you meet your Doodle puppy. Setting the rules early and remaining consistent will ensure you end up with a well-behaved adult Doodle. Because most Doodle pups go to their forever homes at the age of 7 to 8 weeks, they're ready to learn all basic commands right away. In fact, Doodle puppies are most receptive to learning at 6 to 16 weeks of age. They crave direction, and when applied using a positive training method, they learn quickly.

Doodle puppies can quickly learn the following cues: Come, Sit, Down, Take Treats Gently, Housetraining guidelines, and lots of cute tricks, too. But, as puppies tend to have short attention spans, you'll need to keep each training session at no more than 15 minutes each. But, don't worry, you can do these many times throughout the day, which is a great idea as repetition builds understanding.

Adolescents: 4 to 8 months old

Adolescent Doodles are 4 to 8 months old, and they're a handful. Their energy levels are through the roof, and they need training to remain grounded and manageable. If you haven't done the early work and you have an obnoxious teenager on your hands, sign up for a class right away! The longer you wait, the more reactive your Doodle may become.

You can still use a positive training method with an unruly adolescent, but a lot of redirection work will likely be necessary, too (see Chapter 10). Adolescent Doodles are more easily distracted than young puppies are. Everything that moves will grab their attention, and they'll want to investigate what it is. Where Doodle puppies are still a bit insecure and tend to remain near their people, most adolescent Doodles are all about exploring beyond the security of their companions. You'll also notice selective responses in this age group — your Doodle may have responded well to a Come cue when they were 3 months old, but not as readily at 6 months old.

REMEMBER

A *selective response* is knowing what a cue means but not responding to it. If the dog is allowed to ignore a cue, they'll soon not ever respond to it. You need to back up *all* commands (which means you need a way of ensuring your dog follows through with your request); otherwise, your voice and body language will become background noise that will be ignored.

Formal training work is suggested for these adolescent explorers. Training will help them maintain a calm state of mind and keep your frustration levels down as well. *Remember:* Clear communication is key to a healthy relationship.

Adults: Over 8 months old

Regardless of your Doodle's age, they'll enjoy the training process. Dogs of all ages enjoy learning and interacting with you. If you adopted an older Doodle, training will help them settle into your home and their new environment more easily. A daily training session gives your adult Doodle something to look forward to each day — like hearing the ice-cream truck coming down the block when you were a kid. Yes, they do get that excited about it, and seeing you pick up the leash will trigger the happy dance!

You will still need to slowly build on your dog's attention span and work tolerance, but they'll gain those attributes faster than a young Doodle puppy. Your adult Doodle may require a few more repetitions than a younger dog will to fully understand the concepts, but you'll be able to do so with longer training sessions.

REMEMBER

Dogs never stop learning. Even senior Doodles love to participate in training sessions. They may not be able to do flips, but they're very happy to heel, sit, stay and perform other behaviors that are rewarding to them. Dogs enjoy the stimulation of learning, so you should never stop teaching them!

Chapter **2**

The Amazing Poodle

Poodles have ranked in the top ten most highly desired dog breeds for decades. As perfect as they are as purebred dogs, they're also the most popular breed of dog to mix with numerous other breeds, creating so-called "designer dogs," which can cost thousands of dollars. What is it about Poodles that makes them the ideal breed for this purpose?

While Poodles are currently a popular breed to mix with other dogs to create Doodles, this concept isn't a new one. Throughout history, Poodles have been the foundation of many purebred dogs who are registered in worldwide kennel clubs today. From Portuguese Water Dogs to the Curly-Coated Retriever, you can instantly recognize many of the Poodle's influences just by appearance — the curly coat.

Appearance, however, has played only a minor role in the creation of these breeds. Poodles were chosen as foundation dogs for their intelligence and versatility, too. Poodles are ranked as one of the most intelligent breeds in the American Kennel Club (AKC).

This chapter tells you more about the Poodle and why they're such good parents.

Meet the Poodle

Poodles (like the one in Figure 2-1) have high intelligence, versatility, and hypo-allergenic, non-shedding coats. They're easy to train, and they fit into most family environments. Plus, they come in three different sizes (Standard, Miniature, and Toy) to please a large array of preferences. Poodles also have a longer life span than most other breeds, especially Toy-size breeds.

FIGURE 2-1:
The Poodle.

Photograph by Anton Maltsev / 123 RF

There are three Poodle attributes that really stand out when considering them as a foundation for a hybrid Doodle:

>> **Size:** Poodles come in three AKC-recognized sizes:

- *Standard:* Standard Poodles typically measure more than 15 inches at the shoulder. Males weigh 60 to 70 pounds, and females weigh 40 to 50 pounds.

- *Miniature:* Miniature Poodles typically measure 10 to 15 inches at the shoulder and weigh 10 to 15 pounds.

- *Toy:* Toy Poodles typically measure 10 inches or less at the shoulder and weigh 4 to 6 pounds.

There is a fourth Poodle size, the Teacup Poodle, but it isn't officially recognized by the AKC. They're small enough to fit into a pocket! Because their offspring are not consistent in size or conformation, they have yet to be nationally recognized and registered. It can take five generations of consistent appearance to create a recognized dog breed.

» **Color:** Poodles come in a wide variety of coat colors, from black to white and everything in between, including *parti-colored* (multiple colors).

» **Shedding:** The Poodle is one of the few dog breeds that sheds very little. Poodles don't have an undercoat or a long, course overcoat. In fact, their coats are considered "hair," not typical dog fur. As with hair, a few strands may come out here and there, but not in the large amounts seen in most dogs. Because their hair is very tightly woven, much of the hair that *is* shed doesn't leave the dog. (This trait is also why they require regular professional grooming and brushing.)

Besides appearance, personality and instinctual tendencies make Poodles an ideal foundation parent for a Doodle. They're great with people of all ages, other dogs, other pets, and most environmental situations. In a cold climate, you can allow their coat to grow long. In a warm environment, you can trim them shorter. Compared to many other purebred dogs, Poodles have relatively few genetic health concerns, enhancing the vitality of their offspring. And they're highly trainable, making them perfect for a wide variety of jobs.

POODLE ORIGINS

Poodle-type dogs were depicted in Ancient Egyptian and Roman art hundreds of years before the Common Era. In the Middle Ages, a Poodle-type dog came to Europe with the Goths and Ostrogoths (via what is now Russia), who used it for herding their livestock. It was in 1400, however, that Poodles became a recognized breed in Germany, used for retrieving waterfowl. They were called *pudelhund* ("dog that splashes about"). Poodles are often still used as hunting companions for waterfowl sport hunting, retrieving ducks and geese from lakes and other waterways.

In France, Poodles were called *caniche,* from the French word for female duck. The larger Poodles were used in France for waterfowl retrieval. The French then created the size varieties we currently enjoy, with the Standard Poodle remaining the working dogs and the smaller varieties becoming circus performers, farmers' helpers, truffle hunters,

(continued)

(continued)

and, in royal courts, lap dogs. In fact, Toy Poodles were favorites of the Louis IV to Louis XVI regimes.

Over the centuries, Poodles were mixed with water spaniels, terriers, and other breeds to enhance their capabilities for specific jobs. For example, the truffle-hunting Poodle was mixed with terriers to make them more tenacious in their hunt. And they were further specialized into what are now purebred dogs, such as Portuguese Water Dogs (the ultimate water dog and retriever), Curly-Coated Retrievers, and many more. Whenever a breed was created to aid in the hunt, from ducks to truffles, Poodles were often the foundation parent.

Poodles were not only great hunting companions, but also great performers. With their high intelligence and ease of training, as well as agility, they quickly became a favorite of traveling circuses and royal performers throughout Europe. Few other dog breeds had a penchant for doing flips, walking on their hind legs, jumping through hoops, or jumping from tall platforms like the Poodle. As their popularity grew, the smaller Poodle varieties were favored more than the Standard, because they were easier to care for and transport.

In 1874, Poodles entered England, where they were recognized as a breed, with specific standards, within the Kennel Club of England. In 1887, The American Kennel Club recognized Poodles as a breed, using the English standards as a cornerstone of its own requirements. Even though recognized as a breed, however, Poodles were not highly popular until they caught the fancy of wealthy families.

When the Poodle Club of America was formed and Poodles were viewed in both conformation and performance competitions, they gained in popularity. In fact, Poodles have been one of the most frequent Best in Show winners at Westminster and Crufts since 1907.

Poodles don't just win at dog shows. They also continue to work as guide dogs, guard dogs, and wagon pullers. During World War I and World War II, they were used in the field to help soldiers move supplies, carry communications, and sniff out land mines. Due to their fast-growing coats, however, they didn't make the cut for continued use. (It's tough to find a Poodle groomer in a war zone.)

After World War II, Poodles became status symbols, with wealthy families flouting well-groomed pets. In the 1960s, the breed became the most popular dog breed in the United States, and it continues to be one of the top ten most popular American Kennel Club breeds.

Big, Small, Poodles Have It All

As I mention earlier, three Poodle varieties are recognized by the AKC. They were originally created for specific jobs:

» **Standard:** To retrieve downed waterfowl from waterways

» **Miniature:** To flush and retrieve ground birds such as quail in the uplands

» **Toy:** To flush birds and other small game from thick underbrush

Each variety is delineated by size, but they all have similar structural characteristics:

» A square build, with equally proportioned legs to body, with the length of body from the breastbone to the point of the rump equal to the height from the highest point of the shoulders to the ground.

» Dark, oval eyes with an intelligent expression.

» Ears that fold over near the head and are set at, or slightly below, eye level.

» A naturally curly and dense coat all over the body.

» A huge variety of coat colors. Black, blue, gray, silver, cream, and white have black noses, eye rims, and lips, and black toenails. Apricot-colored Poodles tend to have liver-colored noses, eye rims, and lips, and sometimes amber eyes. Parti-colored Poodles can be either black and white or liver and white, with the liver and white Poodles having the lighter colored skin areas. There's also a color combination called phantom Poodles, with coloring similar to a Doberman Pinscher or Rottweiler; they have a predominantly black (sometimes brown) body with a lighter color (usually tan) appearing on their "eyebrows," muzzle, throat, legs, feet, and below their tails.

Poodle Personalities

Poodles are highly intelligent, energetic, and athletic. They were created for long hours of hard work and need a job in order to remain manageable. Although they're generally social, they can be aloof when first meeting people or other dogs but are quick to warm up and initiate play.

Standard Poodles are great with children of all ages and love to get out in the yard and chase toys. And, despite their appearance as froufrou dogs, they'll get down and dirty with digging and rolling around. Standard Poodles love to run, and joining a teenager rolling down the sidewalk on a skateboard is at the top of their to-do list. They don't do well in noisy households, however, and if there tends to be a lot of commotion, they need a place to get away from it all that's quiet. Special care needs to be taken with young babies, and appropriate introductions will lead to a respectful relationship.

The Miniature Poodle and Toy Poodle varieties can do well in most households that are not overly noisy or permissive. They may be small dogs, but they still need to be addressed as dogs and treated as equals, not as the kings or queens of the home. Due to their high intelligence, if they live a permissive lifestyle, they can easily become snarky and demanding.

Common Health Concerns

Although Poodles are one of the healthier breeds of dogs overall, they do have some common health concerns. One is the penchant for ear infections. Ear infections can happen to any dog with a fold-over ear and dog hair within that traps dirt and wax, creating the perfect environment for infections to develop. Keeping the ears free of hair and dirt will easily prevent this from happening.

Other health issues, such as Addison's disease, epilepsy, *gastric dilation* (a twisting of the stomach, sometimes referred to as *bloat*), tracheal collapse, and thyroid issues, can occur as well. Professional breeders generally choose *sires* (fathers) and *dams* (mothers) to prevent these issues from plaguing their puppies. But that doesn't mean that they won't occur to one or more pups within the same litter, because the genes are still present.

Poodles also tend to be sensitive to environmental allergens, which can result in ear and skin infections, as well as *lick granulomas* (irritated spots also known as hot spots) on their feet.

WARNING

Addison's disease may be difficult to diagnose because it appears similar to other health issues. It's caused by insufficient production of glucocorticoid and/or mineralocorticoid in the adrenal cortex, which is near the kidneys. It's more common in the Standard Poodle than the other two varieties. The symptoms include unexplained lethargy, frequent gastric disturbances, and sometimes an inability to handle stress. It can be fatal, but if caught and treated, the dog can live a full life.

Chapter **3**

Considering Your Doodle Options

With all the great Doodles available, which one will most easily fit into your lifestyle? Doodles can come in any size or color, with any personality or degree of athletic ability. It all depends on the parent breeds that constitute the mix.

When choosing which Doodle will be right for you, you'll need to weigh several factors, including your lifestyle and what you're hoping to get out of your relationship with your dog. You may want one for companionship. Or you may want one to help your child negotiate the challenges of a learning disability. Understanding the typical behavioral characteristics, health requirements, and size of your Doodle is important to ensuring you make the right choice.

This chapter walks you through the lifestyle factors to consider, some of the most popular kinds of Doodles, and what all Doodles have in common. Armed with this information, you're sure to find the Doodle who's best for you and your family.

Considering Your Lifestyle

Your first consideration when choosing any dog should be based on your own lifestyle. The size of your home is important. If you live in a city, you may not be able to have a large, high-energy dog like a Standard-size Doodle. Without a securely fenced yard, or lots of time to go on multiple long walks every day, a smaller dog may be a wiser choice. On the other hand, if you live in a suburban or rural neighborhood, any size dog may be appropriate, and your main consideration will be the dog's personality.

It's not just the size of your home (or having a securely fenced yard), however — it's also about the activity level of your family. Many Doodles, like their Poodle parents, don't appreciate a lot of noise, commotion, or erratic schedules. They adore racing around with children or snuggling with a baby, but when the volume of the household is turned up, either by children racing around and screaming or parents' loud, scolding voices, they just want to go hide in a corner. Most Doodles are highly sensitive to sudden environmental changes and inconsistent schedules.

Another consideration is the amount of time you have available to work with your Doodle. Make no mistake, intelligent as they are, Doodles require training. Many Doodles naturally learn things such as people's schedules, their feeding times, when they'll be taken for walks, and when to expect the mail carrier. But they also require education to learn how to understand their environments and respond well when cued.

Another factor to consider is your activity level. Are you an active person? Or do you live a quieter life? An active, social person will probably be happiest with a medium to large dog who loves to run, play fetch, go swimming, or head out on adventures. Someone with a quiet life may be happier with a smaller, less athletic dog, who prefers to snuggle on the couch and take long naps.

Are you getting a Doodle to be helpful to you? Or just to be a companion? If it's the latter, consider a smaller Doodle, such as a Cavadoodle (Cavalier King Charles Spaniel x Miniature Poodle). Although Cavadoodles like a short run once a day, they mainly prefer to remain at your side or on your lap, making them easy to care for. If you're looking for a Doodle to be your service dog, you need to break down the exact service you're expecting from them (see the nearby sidebar).

DOODLE JOBS

Doodles can do all kinds of job. Each breed hybrid excels in specific ways, so if you have a job in mind for your Doodle, get the right kind of Doodle for the job:

- **Assistance:** If you're looking for a dog who can help you get around and fetch heavy objects, you'll want a Standard-size Doodle, for their stout build and strong muscles. Standard-size Doodles are also more energetic and able to work longer. They have better tolerance to weather variations than the smaller Doodles do, and they can help you regardless of climate. They're also intelligent and intuitive, making them great as Seeing Eye dogs, hearing assistance dogs, and assistants to the physically and mentally challenged. They make great health-alert dogs, too, but the smaller Doodle varieties can also excel at that job.

- **Health alerts:** If you're looking for a dog who can alert you to health conditions (such as diabetic shock or epileptic seizures), any size Doodle will do. Just keep in mind that the larger varieties require more exercise and stimulation throughout the day than the smaller dogs do. Generally, a Miniature-size Doodle has the best ability to apply dedication to this job. Because Miniature Poodles tend to be the quickest variety of Poodle to learn new concepts, they're also the most intuitive to a health emergency. They still have enough weight on them to apply pressure to a person who is having an anxiety attack, thereby aiding in helping the person relax.

  Many dogs are great at detecting cancer — some can even be trained for it. Cancer has a specific odor they can pick up. Through repetitive pairing of the odor with a behavior signal, such as placing the dog's nose on the cancer spot, dogs are great at early detection. As I write this, there are groups training dogs to detect COVID-19. So far, they're more accurate in their detection than taking someone's temperature!

- **Emotional support:** Almost any Doodle can perform this job. Just having them around is emotionally supportive. You may go through some stress while they're young puppies (with housetraining, behavior problem solving, and training), but once they mature, they're the perfect companions that you can't live without. You'll need to decide if you want an emotional support dog you can cuddle with in your lap, on your couch, or on the floor. A small Doodle can do all three, but I don't recommend lap or couch time with the larger ones or you're setting yourself up for some long-term problems.

- **Performance:** Doodles are smart, energetic, and highly athletic. This means they can excel at any canine sport. I've successfully shown numerous Doodles in obedience trials, AKC Rally trials, and agility and dock-diving competitions. A well-trained Doodle can achieve very high scores because they strive to do their best. ***Remember:*** You may be looking for ribbons, trophies, and certifications, but your Doodle is enjoying the training journey along the way. Spending time with you, learning new behaviors, and getting lots of activity make a happy Doodle! Performance work is great for any size Doodle.

Doodle Commonalities

All Doodles have similarities, because they all have Poodle parents. In this section, I fill you in on the common traits of all Doodles. In the following sections, I walk you through the differences among the different mixes.

Grooming requirements

All Doodles require regular grooming, including brushing their coats, trimming their nails, and cleaning their ears cleaning (if the ears are droopy and fold over); some Doodles also require attention to skin folds. Most Doodles inherit some of their Poodle parent's coat, which means your Doodle will need to visit a professional groomer regularly.

REMEMBER

There's more to grooming a Doodle than a quick shortening of the coat on their bodies. The feet will need to be cleared of long hair, which can collect debris; the hair inside the ears will need to be removed; the hair around the base of the tail will need to be trimmed; and much more. (Turn to Chapter 8 for more about grooming your Doodle.)

Early socialization requirements

Poodles can be reserved or easily frightened if they aren't exposed to appropriate socialization when very young. Every dog benefits from early socialization with people outside the home, as well as other animals. All introductions to anything or anybody new should be a positive experience for your dog.

Behavioral quirks

All Doodles have a tendency to jump up. If they aren't trained, they'll jump on you, anybody walking into the room, and anybody they meet on the street. Not everybody appreciates this behavior. You can train this behavior out of your Doodle, but you'll have to be very consistent and persistent (see Part 3).

Doodles also like to jump on other dogs. Many dogs are patient with young Doodles, but plenty of dogs aren't so happy being jumped on, whether the Doodle is a pup or not. Pay attention to how your Doodle greets and spends time with other dogs.

Trainability

All Doodles are very trainable. Training should be done while they're still puppies — young dogs learn faster than older dogs do (after all, older dogs have gotten used to running the show, and they're not so eager to give that up). Some

Doodles are more challenging than others, if their non-Poodle parent is somewhat stubborn. Regardless of parentage, however, all Doodles learn quickly when they're under 6 months of age.

Dietary requirements

Most Doodles tend to have bad reactions to specific foods. Poodles are prone to skin disorders, and eating food they can't easily digest or tolerate can cause their skin to develop rashes, flakiness, and itching. Some Doodles also develop ear infections, runny eyes, or *lick granulomas* (irritated spots caused by licking at their skin). You can ensure your Doodle doesn't experience these discomforts, though. In general, feed a diet rich in protein from meat, not carbohydrates or starches. Stick with just one healthy grain and, if possible, organ meats. (You can find more on diet in Chapter 7.)

Exercise requirements

All Doodles have lots of energy, especially when they're young. They need at least one good long walk every day. Some need more, depending on their parent breeds. You can count on the larger Doodles and any with Standard Poodle as a parent to require several hours of exercise every day. Smaller Doodles are fine with one long walk and a couple of indoor play sessions.

Separation anxiety

All Doodles love their families. You're their pack. When they're separated from you, they may become despondent and insecure. Some Doodles become destructive; others bark and whine; some even chew on themselves.

TIP

If you have to be away from home for long periods of time every day, consider taking your Doodle to doggy daycare. There, he can play with other dogs, exercise, and be with other people. Instead of returning home to a stressed-out dog and a destroyed living room, both of you can relax together. Adult Doodles, who are less prone to separation anxiety than puppies, may do fine having a dog walker take them for a walk in the middle of the day.

Meet the Doodles

There are as many Doodles as there are breeds of dogs, but I can't cover all of them in one book, so in this section, I discuss the most popular Doodles. I tell you about their parents, appearance, health, and preferred family situation. Knowing which Doodle is best for you will ensure you choose the perfect companion.

Aussiedoodle

Photograph by blickwinkel / Alamy Stock Photo

Aussiedoodles are created by pairing an Australian Shepherd with a Poodle. There are three sizes of Aussiedoodles, just as there are three sizes of Poodles — Standard, Miniature, and Toy.

Australian Shepherds were created by mixing a variety of herding collies, such as Border Collies and other farm-type Collies from Europe, during the 1900s. There is no consensus, however, on their country of origin. They're ideal stock dogs because of their strong, medium-size bodies and ability to work all day with their human partners.

Aussiedoodles are a mix of two high-energy and intelligent breeds. They're working dogs, in need of a job. Their life span averages between 10 to 14 years of age, and they tend to have few health concerns. They do, however, require a lot of training, consistency, and direction — otherwise, trouble is their middle name.

Size

It's difficult to set an average size of an Aussiedoodle because it's entirely dependent on the parents. The best way of guessing the ultimate size at maturity is to look at the parents. With that in mind, they can be anywhere from 25 to 60 pounds and their height at the shoulder can be 14 to 23 inches.

Appearance

Australian Shepherds have a thick double coat that requires regular grooming to prevent mats. Aussiedoodles have the benefit of the single-coat Poodle genes, but the offspring aren't consistent when it comes to which parent they favor. Often, it's a combination, which means a very thick and curly coat that requires a lot of attention. Their coat can be any variety of colors, including black and white, liver and white, *merle* (a mixture of gray, black, tan, and white or liver-brown with tan and white), or silver and white.

Aussiedoodles are generally solid, medium-size dogs with wide-set eyes, folded-over ears, and a long, pointy snout. Most are born with tails, which may be thick at the base and taper to thinner at the end or thin from base to tip.

Health

Aussiedoodles have a very good health record. Australian Shepherds are a healthy breed, and adding their genetics to a Poodle will minimize the Poodle health concerns. You'll still need to be aware of problems such as Cushing's disease, hip dysplasia, *progressive retinal atrophy* (PRA; a bilateral degeneration of the retina, causing blindness), and possibly a sensitivity to Ivermectin, a common parasite preventive.

Life with an Aussiedoodle

WARNING

The Aussiedoodle can be highly challenging to live with and train. The addition of Poodle characteristics creates a super-active and independent dog.

The ideal environment for Aussiedoodles is one with lots of safe space to run. They don't generally fare well in an apartment or urban setting. A house with a yard, on a farm with a job, or with someone who shares an active lifestyle with their canine companion is ideal. A home with young children and lots of commotion isn't recommended — Australian Shepherds have strong herding instincts, and running children can arouse this instinctive behavior. Like their Australian Shepherd parent, they can be overly territorial, have a tendency to herd anything that moves, and jump up on people. This Doodle is not recommended for a home with elderly folks around, either living in the home or visiting often.

Aussiedoodles require lots of contact with their human companions. They also requires lots of training, using positive reinforcement and motivating them to perform, along with consistency and a job to do. With an Aussiedoodle, you must establish that you're the one in charge.

Bernedoodle

Photograph by Cavan Images / Alamy Stock Photo

Bernedoodles are produced by mixing a Bernese Mountain Dog mother with a Poodle father (of various sizes to produce the Standard-, Miniature-, and Toy-size Bernedoodles). The offspring are laid-back, super cute, sweet, and intelligent dogs who thrive in any environment.

Bernese Mountain Dogs are large working dogs bred to aid farmers by guarding and driving cattle herds in Alpine environments. Stout, hardworking dogs who can do it all, they're happy lying at your feet, playing with children, and cuddling. With a Bernedoodle, you may get an energetic and intelligent dog with a high work drive, though that greatly depends on the dog's size. The larger the Bernedoodle, the more energetic they'll be.

Size

A Bernedoodle with a large Bernese Mountain Dog mother and a Standard Poodle father can range between 23 to 29 inches tall at the shoulder and weigh 70 to 90 pounds. Mixing a Bernese Mountain Dog mother with a Miniature Poodle father results in offspring anywhere from 18 to 22 inches tall and 25 to 50 pounds. And mixing a Bernese Mountain Dog mother with a Toy Poodle father (which is typically done via artificial insemination) can result in offspring ranging from 12 to 17 inches tall at the shoulder and weighing 10 to 25 pounds.

Appearance

Bernese Mountain Dogs are tricolored — black, tan, and white — so Bernedoodles can also be a variety of color combinations, especially when mixed with a Poodle. Bernedoodles also have a wide variety of coats. Bernese Mountain Dogs have a double, thick coat that tends to shed a lot. Mix them with Poodles, and you can have any combination of straight, wavy, or curly Bernedoodles. The more the Poodle parent influences the coat, the less shedding will occur.

This breed mix tends to have large dark to light brown wide-set eyes, a round head and muzzle, and heavy, droopy ears. They also have a solid build, making them strong dogs. Even the minis are solidly built, favoring some of their Bernese Mountain Dog parent's genetics.

Health

Overall, Bernedoodles are very healthy, hardy dogs. Sometimes genetic heritage can't be overcome and they can be prone to hip or elbow dysplasia, skin sensitivities, digestive disorders, and immune system issues. The smaller the Bernedoodle, the closer they are genetically to the smaller Poodle varieties, making them prone to the typical Poodle structural issues, as well as *von Willebrand disease* (a lack of a clotting protein in their blood) and Addison's disease.

Life with a Bernedoodle

Bernedoodles have fantastic temperaments. Because the Bernese Mountain Dog parent is gentle, loving, and willing to do anything for you, you can bet that a lot of that personality will be within your Bernedoodle, too. The rest of their personality, such as activity levels, attention levels, and sociability, will depend on their Poodle parent.

Mixing the Bernese Mountain Dog with a Standard Poodle will result not only in a large dog, but also a dog who may be slightly reactive to new stimuli, such as unfamiliar people, other dogs, or new environments. It may just take a few minutes for the dog to process new things. These larger varieties are also energetic and need of lots of exercise. Mixing the Bernese Mountain Dog with a Miniature Poodle or Toy Poodle will result in an outgoing, social dog who loves attention from everyone. They're equally thrilled with sitting on your lap as they are with chasing you around the yard or playing fetch.

Bernedoodles do well with children and adults of all ages. They're loyal and loving. Exercise some caution with infants and toddlers, though, because Bernedoodles are boisterous when happy, and little ones can easily be knocked down by their exuberance. They're perfect with the elderly.

Cavadoodle (Cavapoo)

Photograph by Sandra Standbridge / Alamy Stock Photo

Cavadoodles (also known as Cavapoos) are the perfect small Doodle. They're a mix between the Cavalier King Charles Spaniel and the Miniature Poodle or Toy Poodle. Both parents have a great temperament, are very intelligent, love to cuddle, and live comfortably in most environments. They adore people of all ages but can be a bit reserved around new dogs, because they know their size and dislike being stepped on or pushed around.

Cavalier King Charles Spaniels were a favorite of England's King Charles, who loved his dogs so much that he took them everywhere he traveled. They were even allowed in Parliament! The breed has remained popular in England, but it didn't cross the Atlantic to the United States until the 1950s.

The first litters of Cavadoodles were bred in Australia in the 1990s, and they were an instant worldwide hit. They're loyal, loving, gentle, and graceful. Living from 12 to 15 years, they make great canine companions.

Size

Cavadoodles can weigh 13 to 18 pounds, depending on whether the Poodle parent is a Miniature or Toy. Their height at the shoulder is 12 to 13 inches, making them a substantial Toy-size dog without being fragile.

Appearance

Cavadoodles are about as cute as a dog can be, with silky, wavy fur, big brown eyes, and droopy ears. They can be any combination of colors, from brown and white, to all tan, or tricolor (black, tan, and white). Cavadoodles have a square build, with curly tails and round heads. Their nose is round and adorable, with super-cute cheeks. Their facial expression is always full of affection and trust.

Health

Cavalier King Charles Spaniels have few inherited health problems, but there are some to be aware of. These include cataracts, epilepsy, PRA, and ear problems (such as frequent ear infections).

TIP

To prevent infections with droopy-eared dogs, be sure to offer a good diet without a lot of carbohydrates or preservatives. Generally, red meats and lamb are easier on their digestive systems than poultry is. Also, clean their ears several times a week with an antiseptic solution to kill bacteria and fungus. Fully dry their ears if they have been swimming or have been bathed.

WARNING

If you smell a foul odor in their ears, take them to a veterinarian as soon as possible. Prolonged and frequent ear infections can lead to deafness.

Other health concerns include heart murmurs, luxating patellas, and eye irritation (because they have large eyes that bulge a bit). It's very important to maintain eye health with saline rinse several times a week and to trim the fur around their eyes to prevent irritation.

Life with a Cavadoodle

Cavadoodles are great everywhere! They tend to be generally quiet apartment dogs, only barking when someone knocks. They can be energetic on hikes and enjoy training sessions immensely. Cavadoodles are great with people of all ages, very patient with youngsters, and enjoy cuddling on your lap. They're also fantastic with the elderly, because they really don't require lots of exercise — they're satisfied with one nice walk a day and regular potty breaks.

Both Cavalier King Charles Spaniels and Poodles are highly intelligent and easy to train, making training lots of fun with a Cavadoodle. Though Cavadoodles are highly intuitive, be sure to educate your pup to help them remain relaxed and understand how to negotiate their environment appropriately. They require daily brushing (because their coats are fine-haired) and a regular schedule for professional grooming to keep their coat trimmed and clean.

Chidoodle (Chipoo)

Photograph by Vincent Scherer / Alamy Stock Photo

Chidoodles are a hybrid dog created by pairing a Chihuahua with either a Miniature Poodle or Toy Poodle. This very small dog is gradually gaining in popularity. Although Chihuahuas tend to be small and fragile, the infusion of Poodle genetics improves the hardiness, life span, and overall health of the offspring.

Chihuahuas have been a favorite in South America since the Toltecs ruled. However, the tiny dog was not quite as small and fragile looking at that time. When the Aztecs took over the area of Mexico in the 12th century, many types of art depicted them as larger and heavier. The Aztecs bred them smaller, closer to their modern appearance. The Chihuahua was considered one of their great treasures. In the 1800s, Chihuahuas were discovered by Americans in some remote Mexican villages in the state of Chihuahua. Since then, they've become a favorite of celebrities and those who enjoy cuddling with these small, sweet dogs.

Chidoodles are intelligent like their Poodle parents (though Chihuahuas are also very bright) and are confident, sometimes assertively so. Their life span averages 12 to 15 years. Despite their outward acts of courage, they're sensitive and they dislike being home alone. Chidoodles also bark a lot, because both parent breeds are quick to react to novel sounds and sights.

Size

Chidoodles can be 5 to 15 inches at the shoulder and weigh 4 to 20 pounds, depending on the size of the parent Poodle.

Appearance

Small, agile, and lively, Chidoodles can have either the erect ears of their Chihuahua parent or the folded-over ears of their Poodle parent. Many have both, depending on their mood and the wind. They often have a back that's a little bit longer from chest to tail base than their legs are from foot to shoulder.

Chidoodles have a variety of coat lengths and styles, from short to long and straight to curly. Regular brushing is suggested to remove debris, and if you intend on lots of cuddles, weekly baths with skin conditioners are a good idea, too.

Health

Chidoodles are a generally healthy hybrid breed, but like all Toy-size breeds, they can be prone to a luxating patella, PRA, epilepsy, ear inflammation, and several skin diseases similar to those found within Poodle genetics. Their sensitivity to specific foods requires you to be creative with their diet, ensuring they don't eat anything that can irritate their gastrointestinal tract or skin.

Life with a Chidoodle

Chidoodles tend to prefer one family member, though they're generally amiable with the entire family. They aren't suitable for families with very young children (because they don't appreciate erratic movement and sounds), but they do well with other household pets. They're suspicious of people they don't know and tend to bark at newcomers at the door or who enter the house.

Chidoodles work well within the confines of an apartment, because they are small, are easily transported, and don't require vast amounts of exercise. But, due to their barking issues, your neighbors won't be happy with you if you aren't home for long periods of time every day and your Chidoodle, who is prone to separation anxiety, barks constantly. Early training, using positive reinforcement methods, is suggested to ensure ease of handling and more confidence with new situations. When mature, and well trained, Chidoodles can be great therapy dogs because they adore attention, but keep in mind, because they tend to attach to one person, their affection isn't always shareable with others.

Cockapoo

Photograph by Farlap / Alamy Stock Photo

The Cockapoo was one of the first designer dog breeds created. They originated in the late 1950s, bred to be companion dogs. They're a cross of the smallest sporting breed, Cocker Spaniel, with a Miniature Poodle.

Because Cockapoo breeders prefer to keep them at around 20 to 25 pounds, they don't breed their Cocker Spaniels with Standard Poodles. Instead, they always breed with the smaller varieties of Poodles, either Miniature or Toy. Cockapoo life spans average 13 to 15 years.

Size

The typical Cockapoo is 10 to 20 inches at the shoulder and weighs 10 to 30 pounds depending on the size of the Poodle parent.

Appearance

Cocker Spaniels tend to be compact, with a slightly sloping back, chiseled facial features, and long, droopy ears. Their eyes are large and almond shaped and look directly forward. Eye color is generally a soft brown, with an intelligent expression. The Cocker Spaniel square back becomes longer with the infusion of Poodle genes.

WARNING

Beware of any Cockapoos who have a less-than-square appearance (longer back with short legs); they may be prone to back problems as they age.

Cockapoos can be any color between white and black. Because Cocker Spaniels vary among white, tan, brown, black, and some parti-colors, Poodles are equally colorful. Because the parti-colors are more difficult to achieve, they're often more expensive.

Their coats vary from straight to curly, but the most typical is wavy. The tighter the wave, the less shedding, because their hair is more like their Poodle parent. Both Cocker Spaniels and Poodles require regular professional grooming. They're small dogs and their long hair picks up debris from the ground, causing tangles.

Health

Cockapoos are one of the healthier types of Doodle. They truly benefit from the hybrid vigor of mixed-breed dogs. Cockapoos still have genetics similar to their parents, so there's always the possibility of having one of their health problems.

Cockapoos are prone to joint issues if they're overweight, ear infections if the ears aren't kept groomed with weekly ear cleanings, eye infections from environmental allergic reactions, and PRA, a common issue with Cocker Spaniels.

Life with a Cockapoo

Cockapoos thrive in any environment, except one where they're left alone for long periods of time or unable to get at least one good exercise period in each day. Cockapoos are rarely overly sensitive or insecure, always ready to make new friends in new places.

Cockapoos are very easily trained, using positive reinforcement. If exposed to anger, harsh handling, or infliction of pain, they'll resort to fear behavior, which includes barking, snarling, and biting. If rewarded for good behavior, they'll constantly strive to repeat it.

Cockapoos adore children of all ages, the elderly, and the physically challenged. In fact, they're great therapy and assistance dogs for those who require help with fetching items or alerting to sounds such as someone at the door or a ringing telephone.

Goldendoodle

Photograph by ESSEXART / Stockimo / Alamy Stock Photo

Goldendoodles are a mix of a Golden Retriever and a Poodle. Golden Retrievers, a mix of a Golden Retriever and a Poodle, are easy to train, loyal, social, and sensitive to the emotions of others. They're sturdy, solid dogs bred to aid hunters in the field. They love running, swimming, and fetching. You can hardly find a more intuitive dog breed. Mix them with a Poodle and you have all those attributes and more.

Goldendoodles are energetic, playful, hardworking, and easy to train. Most are highly social, too. This breed can best be described as always joyful. Their life span averages 10 to 14 years, depending on the size variation.

Size

Male Goldendoodles typically weigh from 65 to 90 pounds, depending on the size of the parents. Female Goldendoodles average 60 to 70 pounds, again, depending on the size of the parents. Mini Goldendoodles (the offspring of a Miniature Poodle and a Golden Retriever) can weigh anywhere from 45 to 60 pounds. The smallest Goldendoodles may top out at 35 pounds.

Appearance

A Goldendoodle's appearance depends greatly on which coat genes were transferred from their parents. Some can have shaggy, barely wavy coats; others sport tight curls. Purebred Golden Retrievers shed a lot, but Goldendoodles shed far less, if at all. A Goldendoodle's coat can be any shade, from cream to black, depending on the Poodle parent.

This breed mix tends to have wide-set brown to amber eyes, folded-over ears, and a thick tail. You'll likely also see webbing between their toes because they're the product of two breeds created for water retrieving. Their barrel (abdomen) tends to be large, with sturdy hips and shoulders. A well-bred Goldendoodle will be as long from their chest to their tail base as they are tall from the paw pad to the top of their shoulder.

Health

Mixing a Golden Retriever with a Poodle does enhance the offspring's overall vitality and possibly results in a longer life span, but there's still the possibility of genetic abnormalities. Golden Retrievers are prone to cancer, hip and elbow dysplasia, heart and lung weakness, environmental and food allergies, von Willebrand disease, and idiopathic epilepsy. Add to this the typical health issues with Poodles (see Chapter 2). A professional breeder will test parent dogs for the majority of these conditions before breeding them, reducing the risk in the offspring.

Life with a Goldendoodle

Goldendoodles need a lot of exercise. If you live in an urban area, this is not the dog to share your life with, unless you have access to a large, securely fenced area and lots of time to exercise your dog every day. They tend to be most at home in suburban and rural areas where there are lots of opportunities to safely exercise. Be sure to babyproof doorknobs, cupboards, and shelves. Goldendoodles can figure out latches, doorknobs, and easily solved puzzles, such as how to jump from ottoman to chair to front paws up on a shelf.

Goldendoodles are great for children of all ages, but beware of allowing your dog to be with your children unsupervised. A large, exuberant dog can knock over little ones and be tempted to grab food from low-hanging hands. Early training is recommended to offer your dog structure and direction, ensuring a more harmonious household.

Goldendoodles are great for any activity. In fact, they thrive when put to work as it is stimulating and fulfilling their need to perform.

Havadoodle

Photograph by Marcello Sgarlato / Alamy Stock Photo

The Havadoodle is a cross between the Havanese and either a Miniature Poodle or a Toy Poodle. The result is a sweet, intelligent, and curious family companion. Havadoodles have a spring in their step and are highly adaptable to any living situation.

TECHNICAL STUFF

Havadoodles are technically not a 50/50 mix of two breeds. The Poodle is already in a Havanese, because it was one of the foundation breeds that created the Havanese, which originated in Cuba.

Havanese have long, silky coats that were designed to insulate them from the heat typical in a tropical environment. But because they were designed to withstand heat, they can't insulate themselves from cold and require coats when walking outdoors in colder climates. Some can be shy, and many prefer to remain close to one person in the family, though they're generally friendly to everyone.

Size

Like their Havanese parent, Havadoodles tend to be 8 to 11 inches at the shoulder and weigh 10 to 16 pounds. This is the ideal size for travel — they fit under a plane seat or in a small carrying case when traveling by car.

Appearance

Havadoodles have full, wavy to curly coats, with a silky feel. Although they have a lively gait, their legs are short. Their backs are straight with tails that curl over, but don't touch, their backs. Their noses are a healthy length to avoid respiratory issues found in many other breeds (or breed mixes). They do have deep chests, with wide ribs and tucked up abdomens.

Their dark brown eyes with almond-shaped lids are sweet, and they also sport black "eyeliner." Their coats can be black, tan, brown, white, or reddish brown. Their ears are fully dropped, with flowing hair all around.

Health

Like many Toy-size dogs, Havadoodles can have a luxating patella, liver disease, heart disease, cataracts, and PRA. These health concerns are present in both parents, so the chances of your Havadoodle experiencing them is not low. Legg-Calve-Perthes disease (a degeneration of the head of the femur bone), hip dysplasia, and hypothyroidism are other possible health concerns.

TIP

Be sure to do your homework with locating a professional breeder. It will pay off by having a higher likelihood of a healthy dog. Professional breeders put in the effort to ensure none of their breeding dogs have these issues because they must pass health screenings for organ and bone issues.

Life with a Havadoodle

Havadoodles can live in any environment, provided they're catered to. They're small, after all, and they need to remain safe and secure, without exposure to severe temperatures, clumsy people, or overbearing pets. They fare well in apartments and houses, and love playing in the park.

Havadoodles may be small, but they still require a few hours of exercise every day, either indoors or within a safely fenced yard or park. Havadoodles aren't generally excessive barkers, but they can become so without appropriate training and socializing. They thrive on reward-based training approaches and learn quickly. They make great emotional support and therapy dogs because they're calm and enjoy attention from everyone. Havadoodles tend to have a preferred human companion and, because they have some Poodle genes, they can sometimes be a little shy about new people. It's best to allow the dog to make the first overtures, to ensure they gain some confidence from meeting new people or other animals.

Jackadoodle (Jackapoo)

Photograph by Gerry Pearce / Alamy Stock Photo

Jackadoodles are a combination of a Jack Russell Terrier with a Miniature Poodle or Toy Poodle. The combination results in a super-cute, highly energetic, and intelligent small dog. Jackadoodles are great family dogs for any age, but they definitely require an active lifestyle. They tend to appear scruffy, like a long-haired Jack Russell Terrier, but with a soft, wavy, and sometimes, curly coat.

Jack Russell Terriers were bred to be working dogs that bolted foxes (as well as other ground-dwelling wildlife, like badgers and groundhogs) from their dens. They were created approximately 200 years ago to aid in the extermination of pesky vermin. Their appearance hasn't changed over the years. They're predominantly white with tan, brown, or black patches, amber to dark brown eyes, wide-set fold-over ears (sometimes upright), and a blocky short body and legs.

Jackadoodles need to stay occupied or they can become destructive. They're also loud dogs that bark to alert, even if it's someone just passing by or when they're playing. They adore learning new skills and excel at anything that involves heavy action, making them ideal performance dogs. Jackapoos can live from 12 to 15 years.

Size

Jackadoodles typically reach 10 to 12 inches at the shoulder and weigh 10 to 30 pounds, depending on the size of the Poodle parent.

Appearance

Besides their normally scruffy to curly coat and short stature, they can come in numerous color combinations. Jack Russells already have the possibility of white, tan, brown, or black, all mixed together or in patches. Poodle genetics offer the possibility of red, brown, silver, and apricot, too. Both breeds are low shedding, so the breed combination is certain to leave very few dust bunnies around. This doesn't mean low grooming, however. Jackadoodles still require a good brushing several times a week, as well as ear cleaning to prevent infections. Jackadoodles with the more Poodle-type coats may require professional grooming every couple of months as well.

Health

Jackadoodles are a hearty, healthy breed mix. Poodles tend to have specific health issues, but Jack Russell Terriers don't have many common health concerns, unless they're poorly bred, in which case any of the following can appear: luxating patella, deafness, arthritis (as a senior or if injured early in life), cataracts (also age-related), or thyroid problems. They also have food sensitivities such as chicken, pork, fish, corn, wheat, and peas. They thrive on a red meat or lamb diet with vegetables.

Life with a Jackadoodle

Jackadoodles may be small, but their exercise needs are big. They're highly energetic and, without appropriate training and exercise, can become very destructive and annoying. Although they do well with active older children, I don't recommend them as a pet for younger children or infants. Jackadoodles are opportunists, and a toddler carrying food is a prime target. They fare well with elderly or mobility-impaired residents, but there must be someone else in the family willing to train and exercise the dog. Suburban areas are the best situations for Jackadoodles. A securely fenced yard is a must — the fence must be at least 6 feet high (because they can jump very high) and the bottom of the fence should be buried (because they love to dig).

Labradoodle

Photograph by yhelfman / 123 RF

Originally bred to aid hunters in the field and retrieve from waterways, Labrador Retrievers prefer being partners with their human companions over being independent. They're hardy, stout, and strong-willed. Long a favorite breed for use in the field, they're also used today as assistance dogs and search-and-rescue dogs.

Labradoodles love their families and enjoy the company of other dogs and people. Nobody is a stranger to a Labradoodle, but they do alert when seeing something new or unknown. Their life span averages 10 to 14 years.

Size

Standard-size male Labradoodles (Labrador x Standard Poodle) can be anywhere from 70 to 100 pounds. Standard-size female Labradoodles can be anywhere from 60 to 78 pounds. Mini Labradoodles (Labrador mixed with a Miniature Poodle) range from 35 to 60 pounds.

Appearance

Labradoodles typically have a shaggy coat that requires regular trimming to remain clean and easily managed. Like their Poodle parents, Labradoodles don't shed much and shed hair can become caught in the coat and create knots. Coat colors range from tan to black and sometimes parti-colored if the Poodle parent is itself a parti-color. Typically, Labradoodles are black, brown, or tan.

They have long legs, long necks, and thin tails, like their Poodle parents. Their eye color ranges from brown to amber and ears fold over. Labradoodle noses can be anywhere from black to light brown to pink, depending on the coloration of their parents.

Health

Labradoodles have the possibility of hip or elbow dysplasia. They have large, fast-maturing bodies and high energy levels. Without a solid bone structure, joints can suffer. Labradoodles are also prone to eye disorders, such as PRA or cataracts. Because Poodles can develop Addison's disease, this can also occur in a Labradoodle. Skin disorders are also possible, such as sebaceous adenitis. Another condition that can occur in Labradoodles is von Willebrand's disease, which appears in both Poodles and Labs.

Labradoodles are prone to ear infections. Lymphoma is also common as Labradoodles reach middle age. Epilepsy is common in poorly bred Labradoodles and even in some very carefully bred dogs. Inflammatory bowel disease (IBD) has been a common issue with Labs and is now often seen in Labradoodles as well.

Life with a Labradoodle

As with many Doodles, there are stark personality differences between a Miniature-size Labradoodle and a Standard-size Labradoodle because the Miniature Poodle and Standard Poodle tend to have different personalities. Miniature Poodles are more confident, learn faster, and are less sensitive and reserved. For this reason, Mini Labradoodles are easier to train, more social and outgoing, and less reactive.

Labradoodles are very active dogs. They need a safely fenced yard or large acreage to satisfy their energy levels. This is not the type of dog to have if you live in the city or in a small home. Don't consider this breed mix unless you have a safely fenced yard, or at least access to one. If you must be away from home for long periods of time, consider doggy daycare.

As a highly active breed mix, Labradoodles are well matched with older children, young adults, and other active families. Be sure to socialize your dog — many Labradoodles can be quite reserved with new people. Keeping your Labradoodle stimulated with a lot of interactive toys, going out and exploring new places, and meeting new people will be important in creating a well-balanced dog.

Maltipoo

Photograph by Jim Vallee / 123 RF

Maltipoos are a cross between a Maltese and a Toy Poodle (or, less commonly, the Miniature Poodle), creating a sweet, cuddly, and intelligent dog who is great with people of all ages and all living conditions. You can hardly find a calmer, more forgiving Doodle than a Maltipoo.

Maltese have been a popular Toy-size dog for centuries. The breed enjoyed the popularity of wealthy Romans in 1500 BCE and its popularity has extended to modern times. Maltese are also part of early Christianity — the Apostle Paul was gifted a Maltese from the Roman Governor Publius. After the fall of Rome, the Chinese kept the breed alive, crossing them with their own Toy breeds, refining the Maltese to their current appearance.

Most Maltipoos are mixed with either Miniature Poodles or Toy Poodles. Because the idea is to keep them on the small side, it's far more common to use the genetics of the Toy Poodle than the Miniature. Their life span averages 12 to 17 years.

Size

Maltipoos are typically 8 to 14 inches tall at the shoulder and weigh 8 to 20 pounds. The size depends on the size of the Poodle parent.

Appearance

The majority of Maltipoos have white fur that can range from the Maltese's long silky coat to the tight curls of a Poodle. They have a small but stout and sturdy body, with dark brown eyes and black nose. Maltipoos have a wide forehead, which also means wide-set droopy ears. They're primarily white, though sometimes they can be gray or tan or have several coat colors.

Health

Like many Toy breeds, Maltipoos are prone to dental problems, as well as Legg-Calve-Perthes disease, *portosystemic shunt* (where the normal blood flow to the liver is reduced or absent), patellar luxation (in which the knee joint disengages), and PRA, as well as epilepsy and *shaker syndrome* (full body tremors that generally manifest by 2 years of age and can cause seizures later in life). A diet rich in red meat proteins will be important to prevent skin disorders due to food allergies.

WARNING

Many Toy-size dogs are prone to leg issues such as Legg-Calve-Perthes disease, patellar luxation, and portosystemic shunt. Pairing *two* Toy-size dogs together can create a higher possibility of these health issues.

Life with a Maltipoo

Maltipoos are great in any environment, as long as they have companionship. They make great apartments dogs, as well as excellent suburban or rural canine companions. They're also great with people of all ages because they're forgiving, even tempered, and patient. But, like many small dogs, if not properly trained, they can become quite annoying with excessive barking, resource guarding, and not responding to cues quickly.

This breed mix loves to play and cuddle. Maltipoos can go from super playful (outlasting most young children) to enjoying a nap on the lap of your elderly parent. They're the Doodles who have it all. This makes them easy pets for any living situation. They also tend to live harmoniously with cats and other dogs, making them an ideal canine for a multi-pet family. Maltipoos are easy to train. In fact, they're quite good with learning complicated concepts and responding to cues in high-distraction areas. This makes them perfect candidates as emotional support, therapy, and assistance dogs for those with hearing or mobility challenges.

Pekapoo

Photograph by Wirestock, Inc. / Alamy Stock Photo

Pekapoos are a result of pairing a Pekingese, a long-haired, short-legged Toy breed with a Miniature Poodle or Toy Poodle. The Pekapoo has been around since the 1950s, as one of the oldest Poodle mixes, way before Doodles were popular.

Pekingese were originally from China, where they were a favorite of emperors and royal households. From the beginning, they were lap dogs and pampered pets. Their round bodies and rolling gait were bred into their structure to keep them from running away from court, but they're also very aware of their surroundings, barking in alarm at any intruders.

Pekapoos live an average of 11 to 15 years. Their life span is affected by maintaining a proper weight, grooming, keeping them out of excessive heat (due to respiratory issues), and handling them careful (they can be horribly injured if they're stepped on). Pekapoos are hardier than their Pekingese parent but still very fragile.

Size

The best way to estimate the size a Pekapoo puppy will reach when mature is to consider their parents. Pekapoos are generally 11 inches at the shoulder and can weigh 15 to 20 pounds. But if one of the parents is a Toy Poodle, instead of a Miniature Poodle, that can reduce the offspring's overall size by a couple inches, to 6 to 9 inches at the shoulder and 7 to 14 pounds.

Appearance

Pekapoos are usually have a more elongated torso, like a Dachshund, though not quite as pronounced. They usually have long, wavy hair, which requires regular grooming. Their snouts are longer than the short-nosed Pekingese, and their ears are bigger though droopy, like both parents. Their eyes tend to be less bulging than those of a Pekingese, making them easier to keep clean.

Pekapoo coat color can favor either parent. Although Pekingese sometimes have face masks (hair a darker color than the rest of their bodies), this trait doesn't appear as often in Pekapoos, who tend to be all one color. Pekapoos can be black, brown, silver, or cream, depending largely on the color of their parents.

Health

Besides being prone to the typical health problems of Poodles — PRA, leg problems, liver problems, and skin problems — Pekapoos can inherit some specific health issues from their Pekingese parents, including heart murmurs, heart failure, organ system problems, eye ulcers, respiratory distress (largely depending on the length of the nose), glaucoma, and eye fluid drainage issues. Many of the Pekingese health problems are related to how they've been specialized over millennia to have short noses, bulging eyes, and unnaturally short legs. The addition of Poodle blood does offer them more vitality, depending on which genes they inherit.

Life with a Pekapoo

Pekapoos adjust well to most environments but thrive in apartments or small homes. They're a favorite of retired seniors and families with older children or respectful young children. Pekapoos need some exercise every day, but not excessive amounts. Most Pekapoos are happiest when nestled on a lap and being stroked.

Pekapoos are super watchdogs and can be great hearing assistance dogs, too. They require early training and socialization, however, or they can bark excessively, engage in resource guarding, and run off after squirrels. Be sure to keep your Pekapoo in a temperature-controlled environment, because excessive heat (including outdoors) can endanger their health. Be sure to take daily walks when the temperature isn't above 80 degrees.

Pomapoo

Photograph courtesy of Brianna Daniel

Pomapoos are the result of breeding Pomeranians with Toy Poodles. Both parents are very small dogs, so you're sure to have a small Doodle as a result. What isn't certain, however, is whether you'll get a full straight coat or one full of curls. Pomapoos are sweet dogs who can adjust to almost any living situation and make great canine companions.

Pomeranians are a genetic mutation of German and Polish sled dogs, such as the Spitz of Northern Europe. By choosing smaller and smaller dogs to breed together, they created the Pomeranian, which averages about 30 pounds. When Queen Victoria came across Pomeranians on a trip to Northern Europe, she brought some home and became a Pomeranian breeder and exhibitor. Through her breeding programs, she further reduced their size to their current stature.

Pomapoos are bold, demanding, and inquisitive. They have a double coat; the undercoat is full and dense, and the outer coat is coarser and longer. Their tails lift up over and onto their backs and are heavily plumed. Pomapoos are affectionate with their families, intelligent, and alert, but they can be reserved with strangers, tend to bark excessively, and don't generally accept new dogs quickly. Early and consistent training is necessary, or they'll bark at everything, engage in resource guarding and fear biting, and be reactive. Their average life span is 12 to 14 years.

Size

Pomapoos average 8 to 10 inches at the shoulder and 7 to 9 pounds, similar in size and structure to their Pomeranian parent, but their size largely depends on the size of the Poodle parent.

Appearance

Though small in stature like their Pomeranian parent, they're finer boned and their fur isn't as thick because their Poodle parent has only one coat instead of two. They tend to have small, dark eyes with black noses, though their nose color can be brown in the lighter-colored varieties. Pomapoo coat color depends on their parents — both have color variations between black, brown, and white. The rarer colors are apricot, silver, or parti-colored and tend to be more expensive. Pomapoos have small, short noses, and ears that can't decide if they're upright or folded over — it depends on their mood and the wind speed.

Health

Pomapoos can be prone to any of the health concerns that are common to both Pomeranians and Toy Poodles. These include the luxating patella, dental problems, *alopecia* (hair loss), as well as the typical allergies of Poodles, but also issues particular to Pomeranians, such as hypothyroid, tracheal collapse, Cushing's disease, pancreatitis, and numerous respiratory concerns. They can also have chronic weight issues, which can exacerbate other health problems. Keeping them at an appropriate weight will enhance their health, resulting in a longer life span.

Life with a Pomapoo

Pomapoos are highly adaptable. They thrive in any environment where they're respected, properly exercised, and well educated. They're the perfect dog for urban living or a small home, because they don't require large yards for exercise (though they do enjoy them). They also fare well in suburban areas but tend to bark a lot at new people and other animals.

If you have young children, always watch them when your Pomapoo is present — a rambunctious youngster can inadvertently injure a small dog. Pomapoos fare well with older children and play well with them for long periods of time, but they're equally happy dozing in someone's lap, making them ideal for elderly people or those who are mobility impaired.

Pugadoodle (Pugapoo)

Photograph by memejojo / Stockimo / Alamy Stock Photo

The Pugadoodle (also known as the Pugapoo) is the resulting of breeding a Pug and either a Toy Poodle or a Miniature Poodle. The offspring of this pairing is a sweet little dog who enjoys the entire family, as well as most other pets. They're outgoing, easy to care for, and not generally very noisy, but they will bark when someone is at the door. When young, Pugadoodles are very energetic, but they mature into proper lap dogs.

Pugs are an ancient breed that can be traced back 2,000 years. They were a favorite of Chinese emperors, who preferred flat-faced dog breeds. It wasn't until 1500, when Dutch traders returned from China with some Pugs, that they began gaining in popularity with Europeans, especially in Great Britain. Pugs are small, short-haired dogs with short legs and wrinkly faces. Their noses are nearly nonexistent, with bulging eyes, small fold-over ears, and strong-willed personalities.

The Pugadoodle has many Pug characteristics, but much of the Pug's structure, which might cause health concerns, is improved upon with the addition of the Poodle genes. Pugadoodles have actual muzzles, allowing for easier breathing. Their eyes aren't as bugged out, which reduces the risk of injury, and their temperaments are less willful. Their life span averages 12 to 14 years, depending on which breed's genetics are more prominent in their DNA.

Size

Pugadoodles tend to be between 10 to 14 inches at the shoulder, depending on the size of the Poodle parent (on the shorter side with a Toy Poodle parent). They're solid little dogs and weigh more than they appear, at 9 to 14 pounds.

Appearance

Pugs have a short, smooth coat, but the Pugadoodle can have either a short, rough coat or a wavy or curly coat. Depending on the dominant parent's genes, the coat can be short or long. The longer the coat, the more often it needs grooming. Their coat color is generally solid, with some having a dark brown or black mask on their faces, like Pugs. Colors range from black to fawn or cream, as well as any combination of shades of brown.

Where Pugs have a flat face, Pugadoodles rarely do. This is a blessing because Pugs have respiratory problems due to their *brachycephalic* (short- and broad-headed) anatomy. Pugadoodles are not a stout as Pugs, but they're still short with solid bodies, and some may have some skin wrinkles around their faces. The majority of Pugadoodles appear scruffy and cute, with dark eyes and black noses.

Health

Along with the typical Poodle health concerns, such as luxating patella, Addison's disease, and skin problems, Pugadoodles can also be prone to eye problems if they favor their Pug parent. Their bug eyes have a name: *brachycephalic ocular syndrome.* If your Pugadoodle has wrinkled skin, they can experience skin-fold dermatitis, which can turn into a bacterial infection known as pyoderma; keeping those skin folds clean will go a long way toward preventing this problem. Also, keeping your Pugadoodle's eyes clean with a regular saline wash may prevent damage from debris.

Life with a Pugadoodle

Pugs were bred to be lap dogs and so were Toy Poodles, though quite a bit more energetic. The Pugadoodle is somewhere in between. You can count on your Pugadoodle being very active and curious as a puppy and more settled into their life as lap dog upon maturity. Pugadoodles need daily exercise and socialization with other dogs. Although they're highly trainable, they can still be independent and willful. Consistency and patience are key to achieving success.

Pyredoodle

Photograph courtesy of Logan Bradley

If ever there was a great Doodle, the Pyredoodle is certainly one of them. Mixing the Great Pyrenees with a Standard Poodle creates a super sweet and intelligent puppy. Great Pyrenees may have a strong guarding instinct and Poodles have a reserved attitude, so, put together, they make well-mannered, great-tempered offspring who are a joy to have in your life.

Great Pyrenees have been helping farmers in Northern Europe since 1800, protecting their livestock herds. These large dogs not only discourage predators, but also fearlessly confront them. Their heavy, multilayer coats protect them from the chill of northern mountain winters and insulate them from heat during the summer. They're family oriented but also very independent. With intruders, they can be ruthless.

Pyredoodles are fantastic companions and adore being part of the family. They're large boned and very hairy, and they can inherit droopy jowls from their Great Pyrenees parent, which means you can expect a lot of saliva flying around when they shake their large heads or drink from their water bowls. Most of the time, they prefer to relax and lay around, but the moment your Pyredoodle senses an intruder, they're alert and on the job.

Size

Great Pyrenees are giant dogs. Mixing them with Standard Poodles doesn't reduce their offspring's size at maturity by much. Adult male Pyredoodles can stand 27 to 32 inches tall at the shoulder and weigh over 100 pounds. Females can be notably smaller, by about 2 inches and 20 pounds.

Appearance

If you want a big, fluffy dog, the Pyredoodle is it! Don't count on a nonshedding dog, however. When Great Pyrenees shake, they create a snowstorm of hair going everywhere; adding Poodle genes reduces that blizzard but won't get rid of it entirely. Pyredoodles have big, blocky heads; large, rounded muzzles; thick, droopy ears; and big, brown eyes. Their paws resemble those of a Sasquatch more than a dog, but that's part of their charm!

Health

Besides the typical Poodle health concerns, Pyredoodles are prone to problems similar to the their Great Pyrenees parent, as well as their Poodle parent, including hip dysplasia, PRA and neurological or immune deficiencies. Cancer is also common in Pyredoodles, as is bloat.

WARNING

Bloat is a common health concern with large, deep-chested dogs. If not caught immediately and treated, it can be fatal. Many pet parents of dogs with these conformation attributes have their dog's stomachs tacked when they're spayed or neutered in order to prevent this deadly situation.

Life with a Pyredoodle

Pyredoodles are large and in charge, and you can bet they'll need to blow off some steam. Play time with other large puppies, a run in the park, or a few days a week at a doggy daycare will meet their needs. They'll be a great alarm dog when someone comes to your house, naturally knowing when to protect your family. Be sure to train your Pyredoodle as a puppy so they understand that they don't own the house and everyone in it. Be observant when they're around small children, older folks, or people with mobility issues — their size can be formidable when they're running or playing. Pyredoodles should not be housed in an urban area. Even a suburban area may be challenging unless you have a large, securely fenced yard. Pyredoodles fare best in rural environments, with lots of room to move around and a quiet home life.

Sheepadoodle

Photograph by MCCAIG / Getty Images

Sheepadoodles are the result of pairing an Old English Sheepdog with a Standard Poodle or Miniature Poodle. Sheepadoodles are one of the larger Doodles, but they are super sweet and make great family companions.

Old English Sheepdogs have been around for hundreds of years. They were bred in England as a drover's helper to drive and guard sheep herds. Some of their genetics include Bearded Collies and Russian Owtchars. They're big enough to be formidable for the sheep and appear like sheep with their bobbed tails; long, droopy ears; long fur; and gray and white coloring.

Mixing Old English Sheepdogs with Standard Poodles makes a great Doodle for families with active lifestyles. They tend to herd a bit, so keep an eye on young children when near the Sheepadoodle. They require lots of interaction and grooming, just like their Old English Sheepdog parents. The average life span of an Old English Sheepdog is 10 to 11 years, but Sheepadoodles tend to live longer thanks to their Poodle parents; Sheepadoodles average 12 to 14 years, with the smaller varieties living longer than the larger ones.

Size

Sheepadoodles reach 18 to 28 inches at the shoulder and 50 to 80 pounds. If an Old English Sheepdog is bred to a Miniature Poodle, however, creating a Mini Sheepadoodle, the offspring are typically less than 20 inches tall at the shoulder and weigh 24 to 45 pounds, depending on the size of the Poodle parent.

Appearance

Sheepadoodles are big, fluffy dogs with big, blocky heads; long, silky ears; big brown eyes; and long muzzles with black noses. Their long, wavy coats can be either the double coat of their Old English Sheepdog parent or the single coat of their Poodle parent. Either way, their coat needs lots of brushing and regular clipping. They can be either solid black, black and white, or gray and white. Some breeders create tri-color, brown, blue, sable, brindle, and merle colorings.

Health

Along with the possibility of the typical Poodle health concerns, Sheepadoodles are prone to hip dysplasia, cataracts, glaucoma, *entropion* (a condition where the eyelid folds inward, causing discomfort and vision problems), thyroid problems, deafness, diabetes, PRA, food sensitivities, and heatstroke. Cancer is also common.

Life with a Sheepadoodle

Sheepadoodles are highly energetic, so they fare best living in an environment where they can exercise a lot. They thrive in suburban or rural areas where they have lots space and time to run. Without appropriate exercise, Sheepadoodles can become very annoying. They tend to be highly boisterous as puppies but do settle down some as adults. They don't do well left alone for long hours and can develop separation anxiety if regularly left alone. They're great with older children and active adults, but think twice before getting one if you have young children, elderly parents, or mobility-impaired residents in your home.

You must train a Sheepadoodle. Begin the process as early as possible and continue through adulthood. A trained Sheepadoodle is a joy. An untrained Sheepadoodle, with nothing to occupy their time, is a disaster. Although they can do quite well as therapy dogs, it's a long road to attain that title.

Be prepared for daily brushing, monthly trips to the dog groomer, weekly ear cleaning, and keeping their eyes clear of debris (including their hair).

Shihdoodle (Shihpoo)

Photograph by Wirestock, Inc. / Alamy Stock Photo

The Shihdoodle is a mix of the Shih Tzu (a Toy breed) and a Toy Poodle, in order to maintain the small size. The result is a great lap dog who is intelligent, confident, and, at times, energetic.

At just 4 to 10 pounds, Shih Tzus were developed as lap warmers for Chinese royalty and pampered as the empire's treasures. Breeders who produced the most beautiful dogs were handsomely paid. The breed was not known to the outside world until the 1930s, when they were shipped to other countries and became popular house pets.

The mixing of Shih Tzus with Toy Poodles or Miniature Poodles results in a cute and sweet canine companion for any environment. It's tough not to cater to their every whim and spoil them, because they're endearing to everyone they meet.

Shihdoodles have a relatively long life span of 13 to 16 years, provided they're fed a high-quality diet and kept well groomed.

Size

Shihdoodles can stand 8 to 11 inches tall at the shoulder and weigh 4 to 16 pounds, depending on the size of their Poodle parent.

Appearance

Shihdoodles' coats can be a variety of colors including white with black, white with tan, white with brown, white with apricot, or just one color, favoring the Poodle parent.

Although they have short noses, they aren't brachycephalic like their Shih Tzu parent, giving them a healthier respiratory system. Their little fold-over ears are wide set, as are their dark eyes and black noses. Their bodies are longer in length than their legs are high, with a little upward swing in the rear and, possibly, a curled tail over their backs.

Health

Shi-doodles can experience any number of health problems common to their parent breeds. These include dental problems, skin problems, hypothyroidism, patellar luxation, renal dysplasia, lung disorders, von Willebrand disease, and spinal disorders. Cleft palate is also a possibility.

Life with a Shihdoodle

Shihdoodles make great canine companions. They're easy to train and intelligent, and they enjoy being with their pet parents. Many Shih Tzus can be stubborn, but a Shihdoodle is unlikely to display this type of behavior due to their Poodle genes.

Shihdoodles love children of all ages and tend to live harmoniously with them, whether in an urban or suburban environment. They're happy to relax on a lap or run in the yard chasing a ball. When trained and mature, Shihdoodles make great therapy dogs. They love attention, and anybody is welcome to participate in giving it.

Sproodle

Photograph courtesy of Anna Hodges

Sproodles are the result of mixing an English Springer Spaniel with a Miniature Poodle or Toy Poodle (they can be mixed with Standard Poodles, but most breeders use the smaller Poodle varieties because the offspring tend to have more family-oriented personalities). The result is a super family dog who is active, intelligent, and low shedding.

English Springer Spaniels are great companions for any type of family. Centuries ago, before the reliance on firearms, Springers aided hunters in detecting, flushing, and retrieving upland game birds, such as pheasants and grouse. They prefer to work closely with their human partners and are easy to train. They can go from working partner during the day to foot warmer at night.

Sproodles are the ideal combination of Poodle and Springer Spaniel, because both breeds were created as hunting partners and family companions. This hybrid is social and easy to train. Whether you want a hiking companion, performance partner, or cuddle buddy, a Sproodle is ready.

Size

Sproodles tend to be 19 to 20 inches at the shoulder and weigh anywhere from 30 to 45 pounds. The Mini Sproodles (with Toy Poodle parents) are noticeably smaller at 13 to 15 inches at the shoulder and 15 to 25 pounds.

Appearance

Their overall square appearance is not just in their bodies, but also in their head shapes. Springers have squarish heads and often pass that trait to their offspring. Sproodle noses may be slightly narrower than the Springer nose, but they're still black (or dark brown if the Sproodle is of the liver-and-white variety). Their beautiful, thick ears droop down, with long, silky fur covering them. Sproodle hair is just one layer, often very wavy to highly curly. Their coloring can be black and white, dark brown (liver) and white, all black, all tan, or tricolor (with black, white, and tan, or brown, white, and tan).

Health

The English Springer Spaniel is a very healthy, hearty breed. In Sproodles, you should be watchful for the typical Poodle health concerns. Their heavy, droopy ears require regular cleaning to prevent ear infections. If poorly bred, Sproodles can be prone to hip or elbow dysplasia or eye problems, such as cataracts.

Life with a Sproodle

Sproodles are great with family members of all ages. They prefer to always be part of the family unit, and, if left alone, they can get into mischief. As an active breed, they require lots of exercise and early training. Sproodles aren't ideal for an urban area or apartment living. A fenced-in yard will go a long way toward keeping your Sproodle in a good frame of mind. Sproodles tend to do well with other pets and are rarely shy with strangers. They're hard workers and enjoy any type of activity where they can run, retrieve, chase, and stimulate their mind (which makes the Sproodle an ideal performance dog).

Whoodle (Wheatenpoo)

Photograph by Deborah Van Kirk / Alamy Stock Photo

The Whoodle is a cross between the Soft Coated Wheaten Terrier and a Standard Poodle or Miniature Poodle. The typical Whoodle is a terrier mixed with a Standard Poodle, but with the popularity of smaller Doodles, some breeders are using Miniature Poodle parents to downsize the offspring.

Soft Coated Wheaten Terriers were developed as all-around farm dogs in Ireland by mixing Kerry Blue Terriers and Irish Terriers. Although tenacious enough to keep the farm clear of rats and other vermin, they also fared well in the farmhouse, keeping people's feet warm. They're high energy and intelligent, with long, wavy fur and natural goatees on their chins.

Whoodles are a very recent addition to the Doodle phenomenon. They're quickly gaining in popularity because they tend to fit in well in numerous environments, from farms to suburban households. Whoodles are great with children of all ages. They're rare, however, and tend to be expensive. Their average life span is 10 to 14 years.

Size

Standard Whoodles (Soft Coated Wheaten Terrier x Standard Poodle) are generally 16 to 20 inches at the shoulder and weigh 40 to 70 pounds. Mini Whoodles (Soft Coated Wheaten Terrier x Miniature Poodle) are smaller, at around 15 inches at the shoulder and 25 to 40 pounds.

Appearance

Whoodles are medium-size dogs with a stocky build. Their long, wavy hair is similar to that of a Poodle in that it's just one layer that continuously grows. The added Poodle genes mean a tighter curl or more wave than the typical Soft Coated Wheaten Terrier. Whoodles can be any color of tan, with brown variations mixed in, or even some white on the chest and feet. Whoodle puppies tend to be darker in color than they are when they mature. They have dark brown eyes and round muzzles with black noses. Whoodles are as close to a teddy bear as a dog can be, especially when they're puppies.

Health

Soft Coated Wheaten Terriers have some unique health risks, including *protein-losing nephropathy* (a kidney disease) and *protein-losing enteropathy* (a gastrointestinal ailment). As with Poodles, Addison's disease can be a genetic health issue. With your Whoodle's fold-over ears and heavy flap, air won't circulate well to dry the ear canals if they become wet and trap debris. Be sure to clean your Whoodle's ears twice a week to prevent ear infections. A good diet rich in red meat proteins will also go a long way toward preventing food sensitivity reactions, which can cause skin irritations.

Life with a Whoodle

Whoodles are a high-energy breed, especially when less than 2 years old. They require the direction and regimentation of training, beginning when they're puppies. A Whoodle who is guided well, with positive associations, will mature into a confident, well-behaved dog who's a pleasure to have in your home. Whoodles need room to exercise and be allowed to do so often. They're highly social and love playing with other dogs, which is a great way to alleviate their pent-up energy and anxiety, preventing destruction due to boredom.

Although Whoodles make great performance dogs in a variety of venues, they aren't recommended for therapy work because they're easily distracted and rarely settle well enough to remain calm for long periods of time.

Yorkipoo (Yorkidoodle)

Photograph by Farlap / Alamy Stock Photo

Yorkipoos may be small, but they have big personalities! They're a combination of Yorkshire Terriers, the smallest AKC-recognized terrier breed, and Toy Poodles. Yorkipoos are athletic and territorial, love to play, and enjoy lap time. Their small size makes them the perfect dogs for urban areas or apartment living, but they also thrive in suburban and rural environments.

Yorkshire Terriers originated in Yorkshire, England, a product of Scottish immigrants who wanted a dog to hunt vermin in the cotton and woolen mills where they worked. They mixed black-and-tan terriers from Scotland (not Scottish Terriers), with Paisley Terriers and possibly Maltese to attain their soft, silky coats. The result is a very tenacious dog, when aroused, and a desire to finish the job no matter the consequences. Yorkshire Terriers mature rarely are more than 6 inches at the shoulder and weigh about 7 pounds. Their coats are considered hypoallergenic because they don't shed much. The coat color is a combination of gray and tan, or black and cream.

Mixing a Yorkshire Terrier with a Toy Poodle enhances their intelligence and athletic abilities. The mix may also add some size to the offspring. Where a Yorkshire Terrier may resource guard or insist on being king of the house, the Poodle genes tamp down those tendencies a bit, giving the Yorkipoo more confidence and ability to share. Both parent dogs have low-shed coats, so this is a great dog to have if you suffer from allergies. Both parents also have a tendency for excessive barking; training and socializing early will reduce this behavior. Yorkipoos can live anywhere from 11 to 15 years.

Size

Yorkipoos are slightly larger than their Yorkshire Terrier parent, because Toy Poodles are bigger than Yorkshire Terriers. They average 7 to 15 inches at the shoulder and 3 to 14 pounds. This greatly depends on the size of both parents.

Appearance

The Yorkipoo can have a slightly wavy, silky coat, or a tighter, curly coat. The coat color can be the gray and tan of the Yorkshire Terrier parent to the Toy Poodle's coloring. Yorkipoos can be small boned, appearing fragile like the Yorkshire Terrier, or a bit more robust, like the Poodle. Either way, you can be certain the Yorkipoo will be small and fit nicely on your lap for a long snooze.

Health

Yorkipoos can suffer from many of the same health issues as Toy Poodles, including Addison's disease, portosystemic shunt, epilepsy, patellar luxation, Legg-Calve-Perthes disease, and hypothyroidism. Mixing two Toy-size dogs together enhances the possibility of any of these health issues being prominent.

Life with a Yorkipoo

Because Yorkipoos are very small, they fit in well in a small home or apartment. They're great with people of all ages, but they don't appreciate a lot of commotion in the household. Also, keep an eye on your dog at all times when they're with young children. Yorkipoos fare very well with the elderly or mobility challenged. They can relieve themselves in a litter box or on a pee pad if they don't have access to an outside relief area. As long as they get a bit of exercise every day, they're happy to relax and cuddle for long periods of time.

As with all dogs, be sure to train and socialize your Yorkipoo when they're young. Puppies learn quickly and enjoy the process. Adult dogs need to be redirected from inappropriate behavior for them to learn some concepts that are very easily taught to a puppy. Your Yorkipoo will be thrilled to chase toys down a hall or in a yard, making them great companions for children of all ages. They're also great comfort dogs — they thoroughly enjoy being fussed over and getting lots of attention!

2

Your Very Own Doodle

Chapter **4**

Pick a Doodle

There's a lot more to finding the perfect Doodle than looking in the classified section of your local newspaper or in a pet shop. In fact, those are the *last* places to look! This chapter helps you locate a Doodle and gives you the information you need to ensure your Doodle will be healthy and fit into your lifestyle.

After you locate a Doodle, you need to make sure they're the right one for your family. Not every dog fits into every home. This chapter gives you the tools to perform temperament tests, so you can be sure you're bringing home a lifelong Doodle companion.

Finding Your Doodle

After you decide on the type of Doodle that's right for you, it's time to find the right breeder. There are three tried-and-true sources for locating breeders: the Internet, Doodle owners, and dog groomers.

Searching the web

The first place you might think to start when you're looking for a Doodle breeder is the Internet. You can search on the type of Doodle you're looking for and the word *breeder*, and you'll find options. Depending on the popularity of the type of

Doodle you're interested in, you might also narrow the search with your state or region. For example, you could search for "Sproodle breeder" or "Goldendoodle breeder Pacific Northwest."

Doodle owners

Most people who own Doodles rave about the breeder they got their dog from. The best form of advertising is a happy customer. Of course, these folks may be a bit biased (as everyone thinks their dog is the best), so you still have to do your research and determine whether the breeder meets *your* standards.

If you have a friend or neighbor with the type of Doodle you want, get to know their Doodle really well, not just in passing along a walk. Ask questions about their dog's health, behavior with dogs and people, ease of training, and behavior in the home and while traveling.

Groomers

Dog groomers see Doodles every day. They know the dogs who are easy to groom and those who are difficult. Generally, the first couple of groomings are challenging, but a wise Doodle learns to go with the flow because their experiences teach them what to expect.

BROKERS VERSUS BREEDERS

Your search results will likely turn up a couple different kinds of sites. Some sites will have one or two types of Doodles; others will have numerous types of Doodles. The former is a breeder; the latter, a broker.

Broker websites offer lots of different types of Doodles, and they ensure that their puppies are not from puppy mills, but brokers still sell large amounts of puppies with little ability to actually visit the breeders or speak at length with them about their breeding program. You'll see pages of puppies listed, as well as their prices. But brokers are *not* who you want to buy your puppy from.

Breeders show pictures and descriptions of their breeding dogs. They also show the parent pairings and samples of their past offspring. Some list upcoming litters. Many have purchase contracts on their sites explaining how to reserve a puppy and their cost. They also offer health guarantees of one to two years. A reputable breeder is what you're looking for. In this chapter, I help you identify which breeders are good and which to steer clear of.

Most groomers know how to handle a wiggly dog or one who is feeling anxious. They also have experience with dogs who may become aggressive when their feet are handled or try to get hold of the brush as it's going through their coat.

Some groomers keep their clients' dogs' information on file. It helps remind them if the dog has any quirks, dislikes, or fears while on the grooming table or in the bath. Some of that information may include the dog's breeder. Also, many groomers tend to have favorite breeds. They probably know the breeders of their favorite dogs.

Groomers don't always know good breeders, but if you know a good groomer, it's worth asking.

Identifying a Reputable Breeder

When you're looking for a Doodle, you want one who will have a long, happy, healthy life. To do this, you can't settle on the first breeder you come across, or the breeder who's closest to you. You may need to spend some time looking before you find the right one, and you may need to be willing to travel some distance to visit the breeder and eventually pick up your puppy.

Looking at the different kinds of breeders

There are several categories of breeders: professional breeders, commercial breeders (also known as puppy mills), and backyard breeders. The following sections explain the differences.

Professional breeders

A professional, reputable breeder cares about the betterment of the breed. Because Doodles are actually a mixed breed, it can be more difficult to locate a breeder who really cares about the betterment of Doodles than it would be to find, say, a Poodle breeder who cares about the betterment of Poodles. Doodle breeders aren't breeding for a specific physical attribute that will enhance a purebred dog the way Poodle breeders are. But Doodle breeders *are* breeding for size, coat color, coat type, and sometimes a sound mind. This last attribute — a sound mind — is one that's in short supply in the Doodle world, so if you find a breeder who specifically talks about this, take note!

In the world of Doodle breeding, health testing of parent dogs is very rare. Many purebred dog breeders do these tests to ensure that they don't breed puppies who inherit bad health traits (such as weak hearts, cataracts, or hip dysplasia). Few

Doodle breeders take the time to test parent dogs, but a breeder who really cares about the dogs they produce *will* put in the effort.

Most reputable breeders sell their puppies with a spay/neuter clause in the contract. This is important to them because they don't want to see their puppies turned into puppy mill victims or fall prey to a backyard breeder's get-rich-quick scheme. Some do it to reduce the chance that you become competition.

Most breeding kennels must have U.S. Department of Agriculture (USDA) certification. In order to get USDA certification, a breeder has to pass a rigorous inspection. All dogs must live in spacious, clean areas and receive good-quality food. Professional breeders automatically do these things anyway, so getting USDA certification isn't difficult for them.

A reputable breeder will screen potential purchasers of their puppies, too. They often have a policy of taking back any puppy who doesn't work out with their families, so they want to take steps to ensure this doesn't happen often.

Commercial breeders or puppy mills

A commercial breeder makes a business out of breeding puppies on a large scale. They often breed more than one type of dog, cut cost corners wherever they can, and rarely back up the dogs they produce. Parent dogs are kept in small cages, often in filthy conditions, and bred until they die. The puppies are sent to brokers all over the world, who sell their puppies to unsuspecting purchasers who have no idea how to choose a reputable breeder.

Sometimes puppies are shipped sick, without the benefit of early vaccinations and wormings. Canine parvovirus (CPV), a deadly condition, is rampant in the kennels, and many of the puppies die during the shipping process. They rarely care who they sell the puppies to, and their health guarantees are generally only 30 days. They don't test the parent dogs for health conditions, and they often can't even tell you the genealogy of the parents. They won't take their puppies back if it doesn't work out with the family. Instead, these unwanted dogs end up in animal shelters, and the breeder doesn't care.

If you were allowed to see puppies at a commercial breeder (often, they don't allow people in to look), you might experience the following:

>> A strong smell of urine or feces and/or bleach

>> Parent dogs nowhere to be seen

>> Puppies not being socialized

>> Puppies being fed a poor diet, resulting in loose stool and bad body odor

REMEMBER

If you purchase a puppy from a commercial breeder, you're supporting the puppy mill, encouraging them to produce more dogs in these poor conditions. You'll also have a dog with numerous health problems, structural issues, and personality disorders.

WARNING

Some Doodle breeders operate commercial kennels and are trying to address the health and well-being of the puppies they produce by offering early training and socialization at a price — usually a *large* price. This training and socialization is merely an add-on to an already expensive puppy. The early training also means that the puppy will remain with the breeder for three more months, missing a very important bonding time with their new families, from 2 to 4 months of age. And you have little knowledge of the methods used to train the puppy. I've seen this firsthand with a Labradoodle breeder who charges $9,000 for a "trained" Labradoodle. The puppies are farmed out to their "trainers" (anybody who signed up for the job), and they use "balanced" training methods. In the dog-training world "balanced" means they're open to the use of choke chains, prong collars, and electronic collars. In all my decades of training Doodles, I've never seen the need to use these training tools to produce a well-behaved dog.

REMEMBER

A professional breeder will properly socialize their puppies until you pick them up at 7 or 8 weeks of age. They do this for free, because they care about how their puppies turn out.

Backyard breeders

Backyard breeders love their Doodles but don't know much about the breeding process. They just want to make more cute, sweet dogs like theirs. Sometimes they do it because they want to make some money. (Doodles sell for upwards of $2,500 each. A litter of six puppies can bring in at least $15,000.) Some backyard breeders offer puppies at less than the normal price of a well-bred dog in order to compete and be more attractive to purchasers.

Backyard breeders haven't educated themselves in how to test parent dogs for physical abnormalities, and they rarely care about the dogs' mental acuity. They also haven't thought about the physical stress involved for the puppies' mother.

Most of the time, backyard breeders provide decent living quarters for puppies, even socializing them with their children. Some provide good diets, but that's not always the case. They're primarily breeding their dogs to make money, and sometimes cutting corners is a choice they make.

They often breed their female dogs multiple times a year, which is physically stressful for the dogs. Pregnancy and birthing puppies takes a lot out of a female dog. Sometimes the mothers lose weight, drop coat, and become very stressed or even aggressive due to their discomfort.

Asking the right questions

When you contact a breeder for the first time, ask the following questions:

>> **How long have you been breeding dogs?** If the breeder tells you that they've been doing it for several years, there's a good chance they're knowledgeable about the process.

>> **How did you choose the parentage for this litter?** The breeder should discuss the good genetic background of the parentage (for example, good health and temperament).

>> **What types of health screenings were done on the parent dogs?** A responsible breeder will have the parents' hips, eyes, and hearts checked for abnormalities. Reputable breeders keep copious records of all dogs crossing their path. The breeders of planned litters generally have health tests performed on the dogs they intend to breed. These clearances give puppy breeders the ability to guarantee the health of the puppies for a period of time, generally up to a year.

>> **Can you give me the names and phone numbers of people who have bought puppies from you in the past?** A good breeder will be proud of their puppy placements. References shouldn't be a problem.

>> **What do you look for in a potential puppy purchaser?** A concerned breeder wants the best homes for their pups and will ask questions such as:

- Will the dog be left home alone for long periods of time?

- Do you have a fenced-in yard?

- Do you have other pets at home?

- Do you have young children?

- What is your lifestyle like? Are you active or more of a homebody?

Many breeders want to make sure their puppies go to the right home for them. Some breeders will help you choose the right puppy for your family because they know their puppies' personalities.

>> **Can you give me a copy of the pup's health records?** All pups should get their first worming at 5 weeks, another at 7 weeks, and their first vaccines at 7 weeks. The puppy pack should also contain proof of the dog parents' health clearances and genealogy.

REMEMBER

These are rare from Doodle breeders, but if they offer it, you've found a serious, reputable breeder!

>> **What are the puppies being fed?** If they're receiving a good-quality food, the breeder cares about giving the pups a good start. (More about nutrition in Chapter 7.)

Visiting a breeder

TIP

When you actually visit the home of a breeder, ask yourself the following questions:

>> **Is the odor overwhelmingly bad, tolerable, or nonexistent?** You want your puppy to come from a place that's clean, so the less offensive the odor, the better.

>> **Where are the puppies being contained?** If they're inside the breeder's home, they're likely to get lots of early socialization, which is very important to their future behavioral development. If they're outside in a kennel or merely with the mother, who is tied up outside, the pups probably aren't receiving the proper handling or care.

WARNING

You may be tempted to purchase a puppy who is living in dire circumstances, but think twice. Not only are you encouraging the situation by rewarding the bad breeder (who will just continue to breed and abuse dogs), but you'll likely be bringing home a dog with numerous health problems, as well as behavioral problems.

>> **How big is the operation?** Is this the breeder's profession? If so, the kennel may be large, but it shouldn't contain more than two different types of hybrid mixes.

>> **Do you see external parasites (such as fleas, flea eggs, ticks, and mange) on the puppies?** If the pups are kept outdoors in unsanitary conditions, they'll probably have one or more external parasites, along with some internal ones.

People who breed dogs professionally normally have the puppy parents — or at least the mother — on premises. These dogs are beloved pets, possibly show dogs, and they're kept in good-size exercise yards. Always ask to meet your potential puppy's parents.

Seeing the *sire* (father) and *dam* (mother) will give you a good idea of your Doodle's future size, appearance, and personality. But your puppy can take on the characteristics — coat color, size, structure, and personality — of either of their parents.

Here's a list of questions ask yourself when meeting the parents:

>> Are you happy with their size?

>> Are you happy with their coat color?

>> Are you happy with their personality?

REMEMBER

Your Doodle puppy is likely to have one, or all, of their parents' attributes, which is why it's so important to meet them. Environment has a lot to do with how a dog turns out, but genetics are the cornerstone of how your Doodle will interact with, and respond to, your family.

Getting health clearances

Few Doodle breeders go through the trouble of taking their parent dogs to be tested for health issues, but those who do really care about the puppies they're producing and should definitely be considered as the breeder for you. This is someone who has integrity and wants the best for the parent dogs, their puppies, and their customers.

The American Kennel Club (AKC) has a breed-specific list of suggested health clearances for parent dogs; you can find it at www.akc.org/breeder-programs/breed-health-testing-requirements. To determine which evaluations are recommended, find the breed of each parent in the list of breed groups (Sporting Group, Hound Group, and so on). The Poodle is listed in the Non-Sporting Group, but Table 4-1 lists the recommended tests for Poodle parents.

TABLE 4-1   **Recommended Health Tests for Poodle Parents**

	Hip Evaluation	Ophthalmologist Evaluation	Progressive Retinal Atrophy (PRA) Test	Patella Evaluation
Toy Poodle		X	X	X
Miniature Poodle	X	X	X	X
Standard Poodle	X	X		

Just as an example, let's say you're getting a Goldendoodle. The Poodle parent would need the health clearance listed in Table 4-1, and the Golden Retriever parent (part of the Sporting Group) would need the following:

>> Hip evaluation

>> Elbow evaluation

>> Cardiac exam

>> Ophthalmologist evaluation

>> Neuronal ceroid lipofuscinosis (NCL) DNA test (**Note:** NCL is a neurological disorder.)

Other health problems — including hypothyroidism, epilepsy, skin disease, and cancer — are common with Golden Retrievers, and a reputable breeder will check the health history of several generations of their breed lines to ensure that there was low to no occurrence of them.

REMEMBER

Despite multiple generations of health clearances, recessive genes can appear in any individual at any time. By purchasing a hybrid dog, you're actually reducing the possibility of breeding two dogs with the same recessive gene that can cause a health problem to occur.

EARLY PUPPY CARE AND EDUCATION

From the moment your Doodle puppy is born, they're learning. The way they experience the world will have an impact on who they become and how healthy they'll be. Responsibility for a puppy begins and ends with the effort and knowledge of the breeder, as well as the health of the mother.

A healthy mother dog will pass on all the antibodies your puppy will need from the time they're born until they've been fully vaccinated. These antibodies are passed through the mother's milk. A mother dog who calmly feeds her puppies will reduce the puppies' overall anxiety. If the mother is the type of dog who wants little to do with her puppies, it will be up to the breeder to hand-feed them. Few breeders will want to go through this process, so they usually only rebreed mother dogs who have a natural parenting ability.

Sometimes, however, an individual puppy will require some extra feeding because they're smaller than their siblings or too weak to remain with the litter. This requires special handling from the breeder. A less-than-perfect puppy may offer early challenges, but the special attention they receive has numerous benefits. They get more one-on-one handling, which translates into a more personable dog. Plus, their nutrition consumption is measured, ensuring they get everything they need to be strong and healthy.

(continued)

(continued)

A mother dog will do the initial puppy cleaning of the amniotic sacs, but most breeders are there to help. There are so many puppies coming that the mother dog can become tired. Having the breeder there will also ensure that the mother dog doesn't accidentally lay down on a newborn puppy. A first-time mother dog may be calmer with the reassurance of someone they know.

When the puppies open their eyes and begin to move around, they'll begin to relieve themselves faster than their mother can keep up with them. At this time, the breeder needs to change their bedding several times a day. At 3 weeks of age, they'll be moved to a larger area where they can move around more. And at 4 weeks, the mother dog will begin weaning the puppies of her milk as the breeder introduces solid, though mushy, food.

As the solid food goes in, more poop comes out. Besides keeping the area clean, there will also be some puppy cleaning to be done. At this point, it's totally up to the breeder because the mother dog will prefer to watch from a distance so the little vultures don't attack her with their sharp little teeth, trying to get milk.

Professional, reputable breeders get very little sleep these first 4 weeks. Many Doodle breeders who have more than one litter a year have help from family or hire people to help out. It all depends on the size of their operation.

When the puppies are 4 to 5 weeks old, it's time for the breeder to take over all the feeding, cleaning, and guidance to create good companions for their customers. And this is where breeders can make a *real* difference.

Puppies need time with their siblings to learn how to interact with each other. They learn proper social skills, such as bite inhibition, what happens when another puppy pounces on them, and how to yip to stop a sibling from getting too rough. They also learn the sound of food coming. They learn about their daily schedule — feeding time, sleeping time, potty time, and so on.

When your puppy is 5 weeks of age, they can also begin to learn the meaning of specific cues. In fact, the entire litter can be taught at the same time. Few breeders train their puppies because they're too busy just feeding and cleaning, but the rare breeder who is creating puppies to promote a specific behavioral attribute will take the time to begin teaching them to come, sit, and walk with them as a group. They also play music and recordings that have the sounds of vehicles, vacuum cleaners, televisions, and other noises that your puppy may experience in the world. Your puppy will be handled a lot, so the act of touching their toes and ears and lifting their tail won't be a novel experience.

These handling and training sessions will take place for the next two or three weeks. Your puppy is being prepared for real life away from their mother, litter, and birth home. At the age of 7½ to 8 weeks, it's time for them to go home with you!

This is an important bonding age, and it continues until your Doodle puppy reaches the age of 4 months. At this age, they should have a good idea about their new family and feel comfortable in their environment.

In order to ensure that your Doodle puppy grows into a sensible, intelligent, and affectionate dog, you need to put in the time to guide them, train them, and encourage them when they seem intimidated.

Reading the puppy purchase contract

Professional breeders nearly always present purchasers with a puppy purchase contract. They care about the future of the puppies they produce. They also want to make sure they won't be held liable for injuries and illnesses unrelated to the dog's genetics.

The puppy contract will clearly state the responsibilities of both parties regarding vaccinations, neutering, spaying, and worming, as well as deposit amounts and overall cost of the puppy. In essence, the contract is in place to protect the dog, the breeder, and the new owner, too.

There's often more to a puppy contract than merely agreeing on a price. Here are some elements you're likely to find on a puppy contract:

>> **Spaying or neutering requirements:** The contract will likely require you to have your puppy spayed or neutered by a certain age, typically 1 year.

>> **Return-to-breeder clause:** Many breeders insist that if the puppy isn't working out in your home, they be returned to the breeder. This prevents the dog from ending up at the shelter or out on the street. Breeders are aware of sudden life changes and they don't want their puppies to suffer because of it.

>> **Pet or show:** This part of a puppy contract typically pertains more to purebred dogs than to hybrids, but breeders want to know what you have in store for your Doodle pup. Most will be thrilled if you have plans for your puppy, including a lot of training and competing in activities like agility or dock diving. Blue ribbons reflect well on their puppies and bring prestige to the breeder.

>> **Health clearances:** This part of the contract is meant to ensure you that your Doodle pup's parents have been cleared of genetic defects, making it unlikely that they'll show up in your puppy. The contract also typically guides the puppy purchaser on when their new Doodle pup will be ready for certain activities (for example, running along the sidewalk for a few miles, or participating in agility activities). Puppies shouldn't be subjected to physical activities that can interfere with their normal growth patterns, and the contract addresses these issues to protect the pup.

Your pup's breeder should be helpful, educational and always available should you have questions about the health, care, and raising of your puppy. If the contract appears combative or restrictive, you may want to look elsewhere for a Doodle puppy.

TIP

You can find a sample puppy contract at `https://animalso.com/wp-content/uploads/2019/10/Puppy-Sales-Contract.pdf`.

Temperament Testing a Doodle

When you've found a dog you think is right for you, you'll want to do what's known as *temperament testing* (testing the dog's temperament and making sure they're right for you and your home). It informs you of the dog's overall personality — how they prefer to be touched, what frightens them, how they feel about being a family member, and whether they'll want to share their toys. It also gives you some insight into what their strengths may be (such as enjoying a game of retrieving or having strong herding ability).

There are five general tests you can perform with your potential pup prior to bringing them into your life. I cover all of them in the following sections.

Be gentle: Testing for touch sensitivity

This test lets you know whether a Doodle has any special sensitivities in specific areas, as well as how they feel about being touched in a dominant manner. It's also a great way to break the ice, because most Doodles *adore* being touched and will quickly become great friends with those who offer it. This test is especially important for Doodles because they can be quite reserved, and that's not a quality you'll want in your future family member.

Here's how to test a Doodle for touch sensitivity:

1. **Begin by touching their chest, then up under their chin, up the sides of their face, followed by touching their ears, head, back, tail, and legs.**

Most dogs, even overly excited puppies, will calm slightly when getting a belly rub.

TIP

Progress slowly and patiently if working with a fearful Doodle. Be patient if they move away and allow them to approach you. Some pups aren't familiar with being touched in certain areas such as their ears, tail, legs, or feet. The breeder is probably spending a lot of time with the puppies, but they won't be giving the pups the same type of attention you will, so this experience may be a new one for the pups you're considering.

2. **When the Doodle has accepted touch on their upper body, move your hands down their legs: Lift their feet (see Figure 4-1), touching their paws and toenails.**

FIGURE 4-1:
Lift the dog's feet and touch their paws and toenails to see how sensitive they are.

Illustration by Barbara Frake

Here are some reactions you may see:

- **The Doodle growls.** If the dog growls, stop all temperament testing and move on to another dog. They may be injured or ill — ask the breeder if the dog has shown any symptoms.

- **The Doodle moves away, growling.** A Doodle who moves away while growling may be aggressive and unsocialized. Don't force yourself on this Doodle — they may display fear aggression. Give the Doodle the opportunity to return to you without force. Again, they may be injured or ill; again, ask the pup's breeder if they've been showing any symptoms.

- **The Doodle cringes but allows you to touch them.** A Doodle who allows you to touch them but cringes may be friendly but also may be fearful. Sadly, this is common with Doodles. Although this Doodle may do well in a quiet home with adult guardians who have lots of patience and time, you'll have to consider your family and lifestyle and see if the Doodle will fare well with you.

- **The Doodle allows touch, but doesn't react.** A Doodle who allows you to touch them but doesn't react may be frightened. They may just take a while to warm up to new people. You may want to sit with them for a while until they get to know you better. They may warm up to you and begin moving into your touch. Doodles can take a while to make a decision about people they just met.

- **The Doodle allows touch and responds by moving closer.** A Doodle who moves closer as you touch will be a great candidate for most environments except ones where they'll be left alone for long periods of time. This is also a Doodle who may display separation anxiety because they have a great need for pack unity. They'll likely work out well in a busy family home where there are family members who would like to include them in their activities. This dog is certainly one to put at the top of your list.

What's that? Testing for movement and object sensitivity

Some Doodles enjoy new sights and sounds; others get nervous in the same situation. Doodles raised with a conscientious breeder will likely be more inquisitive than frightened at seeing something new rolling around, while a Doodle who hasn't had exposure to new things, or had some bad experiences (such as one from a commercial breeder or puppy mill), may become frightened and move away.

This test helps you understand a Doodle's reaction to new things and moving objects. Here's how to do it:

1. **Collect several objects, such as a ball, squeaky toy, and bone. Have a baking pan, car keys, and a heavy book on hand, too.**

2. **Lay all the objects on the floor and allow the Doodle to investigate.**

   Here are some possible reactions you may see:

- **The Doodle moves away.** A Doodle who moves away is very fearful of new things. Unless you're very patient and live in a quiet household, you shouldn't choose this pup. This test is often 50/50 (some fearful, some inquisitive) with a Doodle, unless the breeder has offered enrichment in their playpens.

- **The Doodle has no reaction.** If the Doodle doesn't react, they're indifferent to new things — or at least to *these* new things. If you have very young children or elderly parents living with you, this Doodle may be ideal.

- **The Doodle starts to investigate but stops and moves away.** A Doodle who starts to investigate but moves away will take time to acclimate to new situations. This is your typical Doodle.

- **The Doodle investigates the objects.** The Doodle who investigates the objects is inquisitive but not bold. They'll do well in most any home. Put this one at the top of your list.

- **The Doodle investigates and interacts with the objects.** The Doodle who investigates and interacts is confident. They'll do well in a home with children and an active lifestyle.

3. **One at a time, pick up all the objects and roll them across the floor, observing the Doodle's reactions as you do.**

TIP

Begin with the object least likely to cause a reaction, such as a ball. Then try a bone, a squeaky toy, and car keys. Finish by dropping a pan or book.

Some possible reactions that you may see include the following:

- **The Doodle moves away.** A Doodle who moves away is fearful and shouldn't be in an active home. This Doodle may react fearfully when overwhelmed by new events, sights, or sounds. Most Doodles who receive lots of socialization and exposure to new environments can overcome their fears, but it takes dedication and patience. Be sure you have both if you decide to purchase this dog.

- **The Doodle has no reaction.** A Doodle who has no reaction is a very accepting dog who should do well in most environments.

TIP

Most healthy dogs have *some* reaction, though, so be sure that they at least watched the movement or responded somehow to the sound. Otherwise, you may want to check the Doodle's health.

- **The Doodle starts to chase but loses interest.** This Doodle may work out well in a quiet environment but is unlikely to want to play much with toys. They may like chewing a bone, though. It can also mean they just aren't old enough to enjoy the games yet. Some Doodle puppies like to watch other dogs play with something before they join in.

- **The Doodle chases, grabs, and carries the object away from you.** This Doodle is bold, possessive, and playful. They need to be in a home with structure and consistency. But this is a great trait to see in a Doodle.

- **The Doodle chases, grabs, and brings the object to you.** This dog will be ideal if you have an active family. They love to play, retrieve, and interact with the world. This Doodle is a star!

Who's the boss? Testing for confidence or passivity

This test will help you gauge a Doodle's confident or passive tendencies — very important to understand, because a confident dog may be bolder and more difficult to redirect into an appropriate behavior, whereas a passive dog is happy to have someone be their leader and make all the decisions. One thing to be aware of with Doodles, however, is that their passive behavior can actually be a means of controlling their owners. I've seen this firsthand. The moment their fear or pulling away from something is rewarded (with attention of any sort), the behavior grows stronger and they have their family wrapped around their paws.

There are several ways to test for assertiveness. Following is a list of all three tests.

Always begin with the least-invasive test (Step 1) and work your way to the more difficult (Step 2 and then Step 3). A Doodle should never display impatience that leads to snapping or growling. If this happens, this is not the Doodle for you.

1. **Pick up the Doodle's front end, holding just behind the front legs (see Figure 4-2).**

   Possible reactions you may see in the Doodle include the following:

   - **The Doodle struggles, growls, and tries to bite or mouth you.** This reaction shows a very insecure and possibly assertive Doodle. This is not the Doodle for you. Although they may do well in a home with strict schedules, lots of training, and observation, it won't be an easy relationship from the start.

   - **The dog struggles, but eventually gives in.** This reaction shows a bold Doodle, but not an overly assertive one. They still need a consistent household and may do okay with older children who won't be afraid of them if they jump on or chase the kids.

   Doodles all love to jump up on people and other dogs. Be prepared for this behavior, and make sure everyone is on the same page about insisting on the dog sitting for attention.

FIGURE 4-2:
Lifting the dog's
front legs is a way
to test their
dominance.

Illustration by Barbara Frake

- **The Doodle shows extreme fear and *wall-eye* (in which you see the whites of the eyes) and yips.** This reaction shows a very fearful Doodle. This Doodle should live in a quiet home where their guardians will be patient and understanding. You don't want to see this trait in a Doodle who will be living with an active family. The commotion will be too much for them to handle and they may become a fear biter.

WARNING

I've seen dogs who have this reaction turn from being fearfully submissive to being in charge of their household. This can happen when overly permissive owners give the dog a lot of leeway because they seem afraid. Doodles are smart — they may be displaying the fearful reaction *because* they want to be allowed a dominant role. The bottom line: Let the dog make the first approach, but don't let them run the household.

- **The Doodle gives in readily but moves away when released.** This reaction shows an insecure dog. This Doodle just may not feel comfortable with you yet.

- **The Doodle submits and relaxes, remaining with you when released.** This reaction shows a secure dog. This Doodle would likely do well in any environment, with conscientious children of all ages. They'll learn quickly and enjoy every minute with you. Put them on your list.

If you were able to perform Step 1 without the Doodle showing any aggression, and you feel comfortable with the pup, move on to Step 2.

2. **Sit and stare into the Doodle's eyes. Don't look away first.**

Possible reactions you may see in the Doodle include the following:

WARNING

- **The Doodle stares back at you and growls.** This reaction is one of a very confident, and possibly assertive, Doodle. This is *not* a Doodle you'll want to live with — they'll challenge you every chance they get. This reaction is very rare with Doodles — they don't have overtly aggressive tendencies.

  If the Doodle is showing assertive behavior at this point, you most definitely don't want to move on to Step 3. They may just be stressed in their current situation (separated from their siblings and with someone they don't know), but you have no way of knowing that they won't be similarly stressed at some point after you bring them home.

- **The Doodle stares back at you and doesn't look away.** This reaction is the sign of a confident Doodle. They aren't intimidated by you, and they're comfortable near you. Be sure you intend to do early training and socialization and give this Doodle structure.

- **The Doodle stares at you a moment and then looks away.** The Doodle who stares and looks away is unsure of their position. They may be testy in specific situations, such as when they really want something, but they'll easily back down if their guardian remains assertive and insistent. As you're testing a Doodle, there's not much you can read into this reaction. Something may have moved nearby and the motion caught their attention.

- **The Doodle never looks you in the eye.** A Doodle who never looks in your eyes is very submissive and accepting. This Doodle will do well in most environments. Just be sure they're not overly timid or easily frightened. The other tests will help you decide.

If you were able to perform Step 2 without the Doodle showing any aggression or timidity, you can give Step 3 a try. If the Doodle has shown any assertive behavior in the other tests, do *not* move on to Step 3. Step 3 puts the Doodle in a totally submissive position where they feel vulnerable. You don't want to threaten or intimidate the Doodle because it may cause short-term trauma.

3. **Gently roll the Doodle over onto their back.**

Possible reactions you may see include the following:

- **The Doodle struggles, growls, and tries to bite you.** This is the reaction of a very confident, possibly assertive, Doodle. They're not a good candidate for anyone with children or an active home. They'll do best with a single, consistent owner who will work with them and maintain a structured environment.

- **The Doodle struggles but eventually gives in.** This is the reaction of a Doodle who has some assertive tendencies but who understands when they're not in charge. They'll do well in a home with consistent owners, but not with young children. They'll require a structured environment, early socialization, and consistent training.

- **The Doodle has no reaction and remains on their back without any struggle.** This Doodle will do well in any home. The Doodle feels comfortable and secure in their environment.

- **The Doodle gives in quickly, cries, and moves away when released.** The Doodle who gives in but cries and moves away is submissive and possibly fearful. They should live in a quiet home.

- **The Doodle gives in quickly and remains with you when released.** This Doodle should work well in any home, though they should always be approached in a positive manner and be given lots of praise for everything they do.

I'll get that! Testing for possessiveness and retrieval ability

If you want your Doodle to play fetch with you, the mere fact that they run after the toy is a great sign. But you'd really appreciate them bringing the toy back to you so you can throw it again. It's the give and take that makes the game!

Some dogs have the genetic tendency to play fetch following the rules; other dogs have different ideas. Some dogs would rather just chase the ball and take it elsewhere so that nobody else can play with it. Other dogs think you're nuts if you think they're going to chase that thing when they'd rather be sleeping or chewing on a bone.

This test lets you know which tendency is most likely in your Doodle pup. There are two parts to this test, and I cover both in the following sections.

Give and take

The reaction a Doodle has to this test will depend on the value of the object you give and take away. For example, for some puppies, a squeaky toy may be fun to play with, but a food-filled bone is of higher value, and the Doodle may not give it up easily.

TIP

Begin this test with a toy of lesser value, such as a stick or rubber toy, and gradually work your way toward something of higher value, like a tasty bone.

To do this test, just give the Doodle the item. Then gently take the item away, either offering another one in its place or caressing the dog as you take the object so as not to present a threatening situation.

Possible reactions you may see in the Doodle include the following:

>> **The Doodle growls.** This Doodle is possessive. They're certainly not right for a family with anyone who isn't persistent and patient. And they're not appropriate for a family with children or elderly residents. It's rare for Doodles to display this behavior. Without the proper environment and education, the behavior can get much worse.

>> **The Doodle holds the object but eventually gives it up.** This reaction shows a Doodle who may have some possessive tendencies but will quickly learn to drop on cue, if given a chance to learn the behavior. This Doodle will do well in a home with consistent owners but not with young children, because they have a tendency to pull items from a dog's mouth, which can cause a negative reaction from the dog. Keep in mind, however, that tug-of-war is a favorite canine game and they may just be playing with you.

>> **The Doodle readily gives up the object or drops the object and runs away.** Doodles who have these reactions will work well in any environment, but if the Doodle runs away, you'll need to be patient with them, because they have a short attention span.

Chase and retrieve

To do this test, take one of the Doodle's favorite toys, and throw it a short distance. If doing this at a breeder's location, there may be some toys scattered around the playpen you can use.

Possible reactions you may see include the following:

>> **The Doodle goes after the toy, picks it up, and runs off.** A Doodle who runs off with the toy is independent. They like to chase toys, but they don't want to share them with anyone else.

>> **The Doodle goes after the toy, picks it up, and lays down with it.** This Doodle may not be in a playful mood but definitely wants to possess their toy. This can sometimes happen in large litters. It's a self-defense mode.

>> **The Doodle is curious and goes to check out the toy but then walks away.** This Doodle doesn't have much interest in the toy. Are you sure you chose one of their favorite toys? If not, try again. Remember that young puppies tire quickly, and they may just need a nap before playtime.

>> **The Doodle doesn't go after the toy.** This Doodle just doesn't like toys or doesn't care about that particular toy. Try additional toys until you get some response. If the dog doesn't have any response, they likely either haven't gotten the point of toys or haven't found anything that floats their boat.

>> **The Doodle goes after the toy, picks it up, and returns it to you.** This Doodle is highly interactive and social. They want to play with you and are a natural retriever. They'll likely do well in an active environment with children of all ages and people who spend lots of time with them. This Doodle is displaying all their genetic instincts. Poodles are hunting dogs, bred to retrieve downed waterfowl in wetlands. They're perfect!

Follow the leader: Testing for social skills

If you're testing a puppy, it's highly likely you're doing so at the breeder's home or facility. And although some breeders may have some meandering pets around, such as dogs, cats, or farm animals, it's not something you can count on.

Because you're working with a puppy, they'll be able to acclimate to almost any environment they go to, including one with other pets. So, the main thing you'll be testing them for at this point is whether they have a negative reaction to new people or environments outside their playpen.

TIP

If you're considering an adult or adolescent Doodle, this test will be extremely important. You'll need access to other dogs or animals, if possible. If you're at a shelter, this shouldn't be a problem because many other animals are in the building.

Begin by placing the Doodle in a new place where there may be other animals or other members of your family.

Possible reactions you may see in the puppy include the following:

>> **The Doodle automatically chases the other animals or people.** This Doodle will require lots of redirection during the early months in your home. Proper introductions at the beginning will be paramount, and close observation will prevent a dangerous situation where your Doodle or the other pet gets injured.

>> **The Doodle only goes after other aggressive animals (those jumping, barking or meowing, or growling or hissing as they go by).** This pup will fight if challenged. This behavior would be rare in a young puppy and doesn't bode well for an older dog either. Most Doodles run from an aggressive animal.

>> **The Doodle doesn't show aggression but does show an eagerness to say hello to a quiet dog, cat, or person.** This is a friendly Doodle who should do well in any environment.

>> **The Doodle walks by with no reaction.** This Doodle should do well in any environment.

>> **The Doodle runs by and tries to get away from the other animals or people it sees.** This Doodle should do well in a home with other dogs or cats but should be introduced carefully and with as much positive reinforcement as possible. They probably just need some time to acclimate.

TIP

Some dogs react negatively toward cats but love other dogs. And believe it or not, some dogs love cats and can't stand other dogs. Pay close attention to how the dog reacts to dogs as well as cats — they may be fine with one species and not the other. If you live in an apartment complex with other dog owners, and the Doodle you're considering doesn't like other dogs, you could run into trouble every time you take your dog outside.

Doodle owner

» Preparing your home for your new pup

» Giving your puppy a place to eat and sleep

» Stocking up on the supplies you need to keep your pup healthy and happy

Chapter **5**

Doodle on the Way

Before you bring your Doodle home, you need to get your home ready for their arrival! Your new best friend will require more than just your love, so get ready to make space and stock up on supplies. Dogs are a commitment — both in terms of time and money — but the reward is worth it! In this chapter, I help you get ready for your new Doodle so you can focus on loving them instead of running out to the store.

Before Doodle Day: What to Know Before Bringing Your Dog Home

The excitement of getting your new Doodle is setting in. You're thinking of all the fun activities you'll do together. Although it's great to plan your future, it's far more important to get to work on the present. You'll need to plan all the ways your new Doodle will change your life — for the better!

Doodles are active and curious. They're rarely the type of dog who can be left home alone for long periods of time every day without developing severe separation anxiety. Be sure you're willing to commit to ensuring your Doodle will be relaxed, safe, and stimulated. The following sections give you an idea what to expect.

Financial considerations

Any new baby comes with expenses, and Doodles are no different. The most obvious financial expense will be your dog's veterinary care. Every year, your Doodle will require a yearly physical exam and vaccinations, which can total at least $200 per year, depending on where you live. Besides the normal vaccinations, your Doodle will require neutering or spaying when they near maturity; this procedure can cost anywhere from $250 to $600. Also, plan on monthly heartworm and flea preventives, which average $50 to $75 per month.

Doodles are prone to allergies. Some of them require antihistamine medications or prescription diets, which can add to the overall cost of care. Antihistamines can cost from $50 to $150 per month; prescription diets are similarly priced. You can sometimes avoid these expenses by feeding a high-quality food, however (more on food in Chapter 7).

Your Doodle will require comfortable bedding, a crate, toys, dishes, a collar, a harness, a leash, and identification tags. These supplies can cost hundreds to thousands of dollars, depending on how much you want to indulge your new Doodle (see "Stocking Up on Supplies," later in this chapter for more on supplies).

Depending on your work situation, you may also need to factor in daycare and/or a dog walker. Even if you work from home, you won't be able to be with your Doodle 24/7; if you leave town, you'll need to pay for a dog sitter or boarding. Doggy daycare averages $18 to $35 per day, a dog walker can cost anywhere from $20 to $40 per walk, and overnight stays at a boarding facility can run $35 to $75 per night, depending on where you live.

Your Doodle will require training, too. They're intelligent, but all little ones need an education. If you're able to take the lead on the training process, you can enroll and participate in a group class; group classes can cost anywhere from $120 to $400 per session of, say, eight to ten lessons. Private lessons can run between $45 to $125 per class, depending on location and the trainer's credentials. If you don't have the time or inclination to participate in your Doodle's training, you may consider a board-and-train program (where you send your puppy off to live with a trainer for a period of time); these often run between $1,200 to $6,000, depending on the length of the program.

REMEMBER

These aren't the only expenses your Doodle will bring, but they're the most common to consider.

Time considerations

Dogs require a lot of time. If you'd rather just stare at a screen all day, a Doodle is not for you. Dogs thrive in an engaged, active environment. The following sections list the many ways a Doodle puppy will occupy your time.

Housetraining

If your new Doodle is less than 6 months old, you'll need to structure your day around taking them outside often. Younger Doodles, less than 3 months old, may need to go out every one and a half to two hours. An older puppy, over 3 months old, should be able to hold it up to three hours at a time. Dogs over 6 months old typically can hold it up to five hours, but it's not fair to make them do so — allowing them to relieve themselves every three hours will reduce the likelihood of indoor accidents.

You'll need to allow all this time to take your dog outside to relieve themselves. Especially when puppies are younger, taking them out isn't just a quick in-and-out experience. While you're housetraining, you need to go out with them, encourage them to do their business, reward them for doing it, and come back in — you may have to spend 15 to 20 minutes outside every time they need to go out.

TIP

If possible, get your puppy during an extended break from school or work, if you can't work from home.

Housetraining a dog requires a lot of dedication and good timing. Doodles are intelligent, but they're also living, breathing creatures with physical needs of their own.

Veterinarian visits

You'll need to make the time to take your Doodle to the veterinarian. From yearly exams and vaccinations to the occasional injury, you'll have both scheduled and emergency visits at some point during your dog's lifetime.

Training and exercise

Doodles are very energetic and in need of direction, which means you'll need to spend time exercising and training them. These two activities are a lifetime commitment to your dog. Ensuring your Doodle gets enough time to let loose and to learn is key to a healthy relationship.

Standard-size Doodles require the most exercise time — usually at least an hour or two every day. You can incorporate training into the exercise time so it's it more productive for both of you. Standard-size Doodles need to cover a lot of ground, so having a safely fenced yard or going on long hikes, runs, or swims will keep them in good shape.

Miniature-size Doodles require at least one hour of exercise every day. A hike combined with free play will satisfy their needs.

Toy-size Doodles enjoy racing around, too. If you live in a confined space, consider games of fetch to keep them well exercised. A training session often takes the juice out of a Toy-size Doodle, and they'll likely nap after.

Feeding

Your Doodle will need to be fed two or three times a day (puppies are fed more often; by the time they're adults, twice a day should be enough). Between preparing the food and watching them until they finish, feeding can be a half-hour every time.

TIP

If possible, feeding times should be on a fairly set schedule. Dogs tend to be more relaxed when they know when and where they'll eat.

Sleeping

The younger your Doodle, the more often they'll have to nap. Naps can last anywhere from 30 minutes to two hours, depending on their activity prior to the nap. Nap time is the perfect time for you to actually get something done!

Bedtime may take a few days to set up and can occupy upwards of an hour per night. A new puppy may cry and stress over being left in a crate or other enclosure without their siblings or you there with him. (Follow the crate-training advice in Chapter 9 for help with this situation.) Teaching your Doodle to relax and go to sleep takes some time.

If your Doodle is less than 4 months old, you may need to get up several times during the night to take him out. That means less sleep for you, but a housetrained dog is the reward! You may need nap times for yourself!

Socializing

Socializing is extremely important — it teaches your pup appropriate social skills so they're able to go more places with you and have a richer, fuller life. Having playtime with other dogs and meeting people of all ages will help your Doodle adjust to your family and lifestyle.

You can incorporate socializing into your Doodle's exercise time.

Space considerations

Dogs take up space — there's no way around that. They need a place for their food and water bowls, bed, crate, toy box, and all the toys scattered around the house (dogs don't really put their own toys away — but you could train your Doodle to do that on command, if you have the time to teach it!).

Here are some estimates for the amount of space you'll need for all your Doodle's things:

>> **Food and water bowls (and maybe a mat beneath to catch stray kibble or water slobber):** A 2-x-3-foot space.

>> **Bed and crate:** Toy-size Doodles need 1½ x 2 feet, a Miniature-size Doodle needs 2 x 3½ feet, and a Standard-size Doodle will need anything from a 3 x 4 feet to a couple feet more in either direction. Crate space will be similar dimensions.

>> **A toy box (if you're really organized):** A 2-x-1-foot box. You can count on lots more space occupied by numerous toys around. And you'll need to watch where you step. The importance of lots of toys cannot be overstated, however — the more toys your puppy can access, the less destructive they'll be of your furniture, shoes, and other belongings.

Puppy-Proofing Your Home

Put everything away — and I mean everything! — before your Doodle puppy arrives. Puppies are curious and adventurous. They check out *everything* — books, magazines, eyeglasses, TV remotes, cellphones, tablets, and headphones. If your dog sees something interesting, their teeth will be on it.

Your Doodle isn't necessarily inherently destructive — not any more than a human toddler who tests everything by putting it in their mouth is. Your puppy is just investigating their environment to see what might taste good and what's fun to play with.

In time, you'll be able to get your home life back to normal, but until your new Doodle learns what they can and can't play with, you need to keep your home puppy-proofed. Not only is this better for your relationship with your pup, but it's less of a health hazard for them (some dogs swallow things that can poison them or otherwise wreak serious havoc with their insides).

In the following sections, I fill you in on the major steps you need to take to make sure your home is safe for your new friend.

Removing chewing hazards

Dogs go through several growth and teething periods. Puppies are also exploring their environment and tend to chew anything, especially between 3 and 9 months of age (when they're teething).

At 3 months old, your Doodle will be losing their front teeth and incisors. They'll be wanting to grab hold and pull at objects. They may try to put their teeth around a chair or table leg. The TV remote, if accessible, will also be attractive. Carpet edges can be fun because they may have strings or tufts to pull at. Putting away any loose items can remove some of the attraction, but it's impossible to do that with everything, so you'll just have to be observant and redirect your pup's attention to their toys whenever they go for the couch.

Between 4 and 9 months of age, your Doodle will be losing and regrowing their molars. These tend to be even more uncomfortable than the front teeth as they grow in, and your Doodle will be wanting to chew anything to alleviate the discomfort. Be sure to keep loose items out of reach and continue to keep an eye on your pup at all times. If you see them go for the wrong item, redirect their attention to one of their toys and play with them for a few minutes. The interaction helps reward them for choosing the right toy.

REMEMBER

Empty your trash cans daily, including those in the bathroom and bedroom. The smells from these containers are highly attractive to dogs. The trash can include all kinds of dangerous things, like chicken bones, batteries, and plant cuttings. Even the ink on paper can be poisonous or become clogged in your dog's intestines. So emptying the trash is about more than preventing a mess — it's a safety issue.

WARNING

Electrical cords are a huge hazard with puppies. Not only can a dog pull on them and yank the appliance down on top of them, but if they chew on the electrical cord, they could be electrocuted and die. Either make sure that all electrical cords are up out of your pup's reach or cover them with steel conduit to prevent them from chewing the actual cord. Keeping electrical items unplugged when you're not around to watch your dog is also a good idea.

Put your houseplants in a room where your puppy can't get to them, or arrange them on a high enough platform that they have no access to them. Not only are they attractive to your Doodle, but you'll have a huge mess on your hands if your pup starts to play with them. Plus, some plants can be highly poisonous to dogs.

WARNING

Many household supplies — including bleach, detergents, moth balls, pine and citrus oils, insecticides, rat baits, antifreeze, and batteries — are also very dangerous to your dog. Make sure that they're all out of reach. Because most of those items are stored under the sink, try using a child-proof latch on the cupboard. Some Doodles are able to learn how to open cupboards, so think ahead!

Outside there are other hazards — some poisonous, others merely destructive. Put away the garden hose, any potting supplies, lounge-chair cushions, and children's toys. If you have candles or small lanterns on tables, place them in a safe area as well — especially citronella candles. The only things you can't put away are your landscaping plants and large patio furniture, though if any of the furniture is made of wood, either put it out of reach or cover it daily with a product like Grannick's Bitter Apple. Or you can always keep an eye on your pup when they're outdoors and redirect them away from the furniture and toward a toy.

You can also screen off the patio furniture and other items by placing a removable fence around them. This way, you can allow your Doodle to remain outside without direct observation. If they start to get curious about what's on the other side of that fence, however, you'll need to consider a more permanent solution.

TIP

If you have a garden your dog can access, put a secure fence around it. To keep your pup occupied, place interactive toys outside that area, such as food-filled toys or toys that dispense kibble when moved around. Many dogs like to dig, so a sandbox filled with sand and buried toy treasures can be fun. On hot days, use a water-filled kiddie pool to help your dog cool off — just make sure to supervise your dog around any water, no matter how shallow.

Protecting your furniture

In my house, the dogs aren't allowed on the furniture. I've made this a house rule for several reasons:

>> It prevents my furniture from being destroyed by muddy paws and sharp claws.

>> It maintains my dogs' understanding of their place in my household. Many dogs who are allowed on the furniture feel as though they're superior to everyone else (including the people in the house), and they may growl at others who approach their place on the couch.

>> It keeps my guests from being walked over by my dogs.

>> I've never wanted to have to clean vomit or diarrhea off the upholstery.

TIP

If you'd like to keep your dog off your furniture, and if your Doodle is a pup, have lots of nasty-tasting spray on hand to make sure they don't develop a taste for wood. Several products — such as Grannick's Bitter Apple, Fooey Ultra-Bitter Spray, Four Paws Bitter Lime, and more — are readily available at pet stores for just this purpose.

TIP

If you're bringing an adult Doodle into your home, and you think they might like jumping up on the furniture, you can do a few things to prevent this. In fact, you may want to implement them prior to bringing your Doodle home so they quickly learn that the furniture is off limits:

>> Put things in the way so that your dog can't become comfortable on the couch.

>> Put a ScatMat (an electrified mat that tingles the paws when pressed) across the furniture so if your dog tries to get up, their toes get a tingle. Another great product is PetSafe SSSCAT Spray — it's a cannister of air that's motion activated.

>> Place some pans across the couch so they make noise when jostled, either chasing your dog off the furniture or at the very least letting you know that they're trying it again so you can redirect their actions.

>> Close off the room so they can't access the furniture that you don't want them jumping on.

If you've read all this and you're thinking, "Hey, half the reason I'm getting a Doodle is so I can curl up on the couch with them and watch movies or read a book," you may want to look into furniture covers so your upholstery won't be ruined by their claws. Or you can use a thick throw blanket to cover the areas where you'll allow them to sit. You can also restrict which pieces of furniture they're allowed up on. Maybe you let them up on the couch in the family room, but not on the furniture anywhere else in the house. Whatever works for you — the important thing is to be consistent with your dog.

TIP

Dogs tend to learn best in an all-or-nothing scenario. They rarely understand all the "gray" areas we do. In the beginning, you may want to set the rule of not allowing them on any furniture instead of trying to allow them on a certain couch or chair. This way, they'll learn faster to remain off of everything, unless invited up when they've been good. As you regularly invite them up on the one piece of furniture, they'll begin to assume it's okay for them to get up on that one piece only.

Safety first

A secure yard is very important for your Doodle. They'll need space to exercise and explore. You'll need a place where they can remain safe and secure as they do. If you're in an urban environment, this may not be possible, and you may have to rely on exercising your Doodle on a leash. Many cities have dog parks, though, and I recommend trying to locate the closest one.

Doodles are genetically inclined to require exercise of some sort every day. A fenced yard will ensure that your Doodle remains sane. Even the Toy-size Doodles need to run off some steam sometimes. And a dog park or fenced-in yard will help their mind and body.

TIP

The best fencing is a wood privacy fence. Not only does it offer a solid barrier, but it also keeps other dogs and pranksters from tormenting your dog. With this type of fence, your Doodle is less likely to run the fence, chasing other dogs. The height of the fence you need depends on the size of your dog. A dog less than 10 inches at the shoulder should be fine with a 4-foot-high fence; a dog up to 18 inches at the shoulder should be safe with a 5-foot fence; and any dog over 18 inches at the shoulder, especially one who can jump high as Doodles can, needs at least a 6-foot-high fence.

Alternatives to wood privacy fences include

>> **Chain link:** This is a good way of keeping your dog at home — it's just not as pretty as a nice wood fence and it doesn't give you and your dog the same level of privacy. The same guidelines regarding height apply to chain link as apply to wood fencing. It would be a good idea to also bury a foot or two of the chain link to prevent your Doodle from digging out.

>> **Wire mesh:** This works well as long as it's installed correctly. Wire mesh may be less expensive than wood or chain link, but it's even less attractive than chain link and often not as secure. I don't recommend this type of fencing for anything other than a small dog who isn't prone to digging and jumping. And if you do use this type of fencing, I suggest you bury at least a foot of it to prevent your dog from digging out. Doodles love to dig!

>> **Invisible fencing:** This is great if you live in a neighborhood with rules against fencing. It's also good for fencing in large areas, giving the dog lots of space to run. However, an invisible fence doesn't keep others out, which leaves your dog open to attack from other dogs or people who are looking to steal him. Dogs learn the boundaries of an invisible fence within a week and adhere to them, though some dogs will test the collar batteries now and then to see if they can make a run for it.

Invisible fencing consists of a wire that's buried 1 or 2 inches around the boundary of your yard and attached to a transmitter that maintains the boundary distance, most commonly set at 6 to 15 feet. The dog wears a collar that beeps if they get within 2 feet of the set boundary. If they continue and enter the "no zone," they get a mild electric shock. Be very careful if you intend to use this type of fencing. Remain with your dog until they're aware of the boundaries and feel comfortable enough to use the yard.

WARNING

Doodles are very sensitive and can be traumatized by the shock correction of the invisible fence receiver. This can range from a minor high yip to turning tail and running while screaming. Dogs who are traumatized take a lot of time to recover. Very sensitive dogs will never want to leave the porch again. Make sure to be patient and clear as you train your dog to the boundaries of an invisible fence.

If you don't have the luxury of being able to fence a yard, you'll have to take your dog for walks on a leash. Walks aren't a bad thing — they're actually very positive, because you get to spend lots of time with your Doodle. In fact, even if you have a fenced yard, you should make an effort to walk your dog at least once a day. Daily walks are a special time that your Doodle will look forward to.

TIP

Many neighborhoods have fenced dog parks. These areas are great for letting your dog have the freedom to play in relative safety. They also give your dog a chance to socialize with other dogs and people — a great combination. However, some dog owners aren't conscientious about cleaning their dog's mess or teaching their dogs not to play aggressively. Always keep a watchful eye as the dogs play and remove your dog from any sticky situations. Doodles are easily frightened by overbearing dogs, and a bad experience remains with them for a very long time.

Setting Up Sleeping and Eating Areas

Your Doodle needs a place to sleep where they feel safe and secure. You have a few options, so before you bring your pup home, think about what will work best for you and your dog.

If you intend to allow them in the bed with you, just realize you're setting a precedent — it's harder to force your dog out of the bed than it is never to allow them into the bed in the first place. Sleeping with a tiny, cuddly puppy may sound wonderful, but consider whether you want to share a bed with a full-grown dog.

I recommend setting up a sleeping area that belongs only to your dog. Not only will they feel safe there, but they may go there when they're feeling overwhelmed throughout the day. The bed becomes their safe spot where they can go relax.

The crate: Your dog's first place to sleep

Many dogs who don't yet know the house rules will have accidents indoors or play with something that isn't a dog toy. Until you know for sure that your Doodle won't have an accident in the house or be destructive, contain them in a crate when you're not around to watch them — including during the night. The crate will become your dog's private room where they can go when they want some peace and quiet, as well as a place for them to go to sleep.

Crates emulate a den. In the wild, canines seek shelter in a small cavelike area, where they can feel solid sides around them. Instinctually, dogs prefer a closed-in space where another predator can't access them when they're resting.

The crate should have access to water, a couple of toys, and a comfortable bed. If your puppy is a chewer, steer clear of stuffed beds and go for a blanket instead — you're less likely to be surprised by fluff in the morning.

Be sure to acclimate your dog to the crate using positive reinforcement, teaching them that it's a nice place to be. The crate should never be used as a place of punishment, nor should your Doodle be imprisoned there for long periods of time every day.

TIP

Although a crate offers the safest sleep area, a pen may work for a dog who feels too cramped in a crate. An exercise pen typically consists of eight 2-foot-wide side panels. The pen can be folded for storage or opened, giving your dog 16 cubic feet of space. If your dog likes to climb or is in any way an escape artist, a pen won't be the place to contain them, because they'll easily climb out.

Several types of crates are available, including the metal wire crates and the plastic airline-approved crates. The type you use is a personal preference. Both offer safe containment in your home and give your dog a feeling of safety inside.

Thinking outside the box: Letting your dog sleep outside a crate

WARNING

Don't let your dog sleep outside a crate unless you're absolutely sure they won't get into trouble when you aren't watching.

Start by keeping your Doodle in an enclosed room, such as the kitchen (during the day) or your bedroom with you (at night). When your Doodle proves reliable in these areas, you can gradually open up your house a little more.

Buying bedding

The type of bedding you give your dog depends largely on the situation and size of your dog. For example, a small dog can be spoiled with one of those canopy luxury beds, while a big dog may be most comfortable on a big pillow or hammock-type dog bed.

REMEMBER

Consider the age of your dog prior to giving them access to the bed. Young dogs tend to chew their beds.

The main consideration when shopping for a bed is ease of cleaning and durability. I've found that the beds with a structure made of PVC pipe or aluminum are the hardiest and easiest to clean — you just hose them off. They're great indoors or out, and few dogs will chew them. (I recommend the ones available at https:// kuranda.com.)

A good bed for the crate is a mat-type bed or blanket. Look for something thin enough to go into the washing machine, or a bed that has a removable outer shell.

If you live in an area where fleas are an issue, a cedar-filled bed will help control the pests and protect your pet. Cedar is a natural flea repellent and great for filling up a pillow bed, giving your dog a comfortable place to sleep. This is great for an outdoor bed or if your dog's bedroom is located in the basement or a storage area.

TIP

Don't buy your dog an expensive bed until they've proven that they won't eat it or soil it. At that point, you can go and get that fancy bed you've been eyeing.

Giving your dog a place to eat

The most convenient area to feed your dog is usually the kitchen, because the flooring is easy to clean and most people prefer to keep food in one area of the house. Be consistent with this by always feeding them in the same place. It will help your Doodle know where good things happen.

Dogs should always have access to fresh water. However, if you want to prevent water spillage, offer your dog their water in a raised feeder appropriate to their size. Place the feeder in their eating area. Another idea is to use a stainless-steel bucket. Your dog will need to put their head into the bucket to drink, which will prevent water drops from scattering. Be sure to secure it to something solid, however, because an excited dog can easily tip it over.

Stocking Up on Supplies

Ah, the fun part! You get to go on a shopping spree for your new puppy! Although it's loads of fun to go to a huge pet-supply store, it's also more expensive than shopping via catalog or online. But if you want to take your Doodle along to help choose their toys, brick-and-mortar stores are the way to go.

The basic supplies include a collar (more than one if you want to be stylish), a leash or two, food and water dishes, a bed (see "Buying bedding," earlier in this chapter), and toys. You may also want to get a travel carrier for your vehicle, a home crate or pen, and grooming supplies (see Chapter 4). Prior to bringing your puppy home, you also need to stock up on food (see Chapter 7).

Collars, harnesses, and leashes

Many different types of collars and leashes are available.

The typical buckle or snap-on collar is great for making a fashion statement and for displaying your dog's creds — rabies tag, ID tag, and license. You should never attach your leash to a neck collar because pressure on your dog's throat can cause permanent damage.

If you're looking for a training harness, there are many to choose from. I recommend getting a front-connecting harness, in which the leash is connected to a D-ring at the dog's chest. I suggest finding one that's easily adjustable and doesn't tend to move around your dog's body a lot when in use. My favorite front-connecting harness is the Freedom Harness (www.2houndsdesign.com), though there are several others that may be just as good. (You may also need a head halter down the road — turn to Chapter 10 for more information.)

In terms of leashes, your dog will walk best with a 4- to 6-foot walking leash that isn't overly heavy or difficult to hold. I find that a ½-inch leather leash offers optimal comfort for both the dog and you — and it lasts a long time. Cotton leashes are also generally comfortable, but not practical if your Doodle pulls hard. Nylon is fine for a Miniature-size to Toy-size Doodle.

Dishes and bowls

Which dishes and bowls are right for your dog depends on their size and temperament. Here are a few things to consider:

>> **Size:** If you have a Standard-size Doodle, don't get a dish that's barely big enough to fit their nose. Make sure they can fit their entire face in the bowl as

they eat. On the other hand, you may not want to use a large bowl for a Toy-size Doodle — they'll spend more time chasing down the flying kibble than eating it. For dogs with long ears, get a bowl that's narrow at the top and flares out at the bottom — this will keep their ears from getting into the food. If your Doodle is a puppy, you may want to provide smaller dishes at first and increase their size as your dog matures.

>> **Material:** If your dog is likely to play with their dishes, you don't want anything breakable. Ceramic is out of the question, regardless of how heavy-duty it appears. If they'll chew the dishes, you don't want plastic ones. It doesn't matter if the plastic is very thick — they can get their teeth into it and have a great time demolishing the dish, ingesting plastic along the way. Also, some dogs develop contact allergies (hypersensitivity to plastic).

TIP

Stainless-steel dishes are my top choice. They last a very long time, can't be destroyed (even if your Doodle has all sorts of games planned for their dinner dish), and are easy to clean.

>> **Elevation:** Whether you put your dog's bowls on the ground or in an elevated feeder depends on the size of your dog and how they eat. A Toy-size Doodle will be fine with their dish on the floor. A Miniature-size to Standard-size Doodle should have a raised feeder because it will prevent them from putting their paws in their food and tracking it around the house.

Toys

The types of toys you should get are totally dependent on your dog. Obviously, you want to get a toy that's the right size for your Doodle so they can get the most use out of it — big dog, big toy; small dog, small toy.

SLOW-FEED BOWLS

Many dogs eat too quickly, which can cause digestive disorders, as well as bloat (a potentially life-threatening condition). If you have a Miniature-size to Standard-size Doodle, I suggest you purchase a slow-feed bowl. They have puzzle patterns inside, and your dog will have to work a little harder to get every piece of kibble.

Another way of slowing down the chow is to use a food-dispensing toy, such as a Bob-a-Lot, Buster Cube, or Kong. This approach will add some fun to mealtimes and ensure your Doodle doesn't inhale their food. They really only work with dry food, though. If you use wet food, stick with a slow-feed bowl.

Stay away from anything that can cause choking, diarrhea, or allergic reactions. This means no rawhide bones, chips, or edible toys that contain cornstarch, wheat glutens, or chemical preservatives. I know this rules out a lot of the things that dogs like chewing — some of which even claim to be good for dogs' teeth and gums — but if you don't want to have to take your Doodle to the vet for expensive allergy tests, steer clear of these items.

You can find lots of interactive toys that are safe and fun for your dog. Toys that have hollow areas to put kibble (see the nearby "Slow-feed bowls" sidebar) or squeeze treats (like cheese that comes from a squeeze can) are always popular.

Small dogs may do well with plush toys that have squeakers or even vinyl squeaker toys. However, I don't recommend these toys for dogs over 25 pounds, unless the dog has proven that they won't shred the toy.

Doodles thrive on interactive games. Puzzle toys, where treats are hidden inside, will stimulate their minds. Snuffle mats give your Doodle the opportunity to hunt for food within the folds of the material strips. Doodles have a lot of hunting-dog genetics, so you can fulfill their instinctual need to hunt by putting a plush toy on the end of a long rope and dragging it around.

All dogs do well with real beef shank bones, which have thick walls and are hollow on the inside, offering a great place to stuff food and treats. These toys last for years — they're indestructible. Another great toy is elk antlers, which are pure calcium, great for your dog's health, and take a long time to whittle down (when they get to be small enough for your dog to swallow, remove them — they're a choking hazard). You can find elk antlers available in a variety of sizes, though I recommend the larger ones, even for a small dog, because your dog will enjoy it more and it'll last longer.

TIP

Hollow bones are great for puppies who are teething. They can be filled with canned food and then frozen. Give it to your pup when you can't watch them for an hour or two. They'll stay busy and get some relief for their gums. Another good toy for teething is a frozen twisted washcloth. Numerous toys are available that can be frozen prior to your Doodle playing with them. The cold helps alleviate some of the gum discomfort. Be sure to remove the toy when thawed, however, or it may be shredded.

REMEMBER

There are lots of toys to choose from. Consider the size and temperament of your Doodle before you splurge on items that'll end up in the garbage or lodged in your dog's intestines. Start out with one toy and see how they like it. Then add more toys over time. And when you've accumulated a bunch of toys, rotate them out, keeping some set aside in a closet or someplace where the dog can't get them — then rotate the toys every once in a while, and your Doodle will think it's their birthday all over again!

Chapter **6**

It's Doodle Day: Picking Up Your New Puppy

Depending on where you find your Doodle puppy, you may have to travel some distance to pick them up from the breeder. The first step is to think about how you'll bring your new Doodle home. Then you'll need to set up a schedule for meals and potty breaks so your pup has a routine they can count on. When you walk through the door with your puppy, you'll want to give them the lay of the land. The first night with a new puppy can be stressful — for humans and puppy alike — so in this chapter I walk you through what to expect and set you up for success. A new puppy needs to keep busy with activities you approve of (because if you don't give them things to do, they'll inevitably get into trouble on their own). Finally, getting the whole family involved in caring for the puppy is key — I offer suggestions on how to do that in this chapter.

Travel Considerations

Unless you live next door to your breeder, you'll have to travel to pick up your puppy — whether that's across town, across the state, or across the country. You have two options: plane or car. In this section, I walk you through both, helping you make the trip a smooth one for your new charge.

Flying with your puppy

If you're planning to fly with your puppy, they'll need to be able to fit in a travel carrier under the seat in front of you. Only certified service animals can remain in the cabin with their human companions, and puppies don't qualify. The good news is, even the largest puppies are typically small enough at 7 or 8 weeks to fit in a travel carrier and go with you inside the cabin.

WARNING

The alternative is to have your puppy fly in the cargo hold of the plane. Though it is temperature-controlled while in flight, it isn't while the plane is on the ground. Regardless, flying in the cargo hold is much more stressful for dogs than staying with you in the cabin. With a very young puppy, flying in the cargo hold can be especially stressful. Not only are they in unfamiliar surroundings, but they can't yet hold it for long periods of time. Many types of Doodles can't handle extreme temperatures. Others can become frightened of closed-in spaces after going through this type of travel. In case it isn't obvious, I don't recommend shipping puppies (some breeders will ship a puppy to you) or sending them in the cargo hold of planes.

WARNING

Some types of dogs should not travel by air, period. The U.S. Department of Agriculture (USDA) specifies that dogs less than 8 weeks of age can't fly at all. If the dog is ill, injured, pregnant, or very old, they recommend that they don't travel by air. Also, dogs with very short noses, such as Pugs and Boxers (or Doodles with these genetics), as well as long-nosed dogs such as Collies, are prone to respiratory difficulties, and the UDSA suggests they only travel by air if they can do so in the passenger cabin. Some airlines won't accept short-nosed breeds at all if the temperature exceeds 70 degrees anywhere during the trip (between the terminals and the airplane).

Because you're likely obtaining a puppy from a breeder, you may want to consider a round-trip flight. Most puppies are small enough to fit beneath the seat in front of you, making the situation easier on them as you can allow the Doodle pup time outside the carrier before, after, and in between flights. This means that your

Doodle pup won't have to contain his potty as long. It'll also give you lots of time to bond with your new Doodle as you attend to their needs during the trip.

The following sections offer a few suggestions to make flying with a puppy easier.

Checking out the airlines' requirements

The first thing you need to do when considering an air trip is to determine the airline's regulations. Airlines change their regulations frequently, so check with your favorite airlines *before* buying your ticket.

Buying a travel carrier

The under-seat space on airplanes is approximately 23 x 13 x 9 inches (but check with your specific airline to be sure). Beyond being able to fit in this space, there aren't any other restrictions on the kind of carrier you use. Keep in mind, however, that your puppy won't be allowed out of their carrier during the trip, so just make sure the carrier will be comfortable.

The crate should have plenty of ventilation and a leak-proof floor. Place an absorbent bed on the floor so that your Doodle pup will be comfortable during the flight. The crate door should open easily, but also be secure enough to prevent your dog from escape or from it accidentally opening when it's jostled.

REMEMBER

If you have to send your puppy in the cargo hold if the plane, you'll need an airline-approved crate. These are hard plastic with ventilation grates, and they must meet the standards of the airline. The crate should have a hard shell, so if something accidentally falls on it, your pet will be protected. If the crate (and your dog) are small enough to carry, it should have a strong handle. If your dog is too large to carry, make sure you can either push the crate on wheels or lift it onto a wheeled cart.

Making sure your puppy has proper identification and health certificates

Before you can fly with a puppy, they'll need a complete physical examination. You'll need a copy of their vaccination record, a rabies certificate (if your pup is old enough for one), and a health certificate. Your breeder should gather all this information before you arrive.

If your pup is traveling in the cargo hold, their identification information (and yours) should be placed on the crate, along with any care instructions. When there are layovers or if they're traveling internationally, airline employees will be caring for your puppy and will rely on the information taped on the top of their crate.

TIP

Caring for your puppy before and after the flight

Traveling by air can be stressful for a puppy. Following are some tips for making it better for *both* of you. Ask your breeder if they can help by doing these things:

>> **Before the day of the flight, acclimate your Doodle to the travel carrier or crate.** Make sure they like it before you leave. (Your breeder can get your Doodle used to the crate by leaving it open at the breeder's home and using it as their bed and eating area.)

>> **Don't board the plane with your puppy until the very last minute.** Until then, allow him to be out and about with you, moving around and acclimating to the airport congestion and commotion. Stay upbeat and give them plenty of rewards.

>> **If the puppy is riding in the cargo hold, make sure their water and food bowls are securely fastened to the side of the crate so they don't spill in flight.** If the puppy is traveling in the cabin with you, don't keep water in the travel carrier. You can carry a water bottle and offer them a small cup of it midflight, in their carrier.

>> **Place a couple of their favorite toys in the crate or carrier, as well as some interactive chewies.** Just don't leave them with anything they may choke on, such as rawhide.

>> **After the flight, remove your puppy from their travel carrier or crate (on a leash) as soon as you reach a safe area where they can stretch their legs and go potty.** They'll be eager to go!

>> **After they've done their business, offer them fresh water and food.** Let them move around, play with some toys, and cuddle with you before you leave the airport.

Traveling by car

Traveling by car is the best way of picking up your Doodle from their breeder. This will likely be their first trip beyond the breeder's property, so they may experience motion sickness, anxiety, or stress. If you have a long trip ahead of you, stop every two or three hours for potty breaks, water, and food. (Young puppies need to eat three or four times a day.)

Travel crates are a great way of keeping your puppy safe while in transit., You can also use a booster seat in which your small Doodle can be securely belted in. If your Doodle is large enough, you can use a canine seat belt harness and buckle, preventing them from having free range of the vehicle.

Poop, Pee, Eat, Sleep, Repeat: Setting Up a Feeding and Potty Schedule

Before you bring home your puppy, give a little thought to their routine. Puppies (and dogs in general) are creatures of habit. Figure out what time of day works for you to feed your puppy, and put in place a schedule for taking them out to go potty, too.

Dogs need to know when and where they're going to eat. Being consistent about feeding helps prevent your Doodle from feeling like they can eat anywhere in your home, which can set them up for future anxiety. This is especially important if you have other pets.

Your Doodle's bowls should be somewhere in the kitchen, but not in a direct path with your cooking area. Under a desk, at one end of a kitchen island, or at the edge of the room are generally good places.

WARNING

Don't place the dog's bowl near a trash can. They may think the can is part of their meals.

Stick to a feeding schedule to help your Doodle know they'll be taken care of at a specific time. The feeding times will depend greatly on your own work schedule, as well as the age of your dog.

TIP

Puppies 2 to 3 months of age need to be fed four times a day. At 3 to 4 months of age, they can be fed three times a day. When they're over 4 months of age, you can settle into feeding twice a day.

Potty time goes hand in hand with feeding time, because when your Doodle eats has the most bearing on when they need to go out. If you want a housetrained dog (and who doesn't?), you'll have to adhere to a schedule. Make sure you schedule your Doodle's potty breaks into your day or arrange to have someone available to do it for you.

REMEMBER

The more your Doodle pup exercises, or plays with family members, the more often they'll need to be taken out.

Dogs over the age of 4 months can hold it longer, but they still require potty breaks more often than a dog over 9 months of age. Take your 4- to 9-month-old dog out every three to four hours to be on the safe side. After the age of 9 months, you can wait as long as five hours, longer if you have to, but that isn't kind to do to your dog on a regular basis.

Male dogs require more time to relieve themselves because they have the tendency to urinate several times instead of letting their bladders empty all at once. They also have to relieve themselves more often throughout the day than most female dogs do.

Here's a sample schedule for a dog 3 to 4 months of age:

6 a.m.	Potty break
6:15 a.m.	Mealtime
6:30 a.m.	Potty break and lots of play
11a.m.	Mealtime
12:15 p.m.	Potty break and lots of play
3 p.m.	Mealtime
3:15 p.m.	Potty break and lots of play
6 p.m.	Mealtime
6:15 p.m.	Potty break and lots of play
8 p.m.	Potty break and play
10 p.m.	Last potty break of the day (no need for play)

Dogs over 4 months of age can safely be fed twice a day, as long as they don't have a medical condition that requires the dog to be fed smaller meals more often.

Giving Your Puppy the Guided Tour

When you first arrive home with your puppy, your entire family may be excited, but try to introduce your new Doodle to your home — and everything and everyone in it — in a controlled, calm, and loving manner. Proper introductions will help them settle in faster and feel secure in their new home.

Do this the right way at the beginning to prevent a long-term socialization problem. Doodles are sensitive and easily frightened.

Showing your pup around

Before you get out of the car, put your puppy on a leash. Not only will this prevent them from running off, you'll also want to have some control over where they go after they're inside. Take each room slowly, so they won't feel overwhelmed. Here are some basic steps to follow:

1. **Walk them into a room.**

2. **Let them sniff around the room, still on the leash.**

3. **In each room, cue your Doodle to sit by placing a treat just over their head, between their eyes.**

   If they don't listen, gently place them into position and reward them so they learn the meaning of the word *sit*.

4. **After they sit, praise them, pet them, and give them a treat.**

5. **Move on to the next room.**

   Repeat these steps until you've gone through every room in your house — even rooms you plan on keeping off-limits for your Doodle. This approach will help them feel more comfortable.

TIP
Dogs react to the emotions of the people around them. If you remain calm, you'll help your Doodle puppy feel more relaxed.

REMEMBER
If you have other dogs, put them outdoors when bringing in your new Doodle. This will prevent any territorial disputes and help your Doodle settle in faster. When they're comfortable in your home, allow them to meet other four-legged family members one at a time.

Greeting the family

Everyone probably wants to be the first to greet your new Doodle. But the last thing you should do is let your whole family come up at once. Being swarmed by a bunch of strangers is way too overwhelming for your new Doodle. Instead, make sure that each family member has a treat in hand and then take turns allowing the Doodle to come and accept the treat. As the Doodle eats the treat, pet them gently on their chest and talk to them in a happy, calm tone of voice. When your Doodle is done with the first treat, repeat with the next person until everyone in the family has had a turn. The meeting will be positive, and the Doodle will learn that everyone in your family is a source of all kinds of love and treats.

TIP
To a dog, being the source of treats means good things. You definitely get on a dog's good side through their stomach. Gentle massages are great, too — especially the ears, tummy, and back.

Many dogs feel intimidated when approached from above. Instead, crouch down to your dog's level or sit on the floor and bring your hand in from below, touching their chest before touching their head or back. Be sure your entire family is on the same page with this. Also, move slowly, allowing your Doodle a chance to sniff at your hand, below their head.

TIP

Always closely supervise children as they interact with your new Doodle. They need to be taught responsible handling techniques and that the Doodle should sit for them before giving the dog a treat or petting them.

WARNING

Meeting other pets

Introducing your Doodle to your other pets is something you need to put a little thought into. An unplanned introduction can go very badly for the new Doodle, as well as for your other pets.

Don't make the introductions at the same time you enter your home with your Doodle — it could be threatening to the existing family pets, who may become territorial and assertive. Instead, keep your other animals in a safe area away from where your new dog will be entering and exploring your home.

WARNING

Do the first introductions in a neutral territory, if possible. A great meeting place is anywhere that your current pet doesn't spend much time, someplace where they won't feel territorial. A park or a friend's fenced yard would work well.

TIP

Introductions to other dogs

The best way for dogs to meet is on their own terms. This means off leash (or if you're unsure, allow the leash to drag) in a safely fenced area where they can greet each other in their own way. You'll see lots of rear-end sniffing, nose-to-nose sniffing, *posturing* (walking around stiff-legged, putting a paw over the other dog's shoulders, or fur raising along the spine, among other things), and maybe some whining, whimpering, or barking.

Regardless of what you see, most dogs work it out well on their own without your help. In fact, getting in the way of this initial canine socializing can cause problems because you aren't allowing the dogs to do what they need to do to figure out where they stand within the pack pecking order. After the dogs figure things out, one dog will bow down and invite the other to play. Then they're off and running, lifelong friends.

Following are some signs that the dogs may have some difficulty getting along. If you notice any of these signs, stay calm but separate them immediately:

WARNING

>> One of the dogs is snarling.

>> The dogs rush at each other growling.

>> Both dogs posture and try to get on top of each other.

>> One of the dogs shows complete disinterest and tries to walk away, but the other dog persistently tries to gain that dog's attention. (This is the most common reaction to a new dog entering the home with an existing dog.) This can happen if one of the dogs is very old and has no interest in playing with another dog, but the other dog really wants to play. The older dog may snap at or injure the persistent younger dog, or the younger dog may inadvertently injure the older dog.

>> The dogs stare at each other for a long time, challenging dominance.

TIP

Most Doodles enjoy climbing on top of other dogs. Another Doodle will fully understand this behavior, but many other dogs don't. It's a learning process for these other dogs as they learn to accept this behavior as affection and not a threat.

TIP

A good way of getting dogs used to each other is to walk them together. Initially, have one person walk one dog and another person walk the other dog. Walk the dogs side by side, but make sure they're separated by one or both of the people. When both dogs are paying more attention to their people than to each other, you can bring them closer together while walking. When the dogs can walk in the same direction together, they'll need to learn to pass each other. Start them at a distance where the dogs don't react to each other. Each time the dogs can pass each other without reacting, bring them a little closer together on the next pass by. When both dogs are working well together, they can have the freedom to play together in a neutral area, such as a park or down the road from your house. However, if you're still uncomfortable with allowing the dogs to interact, or you see something in their actions that's bothersome, contact a professional dog trainer or animal behaviorist right away. It never hurts to get a second or third opinion on the dogs' interactions.

PROJECTING A POSITIVE ATTITUDE

When you're helping two dogs acclimate to each other, keep your emotions in check. In order for the dogs to be comfortable, you need to remain passive yet positive about the situation. Your first dog will be directly affected by your emotions, showing edginess if you're pensive or aggression if you're totally scared of the two dogs getting together. The new dog will quickly pick up on this negative energy flowing from you. Keeping your thoughts — and your energy — positive will help the two dogs acclimate to each other quickly. *Remember:* Doodles are very sensitive to your emotions.

Introductions to cats

Introducing your Doodle to a cat can be dicey — some cats won't be as open to greeting your new friend as the puppy is to saying hello, often with enthusiasm, to a running, screeching cat. If your Doodle believes cats are there to be chased, their relationship will be off to a rocky start. And you can pretty much count on your Doodle wanting to chase anything that moves — it's part of their DNA.

TECHNICAL STUFF

All meat-eating animals have a *prey drive,* a desire to hunt that's triggered by something (or many things). For dogs and cats, movement is one of these triggers; scent comes in a close second. Most dogs chase cats merely because they move (usually running away from dogs). The dog isn't chasing the cat because they're hungry — the movement merely triggers the dog's instinctual desire to hunt.

You have to quickly let your Doodle know that the cat is supposed to be a friend, not prey. In order for the pup to get the message, keep the cat still during the initial introduction. Have someone hold your cat as you introduce your Doodle to it. Keep in mind that your Doodle will be very excited and difficult to hold in one place.

Here's how to hold your cat:

1. **Hold the cat's paws in your hands — front paws in one hand, rear paws in the other.**

2. **Place one arm around the cat's haunches to control the movement of their back end.**

3. **Place the other arm around their shoulders for control of the front end.**

4. **Sit and keep your kitty on your lap, holding securely.**

When you're ready to introduce your Doodle to your cat, follow these steps:

1. **Put your Doodle on a leash.**

2. **Allow the dog to push their nose at the cat, with a loose leash.**

   As your kitty remains still, your Doodle's prey drive won't be super strong, but they'll be very curious and push their nose in closely.

3. **Offer both the dog and the cat some tasty treats.**

   This will make the experience of meeting each other a more positive one. It will give them both good associations in each other's presence.

Don't let go of the cat until your Doodle begins to lose interest and turns away. Instead of just letting go of the cat, place the cat in another room. This will ensure that they don't run and trigger your Doodle's prey drive.

It may take several such meetings in order to ensure that the two creatures become friends. However long it takes, the time spent is well worth it. Not having to separate your pets and teaching them to be comfortable together not only gives you less to worry and fuss about, but also gives them the chance to be companions instead of enemies.

Feline/canine companionship rarely entails the rough play that you see between dogs. It's more of a comfort level in each other's presence. But some do become good friends and will play and sleep together.

Taking your Doodle out to do their business

Shortly after introducing your Doodle to your house, your family, and your other animals, you'll need to show them where they should do their business.

Because your Doodle is new to your household you need to show them where to go. Just letting them out the door might may frighten them. They're not yet familiar with the yard, and they'll want to come back inside with you, where they may potty on the floor — not the behavior you were looking for.

Instead, take them to your designated potty zone — on a leash if your yard isn't fenced. Have some treats with you. Wait with the dog as long as it takes for them to go. Your Doodle has been busy with lots of activities, so you can be sure they have to go. Walk around a bit with them, allowing them to sniff. Make sure the leash is very loose at all times.

TIP

When your Doodle does their business, praise them enthusiastically and give them treats. This positive reinforcement tells the dog that you're happy they went outside, in the area where you want them to go.

Until your Doodle is housebroken, you'll need to continually accompany them to the relief zone, giving treats the moment they do their thing.

TECHNICAL
STUFF

Many dogs, especially those new to a pack, will follow the behavior patterns of the established pack (your other dog). This helps them be accepted by the other dogs and, even better, learn the house rules faster.

Helping Your Doodle through the First-Night Blues

The first night in your house may be very frightening. They've found all kinds of new smells, new people, and new companions — it's a lot to take in all at once. Where are the siblings they used to cuddle with? What are all those new sounds?

Your Doodle was probably living with other puppies (or other dogs if they were in a foster environment) and formed strong relationships with them. Dogs are pack animals, social creatures. They want the company of other canines, and they're very lonely when they're separated from them. Your Doodle will likely miss their former family until they feel at home with you.

This situation can be far different if you already have another dog, as long as the other dog has accepted your new dog and is willing to allow them to remain nearby at night. However, if your new Doodle isn't readily accepted as part of the pack, they'll likely pace, whine, and scratch to get to you.

The first tendency of new dog owners is to take their anxious dog into bed with them, thinking this is the best way to alleviate the poor dog's insecurity. Unless you're planning on always doing this, don't. Yes, your dog may sleep better, but you'll regret it later if you really want them to sleep somewhere else.

WARNING

Allowing your Doodle to sleep with you is setting a precedent for the future. Your dog learns that whining and scratching will earn them a place in the *preferred* bed. Plus, it will make them feel empowered, in control of the family instead of merely a family member. This situation can be a dangerous one for a Doodle with assertive or possessive tendencies.

The first night may be difficult for both of you, but setting the house rules early in the game will help your new Doodle learn their place within your family and home. They'll settle in faster, learn their role, and discover the difference between right and wrong.

TIP

Here are some things you can do to help your Doodle in:

>> Sit with them a while at their bed, massaging their chest, back, and ears.

>> Keep the lights turned low, not off.

>> Try to avoid sharp noises.

>> Give them herbal remedies such as valerian root or chamomile tablets an hour before bedtime to help them relax. You can find these at nearly any store that sells vitamins.

> » Flower remedies such as Equilite Herbals, Greenpet Home Sweet Home, or Bach Rescue Remedy are great for helping your dog settle into their new home. You can find these online.
>
> » A toy puppy with a heartbeat sound can be helpful, as is placing a blanket with the smells of their litter in their bed. Familiar sounds and smells are helpful in settling an anxious Doodle.

Before putting your Doodle to bed, give them lots of exercise. A tired dog doesn't have the energy to be stressed.

TIP

Planning Activities to Keep Your Doodle Entertained

Exercising your Doodle is just as important as feeding them. Set aside time every day to play with your dog and work with them.

The amount of exercise your Doodle needs will depend on its age, its Doodle mix, and its personality. But you can be sure that without enough exercise, any dog will engage in the wrong activities — both to get your attention and to occupy their time.

Walking along on a leash is great exercise, especially for an older dog, but younger dogs need more than this.

REMEMBER

Though training exercises stimulate a dog's mind and tire them out, training doesn't totally exercise a dog's body. Dogs need free play — off leash, preferably with other dogs, as long as they haven't ever displayed any aggression to other canines.

A Toy-size Doodle will often get plenty of exercise racing around the house, but that isn't the preferred situation for a Miniature-size or Standard-size Doodle. Having an 80-pound dog racing around an apartment or even a good-sized house can be quite disruptive — imagine them jumping over the couch, running through the kitchen, and barreling over a trash can. Having any dog larger than 10 pounds means lots of exercise — outside, in all types of weather.

A fenced-in yard will help, but your Doodle will prefer to spend much of their exercise time interacting with you, such as going for long walks and playing fetch and chase games. Make time for play!

It Takes a Village: Making Sure the Whole Family Is Onboard

The responsibility for raising a Doodle shouldn't fall on one person's shoulders (unless you're living alone, of course). Although some types of Doodles easily fall into the pattern of favoring one person, it's highly important that everyone in the family share equally in their care, training, and other daily activities.

After all, it's highly likely that your entire family agreed to get a Doodle. They probably all promised to take on some of the responsibilities, too. Sadly, in most families, it all falls onto one individual to do everything. And guess what happens? The dog does anything for, and with, this one person and doesn't care much about everyone else. With some Doodles, this behavior can become more than a nuisance — Doodles commonly develop resource-guarding behavior if given the wrong message.

TECHNICAL STUFF

Resource guarding is an inappropriate behavior associated with an object your dog covets and desperately wants to keep for themselves. These items can be toys, people, locations, or food. Although most dogs have some desire to hoard all available food for themselves, trying to do so with *your* food or another pet's food isn't acceptable. It also isn't acceptable to become aggressive when someone approaches a piece of furniture or wants to move a dog toy. Resource guarding is a learned response. It occurs if a dog is allowed to always have access to places, people, and items without learning that they're to be shared with everyone. Most dogs try to do this while they're still young, and your response will determine whether it becomes a problem.

Sharing the care of your dog, and being consistent with that care, will prevent resource guarding and ensure that everyone in the family is seen as an equal pack member. Every person should be able to do multiple types of activities with your Doodle, from feeding and walking to cleaning the yard and training. Granted, not all ages can do all activities, but the more involved everyone is, the more your Doodle will bond with them.

Here are a few suggestions for involving everyone in the family on feeding, cleaning, exercise, and training.

Feeding times

Decide on feeding times that you know you can maintain on a regular basis. If family members have to get up for school, work, or other activities, choose a time when they won't be rushed. Dogs take time out of your day, so you may want to wake up earlier in order to attend to your puppy's needs.

Create a calendar where you write down each person's name to take turns doing the feeding. These will be your Doodle's favorite times of the day, so it will be rewarding for everybody.

Some pet parents like to feed their dogs just before they eat so that everyone can eat at the same time. This is fine as long as your Doodle eats at their special area and not near the dinner table. You don't want to do anything that will cause the dog to beg for food at the table.

TIP

When you arrange a feeding and potty schedule, write down the times and appoint specific family members to be responsible for those activities.

Potty breaks

Your Doodle will have to go out numerous times per day, so you can easily assign each family member a specific time to take the dog out. If your children are in school, they can do it when they get home. Adults who return from work can do it upon returning home and just before your Doodle's bedtime.

Sharing this responsibility will give each person the chance to have individual time with your dog and work with them on many different behaviors besides just going potty. For example, you should heel with the dog to the door, have them stay at the door as it's opened, heel through to the potty zone, and release them to do their business (see Chapter 10). Then use the potty cue (see Chapter 9).

Your Doodle will enjoy the process, as well as learn the pattern. They'll also learn to communicate with everyone who works with them.

Training and exercise routines

When you take your Doodle to a training class, you'll need to designate one or two individuals to participate in the lessons. It should be the same person or people each time. But these aren't the only family members who will work with your dog. Everyone needs to practice. It's helpful if several people work together to ensure consistency.

Training classes should start as soon as you can enroll your Doodle. Many trainers offer puppy kindergarten classes, American Kennel Club (AKC) S.T.A.R. Puppy classes (www.akc.org/products-services/training-programs/canine-good-citizen/akc-star-puppy), as well as many levels of formal obedience. Not only will training classes help teach your Doodle good manners, but it will give them opportunities to socialize outside the family — a very important activity for the sometimes reserved Doodle.

There are several training games you can play, as a family. Training games further enhance the bond between dog and pet owners. Here are two suggestions:

» **Round Robin:** In this game, everyone should stand in a circle facing each other, about 6 feet apart. Each individual takes a turn calling your dog to come and sit (see Chapter 10). When your puppy is easily running from person to person, you can begin to increase the distance between you. As you gain distance, the fun increases, because your Doodle gets a lot of exercise and learns to respond to everyone involved.

Round Robin should be played both indoors and out, giving your Doodle a variety of settings and teaching them reliability regardless of where they are. Round Robin will teach your Doodle to come when called, whenever and wherever they're cued to do so.

» **Find Me:** As you play the Round Robin game, the person to whom the dog just came and sat in front of should point to the next family member and say their name as that person calls the dog to come. Here's an example:

Susan (pointing to Jeff): "Find Jeff!"

Jeff (bending forwarding and cuing the dog): "Cooper, come!"

Jeff praises Cooper as they're coming, and then cues Cooper to sit. When Cooper sits, Jeff clicks and rewards.

Jeff (pointing to Susan): "Find Susan!"

Susan (bending forward and cuing the dog): "Cooper, come!"

Susan praises Cooper as they're coming, and then cues Cooper to sit. When Cooper sits, Susan clicks and rewards.

This game can be done with the entire family. As you play, your dog is learning to respond to the come and sit cues, and also learning everyone's names.

After this game has been played for about a week, and your Doodle is readily coming to everyone from upwards of 20 feet away, some of you can hide around a corner or door. Your dog will have to work a little harder to find everyone, but that's part of the fun and offers loads of brain stimulation for your dog.

The Find Me game can grow from this point, to randomly sending your dog to find a specific person, to teaching them to take something to someone. You can be sure your dog will adore this game and everyone who plays it with them!

» Keeping your Doodle healthy through regular veterinary care

» Identifying and treating health problems

» Helping your Doodle when they need first aid

» Raising your Doodle the natural way

Chapter **7**

Doodle Care

This chapter explains how to feed your dog a healthy diet, rich in the nutrients they need — and how to avoid ingredients that may be harmful. Then I tell you how to work with a veterinarian to maintain your dog's health through appropriate vaccinations and examinations. I also explain how to recognize and address health problems on your own, as well as how to use natural oils and supplements to maintain your Doodle's health.

Giving Your Doodle the Nutrition They Need

Your Doodle needs a balanced diet for optimum physical and mental health. If you've been in a pet store recently, or even just the pet-food aisle of your local grocery store, you know how many commercial foods are available — and you may have been overwhelmed by all the options. In this section, I tell you what to look for in a dog food, based on your dog's individual attributes.

You don't want to let your dog become overweight, so you need to know how much to feed, as well as how often. If you do some research into this subject (as if you have time!), you'll find varying schools of thought on this topic. I've read the research, but in this section, I cut through all that and give you tips based on my own experience with dogs.

As your dog ages, or if they develop allergies, you may need to remove certain foods from your dog's diet or add certain foods to it. In this section, I explain how to recognize these special needs, as well as what to do to maintain your dog's health through appropriate nutrition.

The basics of nutrition

Your dog has a few important needs when it comes to nutrition. Here's a list of guidelines to keep in mind:

>> **Give your Doodle plenty of water.** Your dog needs to have plenty of water available at all times. Refresh their water bowl twice daily — don't just wait for your dog to empty the bowl. Puppies and their moms tend to drink more, as do working dogs. If it's hot out, your dog will probably drink more than usual.

>> **If you need to change your dog's diet, do so gradually.** Many Doodles have very sensitive stomachs. This is why you don't want to feed them table scraps or whatever food happens to be on sale that week. Your dog's digestive system takes time to adapt to a new food. To switch foods, over a period of two weeks, gradually increase the amount of the new food and decrease the amount of the old food, until you're feeding only the new diet.

You'll probably have to switch foods shortly after you welcome your puppy into your home. Many breeders feed less-expensive food that has lots of grain filler ingredients, because they have many mouths to feed. Begin the transition to the new food about a month after your puppy arrives, when they've had a chance to acclimate to their new environment.

>> **Feed your dog consistently.** Dogs are happiest when they know what's going to happen and when. If your dog is between the ages of 3 and 4 months, feed them three times a day. Most adult Doodles do well with two meals a day. Some veterinarians suggest returning to feeding 3 times per day during your Doodle's growth period — between 4 to 9 months of age, because they burn a lot of energy during that time. In some situations an adult dog may need to be fed more often — for example, if your dog has a digestive disorder or a tendency to bloat, you'll want to feed them three or four smaller meals a day. Many senior dogs are also better served with more numerous smaller meals a day. (If you're not sure how often to feed your dog, as always, check with your veterinarian.)

» **Don't *free-feed* your dog (leaving food out for them to eat whenever they want); instead, control the amount they eat.** If you control how much they eat and when, you'll be able to control their weight better. You'll also have an easier time with housetraining if you control the food.

REMEMBER

Pay attention to your dog's waistline — to be blunt, they should have one. Dogs can develop fat rolls all over their bodies, which not only hinder their ability to exercise but decrease their hearts' efficiency. Reevaluate the amount of food you feed your dog periodically — your dog's needs will vary as they age, as their activity level changes, and as their lifestyle changes.

TIP

When dogs are spayed or neutered, their metabolism slows. When your Doodle fully recovers from surgery, gradually decrease their caloric intake by one-third. You can use filler foods such as green beans and pumpkin to make them feel fuller without the calories.

» **Feed your dog a balanced diet.** I cover the kinds of foods to find your dog in the following section.

» **Make sure your dog's food is "clean" and free of contaminants.** Commercial foods are typically packed to keep contaminants out, but after you open the food (whether a bag or a can), be sure to securely fasten it, refrigerate canned or raw food, and store dry food in a dry location. After your dog has finished a meal, if anything is left in their bowl, throw the food away, and clean the bowl after every meal. (You wouldn't eat off the same dirty plate over and over without washing it, so why should your dog?)

» **Consult your veterinarian if your dog experiences any abnormal conditions.** Changes in appetite, thirst, or behavior may be signs of serious health issues.

TIP

A shiny dog means a healthy dog. You'll know you're feeding your Doodle correctly if they have bright eyes and a shiny coat and maintain a good weight and energy level.

Types of dog food

There are more brands and variations of dog food than I can count. You can find many of them at your local grocery store, online pet shop, discount department store, or pet store. Where you buy your dog's food doesn't necessarily mean it's a better (or worse) food than any other. The only way to know for sure is to read labels.

Most store-bought dog food comes in two varieties — dry and canned — so in this section, I go into more detail on what to look for and what to avoid with these two types of foods.

WARNING

"Wait!" you say. "What about the semi-moist variety?" You may be tempted to go that route, thinking it's the best of both worlds, but here's a serious warning: Stay away. There's a reason that the food is semi-moist — in a word: preservatives. If you feed your dog a food that contains preservatives, you may as well be pumping poison into them. Over time, preservatives affect your Doodle's liver, heart, and other organs. The result is organ malfunction, organ breakdown, and growth of cancerous tumors.

Commercial dog foods aren't your only options. You can cook your own food for your dog. Or you can prepare a raw diet for your dog or have one delivered. Home-made and raw diets offer many benefits, but you have to be careful with how they're prepared, stored, and fed. Feeding your dog a raw diet is extremely difficult and labor intensive, but there are several good commercial raw diet products available in the frozen dog food section of your pet store.

You can also sign up to a pet food subscription service and have custom meals shipped directly to your door. For a custom-designed diet with human-grade ingredients, here are five to consider:

>> **The Farmer's Dog:** www.thefarmersdog.com

>> **Freshpet:** https://freshpet.com

>> **Nom Nom:** www.nomnomnow.com

>> **Ollie:** www.myollie.com

>> **PetPlate:** www.petplate.com

You can choose the meat protein, vegetables, fruits, vitamins and other nutrients. This is an ideal way to feed your Doodle a healthy, safe diet without preservatives, fillers, or ingredients they can't tolerate well.

So you understand which ingredients are best, in the following sections I give you an outline of how to choose the right proteins, carbohydrates, and fats depending on the type and age of your Doodle.

TECHNICAL STUFF

Every dog food package should have the company's phone number on it. If you have concerns with a specific product, you can call and request to speak with the company's veterinary nutritionist. You can find out if the recipe has changed recently or if they continue to perform feeding trials. This is important when dog-food companies merge with other companies. Sometimes ingredients are changed to improve the bottom line — their profits.

Proteins for a lean, strong dog

Doodles thrive on good-quality, meat-based, protein sources. The amount of protein depends largely on the size and age of your Doodle. Puppies require a higher protein content of 22.5 percent, whereas adult Doodles shouldn't have a diet with more than 18 percent protein.

Always check the ingredients of any food you purchase. The meat protein source should be within the first three ingredients in the list. Meats such as lamb, beef, buffalo, or venison are always great protein sources, and your Doodle is likely to tolerate them far better than a poultry protein. Fish and eggs can also be beneficial to your Doodle's health.

TECHNICAL STUFF

Some dog foods add the protein of corn or other carbohydrates into their protein total, but this isn't really accurate, because Doodles don't digest some filler-type carbohydrates very well. These grains merely move through the dog's system and aren't beneficial to the dog's health. In fact, many Doodles have little tolerance for them and can develop skin problems, ear infections, urinary tract infections, and other physical problems.

REMEMBER

Reading the dog food label will save time and money at the veterinarian's office, as well as enhance the overall health of your Doodle.

Carbohydrates for energy

There are healthy carbohydrates and unhealthy carbohydrates. The difference is that the healthy carbohydrates are digestible and beneficial to your dog's health. The unhealthy carbohydrates can cause an allergic reaction or merely move through and out the other end without providing any health benefits at all.

Good carbohydrates are a good source of fiber, which helps your Doodle's digestive and gastrointestinal systems. Good carbohydrates include barley, brown rice, chicory, lentils, and oats. The bad carbohydrates (those that can cause a physical reaction) include corn, rice hulls, wheat, white rice, or white potatoes.

TIP

If the ingredient list on a dog food bag has more than one grain listed, it may have a higher ratio of filler carbohydrates than necessary. Your dog will feel full, but it won't keep them healthy, and it carries the risk of skin and bowel disorders, ear infections, and more.

As a general rule, dry foods have more carbohydrates than canned foods do. It's still important to read labels, though, because some manufacturers use filler ingredients that appear like meat or vegetables and are really neither.

Vegetables are an important part of your dog's diet, as long as they're green vegetables such as peas, green beans, or broccoli. A light dose of carrots is great, as are sweet potatoes.

Fats: Another source of fuel

Fat is a source of energy for dogs, and puppies require a higher percentage of fats than older dogs do, because they burn a lot of calories every day. A good puppy food will have at least an 8 percent fat content, whereas an adult dog food is fine with a 5 percent fat content.

TIP

Steer away from foods that claim they're for all life stages. Different ages require different nutrients.

The fat content should be sourced by meat fats, such as chicken fat. Even better would be fish oil, such as salmon oil. Plant oils aren't nearly as nutritious as the meal-based fats.

THE INS AND OUTS OF GRAINS AND PRESERVATIVES

You've probably noticed grain-free dog foods in your pet store and wondered whether grain-free is better. It really depends on your individual Doodle. If your Doodle can digest some of the good grains — such as barley, oats, or quinoa — they should be in their diet. These grains offer energy and some protein, as well as some fats.

Grain-free diets aren't good for your dog long-term — studies have proven that the fillers used in these diets (such as peas, lentils, and other legumes) may lead to heart disease. Consult with your veterinarian if you're considering this type of diet. In general, you merely want to remain clear of dog foods with the following ingredients: ground yellow corn, corn gluten meal, rice hulls, wheat, wheat middlings, beet pulp, or soy. These are inexpensive fillers and not healthy sources of nutrition.

Other ingredients to avoid are artificial colors, flavors, sweeteners, and preservatives. They have no place in a nutritious diet and can, in fact, be harmful to your dog's health. Some of these types of ingredients (such as butylated hydroxyanisole [BHA], butylated hydroxytoluene [BHT], and ethoxyquin) have been linked to cancer in numerous studies.

Some Doodles have very sensitive stomachs and can't handle a high fat content in their food. Because most puppy diets contain a high fat content, you may want to consult with your veterinarian if you see loose stool. Sometimes just adding digestive enzymes and/or probiotics to your puppy's meals is enough to help them digest that rich puppy food.

Going to the Veterinarian

One of the most important things you can do as the owner of a Doodle is to find a veterinarian you trust. Just as not every doctor is right for you, not every veterinarian is right for your dog. In this section, I walk you through finding a good veterinarian and fill you in on some key issues surrounding your dog's health, including spaying or neutering, getting regular checkups and vaccinations, and controlling parasites.

Choosing a veterinarian

You can find the names and numbers of numerous local veterinarians in your phone book (if you actually still have one) or online. The tough part is deciding which one is right for your dog. Convenience may play a big part in your ultimate decision (you'd probably rather go to a veterinarian who's closer to your house than all the way across town), but the most important factors when choosing a veterinarian should be the veterinarian's reputation, the clinic's facilities, and the veterinarian's specialties.

The veterinarian's demeanor can be equally important. You must have full trust and faith in your Doodle's veterinarian, or you'll always be dubious about their conclusions about your dog's health. You want a veterinarian who's good with you *and* your dog.

REMEMBER

You don't have to get all your veterinary services from one location. For example, I use the services of a local veterinarian for my animals' regular checkups, vaccinations, and stomach upsets. But when it was time for my dog to be neutered, I took him to another veterinarian because he was the only one within an hour radius who performed laser surgery, and that's what I wanted for my dog. Not every veterinarian can specialize in everything — just as not every doctor can specialize in everything.

The best way to choose a veterinarian is to talk to other pet owners in your area. Check with your family members, neighbors, and friends who have pets — they may be able to give you a referral to one they trust, or let you know about those they've had negative experiences with.

Another great way to search for a good veterinarian in your area is to check their reviews on Facebook (www.facebook.com), Yelp (www.yelp.com), Thumbtack (www.thumbtack.com), and other online sources.

TIP

Here's what to look for in a veterinary clinic:

>> **A friendly staff:** The receptionist who answers the phone the very first time you call should be friendly, as should every person you come into contact with at the clinic, from the veterinarian technician on up to the veterinarian.

>> **A clean waiting room and exam room:** If the clinic can't be bothered to keep the areas of the office that you *see* clean, imagine what it's like in the back, where they take your dog for shots or medical treatment.

>> **Efficient recordkeeping:** You want to be sure that your veterinarian has a complete record of your dog's health and can access it at a moment's notice.

>> **Knowledgeable and helpful assistants and veterinarians:** You want to be sure that your questions are treated with respect and that you get the answers you need. You don't want to feel rushed through your appointment or as though the veterinarian doesn't have enough time for you.

When you're looking for a veterinarian, you'll need to decide whether to take your dog to a doctor who works alone or to a larger clinic where multiple veterinarians are on staff. Table 7-1 lists the pros and cons of each.

TABLE 7-1   **Single Veterinarians versus Veterinary Clinics**

Clinic Type	Pros	Cons
Single-vet clinic	Your veterinarian will be more familiar with you and your dog and better able to identify problems when they occur. Your veterinarian will be able to spend more time with your dog.	Your veterinarian will likely not be available in an emergency. Your veterinarian won't have other opinions readily available. Your veterinarian likely won't have any specific veterinary specialties to handle difficult cases.
Multiple-vet clinic	One of the veterinarians will likely be available in an emergency. The veterinarians can consult one another on difficult cases and get better insight into medical conditions. Different veterinarians in the clinic may specialize in different areas, such as nutrition or holistic treatments, and you can turn to whichever veterinarian who has the knowledge you need at the time, with your records all in one place.	You may see a different veterinarian every time you visit, which means you won't develop as close a relationship to your veterinarian as you would otherwise. Each veterinarian will be very busy and may not spend much time with you.

Here's a list of questions you can ask a veterinarian to help you determine whether they're right for you and your dog:

>> **What vaccinations do you recommend and how often should they be given?** Many veterinarians prefer to practice traditional methods — and commonly, dogs have been vaccinated once a year, whether they need the vaccine or not. Newer approaches involve blood tests (called *titers*) to determine whether the vaccine is needed. Titers measure the levels of immune response your dog has.

>> **Where do you send clients who require specialists for their dogs?** You want to make sure that your veterinarian can answer this question and refers their patients to specialists they trust. You also want to pay attention to how far away that specialist is and, if it seems farther than you'd normally want to travel, ask if there's a reason for referring patients so far away. Maybe that veterinarian is the best one in the state, and the local veterinarian only trusts their patients with the best. Or maybe they just don't know anyone else. Obviously, the former would be a better answer than the latter.

>> **Do you offer alternative or homeopathic approaches?** If you don't care about alternative therapies and you're a straight-by-the-book kind of a person, this question won't matter to you. But if you'd like to consider alternative approaches, the veterinarian's answer will make a huge difference. Whether your veterinarian offers these alternatives or not, you want a veterinarian who doesn't dismiss them as wacko.

TECHNICAL STUFF

Homeopathy operates on the assumption that like heals like. Similar to traditional vaccines that utilize killed or low doses of live germs to create antibodies, homeopathic remedies take the same path of administering diluted substances to help the dog heal. The dilution is done in several stages to prevent side effects. These remedies come in tablets, powders, liquids, and ointments. Though they're readily available at health-food stores and online, it's best to consult with a veterinarian who is familiar with alternative medicine in order to know the correct substances, dilutions, and doses to give your dog.

>> **What are your hours?** Make sure that the veterinarian is open hours that are convenient for your life and schedule.

>> **Are you available in emergencies? If not, what arrangements have you made for your patients?** You probably can't expect your veterinarian to be available at all hours of the day or night, but you can and should expect your veterinarian to have a number you can call in case of after-hours emergencies. It may be a 24-hour veterinary hospital in your area.

CHAPTER 7 **Doodle Care** 133

>> If my dog is sick, will you tell me all my treatment options and their costs, and let me make the decision that's right for me financially and emotionally? One of the worst parts about owning a dog is having to make decisions about how far you'll go, and how much you'll spend, to save their life. Some veterinarians believe that anything and everything should be done, and they may make you feel guilty if you question whether a particular treatment is necessary. You want a veterinarian who will respect your decisions and not make you feel like a horrible person for not spending thousands and thousands of dollars to save your dog's life — unless you have the means to. It's bad enough to have to lose your dog without having to deal with a veterinarian's guilt trip in the process.

TIP

Make a list of questions for your veterinarian before you visit so you can get the answers you need while you're there. When you visit the veterinarian, do they answer all your questions in an easy-to-understand manner and make the effort to fully explain your dog's health issues? If not, they're not the vet for you.

Spaying or neutering

Spaying or neutering your dog should be on your schedule. Part of being a responsible guardian of a Doodle is controlling the pet population by spaying or neutering. Allowing accidental breedings is the irresponsible thing to do. Plus, an intact dog can be challenging in many ways:

>> Intact dogs can have a distinct odor, the males upon maturity and the females when in season. It can be difficult to contain a male dog who smells a female dog in season within a 5-mile radius. Instinct drives him to seek her out. And, as the desire to do so strengthens, he may begin to scent-mark your house and property (by urinating on things).

>> Adult intact dogs also experience behavioral changes. They have more difficulty focusing and can become irritable, territorial, or even aggressive.

You may have heard the following myths about spaying or neuter before the age of 1:

>> **Your dog won't grow to their full potential if spayed or neutered.** Dogs actually often continue growing until the age of 2, whether they're spayed or neutered or not.

>> **Your dog will get fat.** Dogs only get fat if they aren't exercised.

>> **Your dog will develop arthritis if neutered before the age of 1 or 2.** Early onset of arthritis only occurs when a dog has been injured while young. It has nothing to do with spaying or neutering.

If you got your Doodle to be a pet, you don't need to wait until they reach full sexual maturity, especially when allowing them to do so will bring about some behavioral changes that can make the dog more challenging as a pet. Neutering between 6 and 8 months will prevent these behavioral issues.

The spaying or neutering procedure really doesn't take much time, but it *is* surgery, so your veterinarian will recommend not feeding or giving your Doodle any water starting about 12 hours before the surgery. (If your veterinarian's guidelines differ from these, of course, do what your veterinarian says.)

After surgery, you'll need to keep your dog quiet for a couple days, to give them some time to heal. Don't let your dog jump or race around within a week after surgery.

Some dogs will lick or bite at the incision area as it heals, because it can be very itchy. You can prevent this biting and itching in a few ways:

» **Put a soft or hard plastic Elizabethan (cone-shaped) collar on your dog.** With one of these contraptions on, your dog won't be able to reach to bite at the incision area. They'll try, of course — and they'll bump that collar on everything they pass. No dog likes wearing one of these collars, but keeping them from biting or licking their incision is critical, so just remember that it's only for a week or so.

» **Rub a product called Grannick's Bitter Apple around the area.** I usually apply antibacterial cream around the incision area, and then I apply the Bitter Apple on top of that. With such a horrible flavor, your dog is sure to not mess with the incision area. You'll need to reapply the Bitter Apple every day.

No matter what, keep the incision area clean. After your dog goes outside (and remember to keep the play to a minimum), clean the area with a disinfectant solution such as NOLVASAN Solution, and then reapply the antibacterial cream and Bitter Apple over that.

Going for regular checkups and vaccinations

Yearly vaccinations and examinations are important for your Doodle. This is especially true for dogs under 6 years of age — they have lots of energy and are inquisitive, so they often get into things that may cause a parasite infection or illness. Regular checkups, with fecal tests, can identify an infestation or infection that you never knew existed. Your dog's veterinarian will customize vaccinations according to your dog's age and overall health.

Vaccinations

Puppies and adult dogs require different vaccination regimens. Because puppies are just starting out, they need an initial set of vaccinations (which they get from their breeder) followed by booster shots in order to attain a high level of resistance to common illnesses. When your Doodle celebrates their first birthday, the yearly vaccinations are the boosters needed to maintain a healthy resistance.

PUPPY VACCINATIONS

When you get your puppy, they should have had at least the first set of vaccinations. These include the initial parvo and distemper vaccination at the age of 6 weeks. Most puppies are allowed to leave their breeder between 7 and 8 weeks, after they've had a chance to learn some social skills from their littermates and mother.

There will be two more booster shots that first year for distemper and parvo, as well as hepatitis. The vaccinations are normally given at 10 and 12 weeks. At the age of 4 months, your Doodle pup should get a rabies vaccination, which is good for one year. A year later, the next rabies vaccination will be good for three years.

TECHNICAL STUFF

The reason your puppy needs a series of vaccinations is because the antibodies they got from their mother can interfere with their ability to create their own immune system to overcome the declining maternal antibodies. This is the reason the booster shots are done every three or four weeks, to gradually build your pup's immunity to these diseases.

ADULT DOG VACCINATIONS

Most adult dogs get a set of annual vaccinations, along with a three-year rabies vaccination. The only vaccination required by law is the rabies one. Many municipalities require proof of vaccination in order to obtain licenses, allowing your dog to go to dog parks, live in apartment complexes, or be in any social environment.

To understand which vaccinations are vital versus recommended, you should have an idea of which are core versus non-core. Core vaccinations should be given to all dogs, whereas non-core vaccinations are based on where you live, where you travel, or your general lifestyle.

The core vaccinations are the following:

>> Distemper

>> Hepatitis

>> Parvo

>> Rabies

The distemper, hepatitis, and parvo vaccinations are often blended and applied through one injection. The rabies shots are always separate.

Here are the non-core vaccinations and some information on why you may want to consider them:

>> **Bordetella:** The respiratory infection of Bordetella, also known as kennel cough, is easily transmitted from one dog to another. There are 14 types of kennel cough. Though the Bordetella vaccine only covers a percentage of these, it greatly reduces your dog's risk of contagion. For this reason, it's normally required at dog daycares and boarding facilities.

>> **Canine influenza:** The newest vaccination, which should be administered yearly, is canine influenza, the dog flu. Canine influenza is becoming more prevalent in most areas and is highly contagious. It can also be fatal if not treated promptly. You may want to request this vaccination if your veterinarian doesn't offer it.

>> **Leptospirosis:** Leptospirosis is a common bacteria in ponds and wild animal droppings. If you take your dog to a farm, hike in the woods, or merely live near an area teeming with wild animals such as deer, rabbits, turkey, or bear, your dog is at high risk.

>> **Lyme disease:** Lyme disease is highly prevalent throughout the world. It's transmitted by deer ticks, usually associated with white tail deer, but also with many other wild and domestic animals. Many dogs get Lyme, and their owners don't know it. They show no signs of having it until it becomes a heavy infection. Although Lyme disease can often be treated with antibiotics, it rarely goes away completely and can cause problems as your dog ages.

TECHNICAL STUFF

Many types of tick-borne diseases can be subclinical, meaning they don't show signs until a heavy infection or another illness is present.

>> **Parainfluenza:** Parainfluenza is another respiratory infection easily transmitted from one dog to another. It causes a bronchial infection and results in kennel cough. Parainfluenza originated in horses, but it crossed over into dogs in high-population kennels, such as racing Greyhounds. In 2004, parainfluenza was found to have mutated into a highly infectious canine virus.

If your puppy will be exposed to areas where there are wild animals, or if you travel, go to dog shows, dog parks, or on walks in the woods, all these vaccinations are recommended. In fact, most dog boarding facilities require them.

If your Doodle is primarily a house dog and only goes out to do their business in your yard, they may be safe enough with just the core vaccinations. Keep in mind, however, that your dog doesn't live in a vacuum, even indoors. Fleas, ticks, and other germs can get inside on the soles of shoes, through open windows, and on other pets that come and go.

Many veterinarians routinely offer the core vaccines, but depending on your veterinarian, you may need to request the non-core ones.

Regular checkups

Regular checkups aren't just about vaccinations. They should also entail a fecal exam (to check for parasites, including giardia, as well as coccidia) and a blood test (to check for heartworm and tick-borne illnesses).

When you bring your Doodle to your veterinarian for a yearly exam, your veterinarian will examine their abdomen for lumps and sensitivity, take their temperature, and check their eyes, ears, teeth, and throat. Some veterinarians like to watch the dog in motion; others manipulate their legs and neck, checking for signs of injury or sensitivity.

At your puppy's first physical exam with your veterinarian, they may order a *baseline test* (a simple blood test that gives your veterinarian an idea of what constitutes normal function for your dog). If you have one done while your dog is healthy, it'll be a great way of informing your veterinarian of age-related or illness-related changes in your dog down the road.

I always have baseline tests done on my dogs prior to spaying or neutering, to make sure my dogs didn't have any heart or blood problems that may risk their lives while on the operating table. Most veterinarians require this anyway. As a dog ages, baseline testing should be done yearly to diagnose any life-threatening or debilitating diseases at an early stage.

Controlling parasites

Modern veterinary medicine now offers many ways to prevent parasite infestation. On your first visit to the veterinarian, be sure to discuss this subject. Your veterinarian will prescribe the appropriate preventive for your Doodle's size and age. The main parasites that must be prevented are heartworm, whipworm, roundworm, hookworm, and tapeworm. Any of these can cause severe illness or death. All of them are contagious in some form or another.

For heartworm prevention, you'll give your Doodle a monthly tablet prescribed by the veterinarian. For flea and tick prevention, any number of oral chewables and topical oils are available; you typically give them monthly. Talk with your veterinarian to find out exactly which parasites each product will repel or kill, and go with their recommendations.

Some breeds of dogs don't respond well to flea, tick, and parasite prevention products. Most veterinarians are aware of this, but do some research to make sure that your Doodle mix won't have a bad reaction to the medications.

If you're using a topical deterrent, such as Frontline, and your dog gets bathed a lot, you'll want to reapply the topical preventive more often than the package suggests. A topical such as Revolution, on the other hand, goes into the bloodstream and doesn't require reapplication more than once a month.

Recognizing and Addressing Health Issues

Not every dog is in perfect health all the time — just as not every human being is in perfect health all the time. Though some dogs display health sensitivities as pups, others may not develop them until they get older. In the following sections, I walk you through some of the most common problems dogs develop and tell you what to expect in terms of treatment and prevention. Many of these health concerns are common in Doodles, and they can be indicative of a more serious issue. It's important to delve into the problem and discover the source.

Itches, bumps and spots: Skin disorders

Dogs are commonly allergic to flea and tick bites. One bite is all it takes to drive your Doodle crazy. Multiple bites will cause their fur to fall out, their skin to thicken and redden, and constant scratching, biting, and discomfort.

Skin allergies also occur when dogs eat something that doesn't agree with them. Some have allergies to lawn treatments or specific types of grasses or plants, for example.

The only way to determine the exact cause of the problem is to take your Doodle to a veterinary dermatologist for testing. Knowing what's causing the problem will help you remove it from your dog's environment and speed the healing process. Plus, it'll help you prevent your dog from having the same reaction again.

Most allergy tests require a vial of blood to be drawn. The blood is sent out to a lab where it's tested. Within a week or two, you'll get the results as well as a list of safe foods for your Doodle. Doodles are notoriously allergic to several types of foods and environmental allergens, so I highly recommend this process — it'll save you a lot of stress, time, and money.

A more accurate allergy test is via intradermal skin testing where allergens are injected into the skin. The dermatologist can then identify all the specific items that your Doodle can't tolerate. This test can detect a less severe allergic reaction than a blood test can.

Food allergies

With all the ingredients that go into commercial dog foods, it's no wonder that some dogs have allergies — with every additional ingredient, there's an additional item that the dog may be allergic to. From dyes and preservatives, to using multiple grains as fillers, any number of these can cause dry skin, itching, runny eyes, and behavioral anomalies, such as hyper or aggressive behavior due to overall discomfort.

Your veterinarian will have some suggestions of food brands or homemade meals that will help pinpoint the source(s) of your dog's allergies and offer your dog a wholesome diet. Consult with a holistic veterinarian or veterinary dermatologist about food allergies, too — they'll have some good insight into the most common foods that cause allergic reactions in dogs, such as beef, chicken, corn, rice, and wheat, among others.

Finicky or piggy: Eating disorders

More dogs have obesity issues than poor-skinny-waif problems. I've seen my share of barrel-shaped Doodles. Just as humans tend to overeat, many dog owners overfeed their dogs. Overeating is just as dangerous for canines as it is for humans.

Ask your veterinarian if your dog is at a healthy weight. You should be able to detect a waistline — an indentation between your dog's ribcage and hips. If you can't, or if your veterinarian says your dog is overweight, here are a few things you can do to ensure your Doodle remains fit and healthy:

>> **Change their diet to a lower-calorie one.**

>> **Reduce the amount you feed them by half and substitute the other half with raw vegetables.** This solution gives your dog the fiber they need without the calories they don't need. Canned pumpkin and green beans are great options.

>> **Make sure they're getting enough exercise (see Chapter 3).** Doodles are normally very active and require lots of exercise for both their body and mind.

WARNING

If your dog is underweight or stops eating, take them to the veterinarian right away. Dogs often refuse to eat when they're very sick. Have your veterinarian examine your dog to find out what's going on.

Doodles don't have to be severely sick to refuse to eat, however. There are other reasons, too, including the following:

>> Not getting enough exercise

>> Stress

» Anxiety

» Not liking plain kibble

» Having an upset stomach

If there's absolutely nothing wrong with your Doodle and they still don't want to eat, try adding some flavorful gravy to their meals. Adding canned food and mixing it into the kibble can also be helpful in generating interest. Maybe just changing their food altogether to something that's richer, more aromatic, and more flavorful will do the trick. Some pet parents of Doodles will add real cooked meats, vegetables, or gravy to the meals. Just be careful, however, because Doodles are very intelligent — if they realize that skipping a meal means that the next one will be fit for a king, they'll do it.

Born with it or accidental: Skeletal issues

Skeletal disorders can be caused by accidental injury or genetic inheritance. Either way, your veterinarian will need to do a thorough exam and take X-rays to discover the source of discomfort.

Because Doodles are a mix of two breeds, you'll need to be aware of skeletal issues that may be common on both sides of the parentage. Toy-size Doodles tend to have knee and hock problems. Standard-size Doodles may be prone to hip or elbow dysplasia. Doodles with long backs may be prone to spinal disorders. The only way to ensure a better-than-average likelihood of few skeletal disorders throughout the life of your Doodle is to do lots of research into the parent breeds, as well as their breeders. (You can find out about health testing of parent dogs in Chapter 4.)

If a skeletal disorder is *degenerative* (that is, it happens over time, as the dog ages — such as osteoarthritis), the inflammation can be controlled by several different prescription medications. The one your veterinarian recommends will be based on the dog's age, size, and possible breed combination — not all medications work well with all dog breeds. There is rarely a way to prevent age-related skeletal disorders — it happens to all of us. Bodies simply break down as they age, and Doodles are bound to injure themselves through their active antics at some point, which can cause physical problems later in their lives.

You can give supplements such as glucosamine and chondroitin when your Doodle becomes a senior or if they suffer an injury earlier in their life. This supplement will help control the fluid levels between the joints and reduce inflammation in the tissue surrounding the joints. If your veterinarian isn't familiar with these supplements, talk to a holistic veterinarian or find another veterinarian who is. Changing your dog's diet can also be helpful. For example, a diet high in omega-3 fatty acids (such as salmon oil) and low in carbohydrates can reduce inflammation.

Common food sensitivities

Not all foods are right for all dogs. As dogs age, or even due to genetics, some dogs need special diets to stay healthy and happy.

TIP

Here are a few signs telling you that what you're currently feeding may not be right for your dog:

>> Your dog is scratching a lot.

>> Your dog tends to get frequent ear infections.

>> Your dog has really bad gas.

>> Your dog has loose, light-colored stool or diarrhea.

>> Your dog has *lick granulomas* (raised reddish skin due to the dog repetitively licking and biting that one spot) on their legs.

>> Your dog's coat is dry, dull, and coarse.

There's really no way to know for sure which specific ingredient is causing your dog distress without narrowing it down by feeding fewer ingredients. Because the most common allergy is to specific meats, that's the first item you should change. The most common switch is from chicken or beef to duck, fish, lamb, or venison.

Another common allergy is to grains, such as corn and wheat, which are common fillers in commercial kibble. Many dogs have allergies to these grains, which manifests itself in an itchy coat, watery eyes, ear infections, and lick granulomas. Rice can be another culprit; you can easily remove rice from your dog's diet to see if this was the cause of their allergic reactions.

Try eliminating some of these common allergens before giving your dog prescription medications, which treat the symptoms but not the source of the allergies. Elimination diets take time (10 to 12 weeks) to see results.

WARNING

Dogs suffering from physical ailments, such as cancer, diabetes, or organ malfunction, need prescription diets from a veterinarian. For example, you may need a low-sodium prescription diet if your dog suffers from heart disease, a prescription diet high in complex carbohydrates for a dog with diabetes, or a low-protein prescription diet for a dog with liver problems. Only a veterinarian can test for these disorders, so you'll serve your dog best by getting the correctly formulated diet that your veterinarian provides.

Itches, bumps and spots: Skin disorders

Skin disorders are very common with Doodles, especially if they're given the wrong diet, have environmental allergies, become stressed, or are bitten by bugs. The following section walks you through the most common ones.

Sebaceous adenitis

One of the most common skin disorders for Doodles is sebaceous adenitis, which is generally genetic, passed down in the Poodle genes and tough to avoid when breeding anything with Poodles, especially those that are of Standard size. Sebaceous adenitis is generally a cosmetic disorder with hair thinning and loss that begins at the dog's head, neck, and back. The skin beneath the hair loss areas will become scaly and dry, as the sebaceous glands malfunction. The dog may emit a musty odor. Long-haired dogs can get secondary epidermal infections because their hair blocks airflow to dry up the lesions.

TECHNICAL STUFF

The sebaceous glands in your Doodle's skin produce an oily substance called *sebum.* This skin oil provides your dog's skin and coat with moisture and emits chemicals that coincide with your dog's emotional state. For example, if your dog is feeling distressed or aroused, other dogs can smell this emotional state via the sebum emitted from their sebaceous glands.

If you see any signs — hair loss, itching, scaly skin, take your dog to the veterinarian for testing. They'll likely take a skin biopsy and run fungal and bacterial cultures to check the source of the disorder.

Luckily, although sebaceous adenitis is not curable, it is not fatal and it's very treatable, allowing your Doodle to live a normal life span. The care includes keratolytic shampoos, emollient rinses, and regular oil baths and sprays to improve your Doodle's skin and coat. There are also prescription treatments, such as Apoquel. You can also give your dog supplements to help keep their skin and coat healthy; these include vitamins A, C, and E, as well as omega-3 and omega-6 fatty acids. Your veterinarian can prescribe antibiotics for lesions and corticosteroids to address the itch.

Demodicosis

In demodicosis, skin mites can cause itching, hair loss, and inflammation. It's easily treated with topical and oral medications, but only your veterinarian will be able to detect the mites via a skin scraping and looking under a microscope. Many dogs get the mites from their mother, though rarely do they cause problems later on. It is not transferable to other pets and people. It only affects dogs who already harbor the mites and have a weakened immune system.

Sarcoptic mange

Sarcoptic mange is very contagious to other dogs and humans. The symptoms are similar to demodicosis, but it isn't as common. Skin scrapings also aid in diagnosis of this problem.

Skin tumors

Labradoodles and Goldendoodles, as well as several other types of Doodle, are prone to skin tumors. These tumors can originate in the anal glands or appear in numerous other areas on your Doodle's body. Some skin tumors are benign (not cancerous); others are malignant (cancerous).

WARNING

To prevent a skin tumor from progressing from benign to malignant, always be aware of your dog's natural contours. When you feel anything new (especially if it's growing quickly), take your dog to your veterinarian for surgical removal.

Dry skin

Dry skin is a common condition with Doodles. Normally, you can figure out the cause, such as a vitamin or mineral deficiency, poor diet, too much bathing, harsh shampoo, or an illness. A malfunctioning thyroid gland can also be a source, but your veterinarian will need to run a blood test to determine if that's the cause.

Flea-related issues

Flea bites can create all sorts of problems for your Doodle, such as flea allergy dermatitis, abrasions, and *hemobartonella* (a condition in which organisms in the flea's mouth go into the dog, causing anemia). Be sure to use a monthly flea and tick preventive.

Offering First-Aid to Your Doodle

You can't care for your dog like a veterinarian can, but there are actions you can take when your Doodle is injured or ill. Often, these first-line responses can make the difference between life and death. Having the supplies to address whatever issue comes up is the first step. Second is knowing how to identify a problem. Finally, having your veterinarian on speed dial can ensure you get help quickly.

Assembling your canine first-aid kit

Following are all the items you need in a basic, in-home first-aid kit. Though you may not need all the items listed here at any one time in your mixed breed's life, it's a good idea to at least own them and know where you keep them.

>> First-aid book

>> Adhesive tape or self-sticking Vet Wrap

>> Cotton balls

>> Square gauze pads, 3 x 3 inches

>> Instant hot/cold packs

>> Cotton-tipped applicators (like Q-tips)

>> Antibacterial ointment (like Neosporin or Bacitracin)

>> Bitter Apple cream and/or spray

>> Hydrogen peroxide

>> Clotisol (clotting cream)

>> Activated charcoal (in case of poisoning)

>> Tweezers and small, sharp scissors

>> Thermometer (**Note:** A dog's normal temperature is 101 degrees. You can buy ear thermometers for pets at most major pet-supply stores.)

>> Aloe-vera gel (to sooth scrapes and cuts)

>> Canine antidiarrhea medication (such as Metronidazole, an antibiotic available from your veterinarian) (**Note:** Human over-the-counter antidiarrhea medications often don't work at all with dogs.)

>> Disposable gloves

>> Muzzle (**Note:** Many injured dogs bite first and ask questions later.) You can make a quick muzzle out of a gauze roll, if necessary.

TIP

You can make a quick muzzle out of your leash by wrapping it around his muzzle and then behind his ears.

>> Something you can use for a stretcher, such as a board, blanket, or floor mat

If you're hiking, camping, boating, or engaging in some other outdoor activities with your Doodle, place the following items in a zip-top plastic bag and toss it in your backpack:

>> Fresh water, at least 1 pint

>> Antiseptic wipes

>> Sterile gauze pads

>> Antibacterial ointment

>> Vet Wrap

>> Bite/sting stop

>> Tweezers

If you're interested, you can take courses in first aid and canine CPR. Books such as *First Aid for Dogs: What to Do When Emergencies Happen,* by Bruce Fogle, and *The First Aid Companion for Dogs & Cats,* by Amy D. Shojai, are also good sources.

Knowing what to do in an emergency

Dogs tend to be inquisitive, which can often get them into trouble. Doodles often react before thinking things through, and even then they don't consider the implications of their actions. No matter where you live, your dog could have an accident, get sick, or get hurt. Few dogs go through life without *some* physical trauma.

In the following sections, I cover the majority of situations, how to recognize emergencies, and what to do if they happen to your dog.

Bloat

Bloat is a swelling of the stomach from gas, fluid, food, or all three. It tends to occur in dogs with large chest cavities, like Pyredoodles or large Labradoodles, who also tend to eat their food too quickly.

TIP

Doodles prone to bloat should be fed several small meals a day and not exercise for an hour after eating. Or use a slow-feeder dish, which will increase how long it takes for the dog to eat, reducing the incidence of bloat.

The symptoms of bloat include pacing continuously or lying down in odd places, panting, whining, salivating, and being agitated. The dog may vomit without anything coming up. They'll drool excessively, make retching noises (without being able to vomit), and have swelling in the abdominal area.

WARNING

Bloat is potentially fatal, and you can't do anything for your dog to help other than recognize the symptoms and get them to the veterinarian *immediately.* Surgery must be performed within six hours to save the dog's life. Bloat has a 30 percent to 60 percent fatality rate, mostly due to dog owners who either don't recognize the symptoms or are too slow to react.

You can preempt the possibility of bloat by asking your veterinarian to surgically tack your dog's stomach in place. Discuss this option with your veterinarian if you're interested.

Broken bones or dislocations

You can never be sure whether your dog has broken or dislocated a bone without the help of your veterinarian. The only symptoms you'll be able to recognize are your dog being unable to use a limb or the limb appearing to be at an odd angle. If the dog has a rib, shoulder, hip, or back fracture, they may not move at all.

If bleeding is involved, apply direct pressure (see "Puncture wounds," later in this chapter, for tips on controlling bleeding), but *don't try to fix the fracture.* Protect the area with cotton padding. If it's a limb, apply a splint of some sort (two long pieces of wood) and secure them with a bandage such as 3M Vetrap. Carefully place your dog on a makeshift stretcher — a rug, blanket, or wide board will work — so they won't further injure themselves by moving. Take them to the veterinarian immediately.

WARNING

Some injured animals are prone to aggression, due to stress and pain, so I recommend muzzling your dog before applying the splint. Not only will this prevent injury to you, but it will prevent further injury to the dog.

Burns

You'll know your dog is burned if you see singed fur, blistering, redness of skin, and/or swelling. Flush it with cool water and apply aloe gel. Then get to the veterinarian immediately for complete treatment, which will likely include antibiotics to prevent infection. If you have someone who can drive while you flush your dog's injury with cool water, that would be ideal. If not, just put your Doodle in the car and get to the veterinarian right away.

Some light-colored Doodles can get sunburn on their muzzles. Their pink skin may be sensitive and in need of sunblock if you expect to be spending time outdoors with them. Be sure that the type of sunscreen you use isn't toxic for dogs. Zinc oxide and titanium dioxide are fine, but avoid sunscreens with oxybenzone in them — they're known to cause allergic reactions in dogs. Look for a gel-type sunscreen — lotions, sprays, and sticks won't get past the hair or fur on your dog's nose.

Choking

You'll recognize the symptoms of choking by noticing that your dog is having difficulty breathing or swallowing. They may paw at their mouth, and their lips and tongue could turn blue from lack of blood flow.

Look inside your dog's mouth and throat. Clear it by using pliers or tweezers — if you stick your finger down their throat, you can easily lodge the object farther down.

If the object is too deep and you can't get it, perform the Heimlich maneuver by putting your hands on either side of your dog's rib cage and applying firm, quick pressure. Or place your dog on their side and press against their rib cage with the palm of your hand. Repeat until the object is dislodged.

TIP

Get someone to take you and your dog to a veterinarian as you're doing the Heimlich. You may not be able to totally dislodge the entire object, and the sooner you can get veterinary attention, the better chance your dog has of surviving.

Cuts

Wash the area with cool water and mild soap; then pat dry. If the cut has stopped bleeding (and after the area is dry), apply an antibacterial ointment and then spread a little Grannick's Bitter Apple ointment around the edges (*not* in the cut) to prevent your dog from licking off the antibacterial ointment.

If the wound is deep or doesn't stop bleeding, apply a pressure bandage and take your dog to the veterinarian immediately. It's likely to require stitches or staples, as well as drains to prevent a buildup of bacteria.

Diarrhea

If your dog has diarrhea, the best thing to do is withhold food for 12 to 24 hours. Give them plenty of ice cubes and water — they'll need to stay hydrated.

Some dogs get diarrhea after eating something that doesn't agree with them, so after that initial 12 to 24 hours, keep your dog on a bland diet of boiled rice and ground beef (as long as they're not allergic to these ingredients) for a couple days and gradually transfer them back to their normal food.

If the diarrhea doesn't end within a day, take your Doodle to the veterinarian and bring a stool sample with you for testing. If the consistency of the diarrhea is mucousy, if it's light in color or tar black, or if it contains blood, take your dog to the veterinarian immediately.

Loose stool can also be a sign of an allergic reaction or stress. Always aim to discover the source of the problem, and don't settle for treatment that's temporary.

Heatstroke

WARNING

Heatstroke happens when a dog becomes too hot. The symptoms of heatstroke include difficulty breathing, vomiting, high temperature, and collapse. If a dog suffering from heatstroke isn't treated immediately, it can be fatal.

The best treatment is to immerse your dog in a tub of cool water. You can also gently soak them with a garden hose or wrap them in a cool, wet towel. You'll need to lower their temperature gradually, so don't put them in a tub of ice — this could go in the other direction and cause hypothermia or shock. If they'll drink, give them some electrolyte-supplemented water, such as smartwater.

Take their temperature often and stop the cooling process when their temperature reaches 103 degrees. If you aren't sure how to proceed, or you have any questions or concerns, immediately take your dog to the veterinarian.

If your Doodle has a short nose (such as a Pekapoo or Shihdoodle), heavy fur, or large structure, don't exercise them at all in hot weather conditions — their body can't handle it. For other Doodles, keep exercise on hot days to a minimum. Stick to allowing your Doodle to run in early mornings and late evenings during summer months to prevent any temperature-related illness.

Hypothermia

Hypothermia happens when a dog becomes too cold. It's most common in small dogs or those with a short coat and no body fat. Toy-size Doodles can be prone to this issue. The symptoms of hypothermia are similar to heatstroke (see the preceding section), except the dog will be shaking to try to stay warm, and they're not likely to vomit. Their limbs will be stiff with cold.

Wrap them in warm blankets and rub them vigorously to maintain a healthy blood flow to all parts of the body. Place them on a heating pad, but be sure to put a towel or blanket between your dog and the pad to prevent burning.

As with all emergency situations, take your dog to the veterinarian as soon as you can.

If you have a Toy-size Doodle, never leave them outdoors for a prolonged period of time during winter weather conditions, especially below 35 degrees.

Poisoning

Dogs will eat nearly anything, so poisoning is always a possibility. It may be mild (from eating fallen nuts) or severe (from eating garden poisons or antifreeze). The symptoms of poisoning include vomiting, convulsions (in severe cases), diarrhea, increased salivation, weakness, depression, or collapse. In severe cases, if it isn't caught in time, poisoning can be fatal.

Give your dog activated charcoal mixed with a small amount of canned food in the case of poisoning.

If you saw what your dog ate, write it down and try to note the amount they ingested. Call the ASPCA Animal Poison Control Center at 888-426-4435 (a fee of $55 may be charged to your credit card) and give the operator the information. Or, if you prefer, call your veterinarian.

Don't induce vomiting unless your veterinarian directs you to do so. If the poisoning is topical (on the skin or coat) from substances such as oil, paint, or chemicals, wash the skin or coat with a mild soap and rinse well.

Puncture wounds

Punctures commonly occur when animals fight. They also happen when dogs go after wild creatures with sharp teeth. If your dog has gotten into a fight, you may not be able to see all the puncture wounds unless they're actively bleeding.

Apply firm, direct pressure over any bleeding areas until the bleeding stops. Hold that pressure for ten minutes, and don't bandage it, because the wound needs air circulation for proper healing. Then take your dog to the veterinarian for a thorough investigation and treatment.

Many veterinarians will first shave the fur around the wounds and possibly put drains in place to ensure the wounds don't become infected and can heal properly from the inside out. The drains normally remain in place for three days, at which point they're removed and the wounds are kept clean and dry for another week. Your dog will likely be on antibiotics for a period of time.

TIP

Be sure to check your Doodle's entire body for any swelling in areas where you didn't see a wound. Sometimes puncture wounds aren't obvious right away, but over time they swell as they become infected.

Run-ins with wild animals

If your dog has a run-in with a wild animal, clean the wound with large amounts of water and dab it with hydrogen peroxide. Any large, open wound should be wrapped to keep it clean. If it's a puncture wound or bleeding profusely, apply pressure until the bleeding stops.

Take your dog to the veterinarian. Saliva has a high concentration of bacteria, so your dog will need to be given antibiotics to prevent infection.

If your dog has a run-in with a porcupine or foxtails, take them to the veterinarian to have them removed. Don't try to remove them yourself.

Seizures

Some dogs inherit epilepsy; others develop seizures due to toxicity or illness. The symptoms include salivation, disorientation, violent muscle spasms, an inability to control their excretions, and sometimes, loss of consciousness.

The first thing you should do if you see these symptoms is move furniture or other objects away from your Doodle so they don't get injured. Don't try to move your dog.

Don't put yourself at risk during your dog's seizure. Dogs are apt to lash out without control while having a seizure, so don't try to restrain them. Time the seizure so you can tell your veterinarian how long it lasted. Most seizures last approximately one minute.

WARNING

If your dog experiences more than three seizures within a 24-hour period, take them to the veterinarian immediately; they may have been poisoned and will need immediate treatment. On your trip to the veterinarian, try to keep your dog quiet. Speak in a soothing tone and try to prevent them from seeing anything that might excite them (like another dog).

If the seizure is due to epilepsy or another illness, your veterinarian can prescribe a daily medication to minimize the incidence and severity of the seizures.

Shallow wounds

Do you go to the doctor every time you cut your finger? Probably not. Unless your wound is deep, you probably just apply hydrogen peroxide and antibacterial cream, slap a bandage on it, and go on with your life. If you've got these items for yourself, you have all you need to treat your dog's minor wounds.

Always clean a cut or abrasion thoroughly with mild soap and warm water to remove any dirt and debris. Then pat it dry. When it's dry, apply antibacterial ointment.

TIP

Some dogs will lick off the ointment, so to prevent this, either apply a bandage or, if the area can't be bandaged, apply Grannick's Bitter Apple around (but not on) the wound. They'll be less likely to lick off the antibacterial cream again.

Shock

Shock can occur after a serious injury, fright, or a reaction to extreme temperatures. Shock is the body's way of protecting itself from trauma, but it can also threaten a dog's life. The symptoms are irregular breathing, white gums, and dilated pupils.

You'll need to keep your dog gently restrained, warm, and quiet. Also, elevate their lower body.

Take your dog to the veterinarian immediately. Only your veterinarian is equipped to treat your dog for shock.

Snake bites

Snake bites are extremely dangerous. There are many venomous species that, with one bite, can damage your dog's nerves or body tissue on contact. Many types of snake bites can be fatal to dogs.

If your dog is bitten by a snake, the skin will swell quickly. You'll notice a skin puncture. Sometimes the skin in the area of the puncture will turn black. The dog will display pain in the bitten area. All you can do is clean the area and rush your dog to the veterinarian to be treated. They'll likely prescribe antibiotics to prevent an infection, as well as cold compresses to reduce inflammation.

Snake bites often haunt dogs later in life when the joints near the bite become arthritic.

Vomiting

Dogs vomit a lot — from mother dogs regurgitating meals for puppies to older dogs who enjoy eating grass, vomiting is part of a dog's life. You don't need to be concerned about vomiting unless your dog is doing it many times throughout the day, or more often than normal.

TIP

Pay attention to the consistency of the vomit. If it's mucousy, there may be a serious problem. If it's merely a meal that was eaten too quickly, it's probably not anything you need to see a veterinarian for. If your dog is vomiting their meal, isolate them from other pets to prevent possible contagion. Withhold food and water for 6 to 12 hours, but make sure they gets some ice cubes. When the vomiting stops, gradually introduce water and then food. Take your dog to the veterinarian to have them checked for disease or any other possibilities. There are medications that can reduce nausea, making your dog more comfortable.

WARNING

If they continue vomiting with nothing coming up, they could be choking. Head to the veterinarian immediately.

Nature's Way: Exploring Natural Foods and Supplements

Most high-quality dog foods have all the vitamins and minerals your Doodle will need. There are times in your dog's life, however, when a few extra supplements can help with keeping their stomach settled, reduce stress levels, or help them focus on their learning skills.

There are also herbs to aid in freshening a dog's breath, reducing gas, or mitigating other digestive issues.

Oils keep your Doodle's coat shiny and soft, and can often help when there are skin irritations or to soothe the skin after a bath or bug bite. They can also help maintain organ health.

The following sections cover these additional supplements, how they work, and when to use them.

Vitamins

Most high-quality dog foods have the appropriate amount of vitamins because they have to abide by the rules of the Association of American Feed Control

Officials (AAFCO; www.aafco.org). Some Doodles require a little bit more, especially if they have a skin disorder or organ malfunction.

Before giving your Doodle any additional vitamins, consult with your veterinarian. Some vitamins — such as iron, calcium, vitamin A, and vitamin D — can be detrimental to your dog's health if they take too much. Overdosing on any of these vitamins can lead to hair loss or even organ shutdown.

Prescription diets, tend to have a formula that addresses specific health issues. They have a specific balance of vitamins and other supplements.

Herbs

Just because something is an herb doesn't mean it's completely safe. Certain herbs can have bad interactions with medications. Others simply don't do much to help your dog.

Again, consult with your veterinarian about herbal supplements prior to giving them to your Doodle. Here are some herbs you may want to discuss with your veterinarian:

>> **For stress:** Chamomile, kava kava, lavender.

>> **For upset stomach:** Dill, ginger, parsley, slippery elm.

>> **For bad breath:** Apple cider vinegar, lemon, spirulina. A dental chew that contains cinnamon, clove, or chlorophyll is also helpful.

Even better than herbs for stress is dog-appeasing pheromone (DAP), which is available in a spray, a diffuser, or a collar.

Oils

Essential oils should never be given orally to your dog. Some can be quite toxic, in fact.

Here are some oils that can be harmful, if ingested:

>> Anise oil

>> Cinnamon oil

>> Clove oil

- Eucalyptus oil
- Garlic oil
- Pennyroyal oil
- Pine oil
- Tea tree oil
- Wintergreen oil
- Ylang-ylang oil

TIP

As a general rule, unless it's a vitamin E supplement (usually an oil-filled tablet), don't give oils orally.

There are some great skin oils that can be helpful to apply externally and as a supplement to a Doodle with dry skin:

- Coconut oil
- Fish oil
- Flaxseed oil
- Primrose oil

REMEMBER

As with any food additive, check with your veterinarian to ensure that your Doodle receives the right amount or that you apply it to the skin or coat correctly.

Chapter **8**

The Dapper Doodle

From the tops of their heads to their fluffy feet, Doodles require regular grooming. Because they're part Poodle, you'll need to schedule regular professional grooming sessions. But that's not enough. Doodles have weekly and daily grooming needs as well. In this chapter, I walk you through how to clean your Doodle's ears, trim their nails, brush their teeth, and maintain their coat. I also walk you through what goes into professional grooming, so you know what to expect.

The Better to Hear You With: Cleaning Your Doodle's Ears

Everything from mites and dirt to bacteria can cause ear infections in a dog. If you don't give weekly attention to your Doodle's ears, they may be more prone to getting ear infections. And ear infections aren't just minor annoyances — they can cause hearing loss, damage to the middle ear, and/or fever from a bacterial infection (see the nearby sidebar, "Handling an ear infection," for more on the symptoms and treatment).

To prevent infection, clean your dog's ears once or twice a week. You may also need to clean your dog's ears after bathing or swimming. Water tends to remain in the ears, especially if the ears have a fold-over structure. Upright ears allow moisture to dry out quickly, so if your Doodle's ears are upright, you'll only need to do a minor ear cleaning.

Doodles who have Retriever or Spaniel heritage may have smaller ear canals than other dogs, making them ripe for contracting infections. This special structure, combined with the heavy, fold-over ears, causes the ears to retain moisture, dirt, and bacteria.

To clean your dog's ears, you'll need to start by acclimating them to all forms of grooming from the moment you bring them home. Begin by rubbing your Doodle's ears as you pet them. Dogs *love* having their ears rubbed, so your dog will not only allow it but appreciate it. As you rub, manipulate the ears so you touch all parts of them. Your Doodle will especially enjoy when you massage the base of the ears.

If your Doodle tends to get playful when you try to manipulate their ears, keep them busy with a *lick mat* (a silicone mat that sticks to smooth surfaces and on which you can place a yummy treat like peanut butter — you can find lick mats at most big pet stores). Your dog will be so busy licking the food that they won't notice you working with their ears.

Here are basic ear-cleaning procedures to follow:

1. **Squirt a couple drops of herbal ear cleaner into your dog's ear.**

2. **Rub the ear for a couple seconds to loosen any dirt and grease.**

3. **With a soft cloth wrapped around your index finger, gently remove the loosened dirt from the outer canal features and inside the ear flap.**

4. **Repeat with the other ear.**

Never clean deep in the dog's ear canal. You can damage the dog's ear and hearing that way. If you think something may be stuck deeper inside your dog's ear, have your veterinarian do a thorough cleaning and exam. If you have any concerns about your ability to perform ear cleaning, have your veterinarian show you the process.

Doodles have lots of hair in their ears, which can clog the air flow that's needed to keep the ears free of moisture. From time to time, tweeze these hairs — only those that come out easily — so that the outer ear can remain dryer. If you're not sure how to do this, take your dog to the groomer to have it done professionally.

HANDLING AN EAR INFECTION

Most dogs with ear infections show clear signs of irritation. They shake their heads, rub their ears against solid objects, or use their paws to scratch at their ears. If the infection gets worse, you'll likely smell a foul odor coming from the ear and see small granular dirt particles and a reddish waxlike substance; the ear may be warm, too. If the infection has been going on for a while, you may notice a topical rash from your dog's constant scratching.

If your dog is exhibiting these symptoms, your veterinarian will need to inspect the ear and possibly take a sample of the infectious material. The prescribed cure is anything from ear ointment to antibiotics, depending on the cause of the infection.

Mani-Pedi Time: Trimming Your Doodle's Nails

Dogs' nails grow quickly and need to be trimmed every three to six weeks. If your dog spends most of their time on soft surfaces (such as dirt, grass, or sand), they may need their nails trimmed more often. Even if you walk your dog on sidewalks or along the street, you'll still need to trim the nails on the sides of the feet, as well as the dew-claw nails.

Regular pedicures prevent the *quick* (the pink inside the nail) from growing long and risking being nicked when trimmed. A nicked quick bleeds a lot and can be painful to your dog. Frequent trimming keeps your dog comfortable. Chronic long nails will create joint problems in your dog's feet — the constant upward pressure of the nails can result in arthritis, making it painful for your dog to walk. Also, long nails tend to get caught on things and break or tear.

As your dog ages, the quick naturally gets longer. The only way to control that is to have your veterinarian clip the nails a little shorter. It's highly possible that during that procedure the quick will be nipped a bit, but your veterinarian will have styptic powder and other supplies necessary to handle this possibility.

If you don't feel confident trimming your Doodle's nails, don't feel bad about it. It's a challenging process, and one misstep can be painful for your dog. You can always take your dog to a groomer for regular nail trims. If you prefer to do it yourself, though, start by touching your Doodle's feet a lot from the moment you bring them home. Gentle touching and massaging of the feet helps a dog relax and accept having them manipulated while getting their nails trimmed.

There are several ways to approach nail trimming, but early preparation is the best. Training teaches your dog about their environment and how to behave within it. Here's a way to teach your Doodle to accept getting a pedicure:

1. **Teach your dog some basic obedience, such as sit and down stays.**

2. **Teach your dog to give a paw or shake.**

3. **Gradually hold the paw a couple seconds longer with each successful shake offer.**

4. **When you can hold the paw, and your dog remains calm, introduce them to the clippers or Dremel tool.**

5. **Make noise with the nail trimming tool, near the dog's feet. As the dog remains calm (or at the very least doesn't pull their foot away), mark with a click and reward.**

   Do this often, for at least 5 minutes, so your Doodle has positive associations with the sounds of the clippers or Dremel tool.

6. **When the dog is calm, you can begin clipping or sanding down her nails.**

   If the dog starts to wiggle, have someone help you. One of you can hold the dog's attention with a lick mat or target stick and offer frequent rewards, while the other clips or sands the nails.

If your Doodle already has a fear of getting a pedicure and needs one immediately, you'll need to have someone hold the dog for you as you trim their nails. There are two ways to immobilize a dog:

» Lift with one arm wrapped around their chest and the other around their rump, leaving their feet dangling, giving you access to the nails.

» Hold their body close, with one leg held securely, giving access to that foot's nail.

TIP

Before clipping the nail, look at how it curves. If your dog's nails are white, notice how far around the curve the quick goes (see Figure 8-1). This will guide you on where to clip — you want to remain at *least* ⅛ inch away from the quick to avoid injuring your dog.

Be sure to give your dog frequent breaks to relax after each paw has been attended to. Also, click and reward throughout to help your Doodle have positive associations with the process.

TIP

Have some styptic powder handy to help stop any accidental bleeding that may occur from cutting too closely. You can find it at most pet stores.

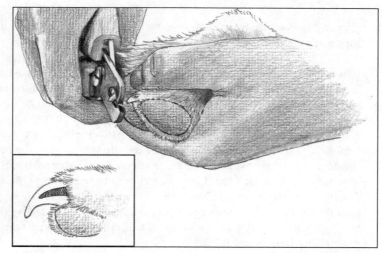

FIGURE 8-1:
Look carefully at where the nail hooks. This is where you'll want to apply the nail clippers in order to avoid clipping too closely.

Illustration by Barbara Frake

If your Doodle has dark nails, you won't be able to see the quick as easily, so you should use a Dremel tool to file them, instead of nail clippers. A Dremel tool is less likely to cause injury, because you can gradually remove excess nail growth without accidentally clipping so close as to cause your dog's nail to bleed. A Dremel takes a bit longer, but your dog will be less likely to have a bad experience. Just hold the nail so it doesn't vibrate when sanded with the Dremel.

REMEMBER

Keep all grooming activities positive. Do everything in small increments, slowly acclimating your dog to the process. This will make your Doodle a more willing and patient partner.

Say Cheese!: Keeping Your Doodle's Teeth Healthy

Brushing a dog's teeth is a part of routine maintenance that many dog owners overlook. But if you think about it, your dog's teeth are as important to their overall health and well-being as your own teeth are to yours.

Would you skip brushing your teeth for a couple days? A week? A year? Absolutely not! And it's not just because teeth that haven't been brushed cause bad breath. Without regular brushing, you can develop gum disease that may cause you to lose your teeth and can even harm organs such as your heart. The same goes for dogs!

If your dog loses their teeth at a young age, it will shorten their life span because they can't eat as they should.

When you introduce your Doodle to dental cleaning, keep it positive! Use a meat-flavored toothpaste (they come in beef, poultry, and liver flavors) that your dog will love, along with a long-handled toothbrush or a finger brush.

Place a little paste on the brush and begin brushing the front teeth. These are the easiest to start with because they don't require you to push the brush farther into the dog's mouth. Brush in a circular motion so you cover each tooth. Remember to brush the back of each tooth (the side closest to the tongue). Be sure to give your dog frequent breaks to lick the paste off their teeth, which will keep the experience positive for them. When your dog is relaxed, work on the teeth farther back in the mouth. Gently pull the dog's skin away from the teeth, so you can access the teeth more easily (see Figure 8-2).

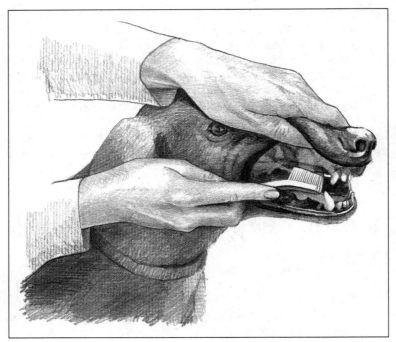

FIGURE 8-2: Brushing your dog's teeth is a vital part of keeping them healthy.

Illustration by Barbara Frake

Talk to your veterinarian if you're at all unsure that you're brushing your dog's teeth correctly. They'll be happy to show you the right way to do it.

Even if you do brush your dog's teeth regularly, they should get a yearly checkup with your veterinarian, who can locate any unhealthy teeth or gums that may require attention. Some dogs are prone to tartar buildup and require a full dental cleaning once a year, even with regular cleaning by their owners.

Lookin' Good: Coat Maintenance

Doodles require daily brushing and regular professional grooming sessions. Otherwise, debris collects in the coat and tangles occur. Some tangles can form down to your dog's skin, causing discomfort.

A daily brushing is bonding time. You hold your Doodle close to you, speak soothingly, and brush them all over. Doodles *love* to cuddle, and the daily brushing becomes another great opportunity to do so.

TIP

Even though you may not think your puppy needs grooming, you should begin acclimating them to the grooming process early. Dogs learn best when they're puppies, and if your Doodle learns that grooming will be part of their everyday life, they'll easily accept the process. Training older dogs to accept grooming can be challenging.

Most Doodles enjoy being brushed along their necks, shoulders, backs, and upper legs. But don't forget to brush their face, ears, feet, and tail, too. Most Doodles don't love having their tails brushed, but you can condition them to accept it. Take your time and use positive associations so your Doodle learns to enjoy every part of the brushing process.

TIP

Doodles have anything from tight curls to long waves, so there are many ways to approach brushing them. Generally, a *pin brush* (the type with plastic bristles and rounded ends) works very well. You can use it on any part of the body to clear out tangles. If you want to fluff up your dog's coat, use a slicker brush. I don't recommend slicker brushes for everyday brushing, however, because their sharp pins can scratch a dog's sensitive skin, making them not appreciate being brushed.

I suggest using a metal comb with rotating teeth for the long hairs of your Doodle's tail, ears, and face. Because the face has very sensitive areas, a comb gives you more direct control than a pin brush does.

Don't forget to brush your Doodle's underbelly and the insides of their thighs. The hair in these areas is very fine and prone to tight tangles. Daily attention prevents tangles and keeps your dog comfortable. Long hair around the genitals can trap urine and feces, as well as bacteria, so professional groomers often shave these areas to keep them clean.

THE DAILY ONCE-OVER: CHECKING YOUR DOG FOR PROBLEMS

Make it a point to go over your dog daily and check for injuries, cuts, bruises, parasites, and suspicious lumps. As your Doodle ages, this daily check becomes more important. Dogs rarely let you know that they aren't feeling well or are in pain — in fact, the dog's nature is to *not* show weakness, so you'll be the last to know when something's wrong.

Daily checks will help you discover something that may be the beginning of a problem — for example, a wound that may become infected, a lump that may be the beginning of cancer, or a flea that will bite and cause your dog to have an allergic reaction. All these things, and more, can be detected by a daily once-over.

Here's a great way to do a thorough daily check while also giving your dog a great massage:

1. **Using your fingertips, rub the dog's nose in a circular manner.**

   This will allow you to feel any scabby skin or lumps while giving your dog a very relaxing massage.

2. **Move up the head, around the forehead, cheeks, lower jaw, and base of the ears.**

   Familiarize yourself with your Doodle's dimples, moles, and whiskers. Often there is lumpy skin around each whisker. As they age, their skin may become a little lumpy from fatty pockets. Daily checks will enable you to detect abnormal growth of these deposits.

3. **Look inside the ears, and rub the ears from base to tip.**

   This will help locate any extra dirt or grease, as well as ticks. Ticks often latch on to the inside of the ear flap because the skin is moist and warm there. The ears also tend to brush against foliage where ticks are waiting for hosts.

4. **Move down the neck, still using your fingertips (though you can begin to apply a little more pressure).**

   The skin on the neck is a bit tougher than it is on the face, and you'll have more fur to go through as well. This is another place where ticks like to attach to dogs.

5. **With the dog's head and neck checked, move your hand along the center of their back.**

   You can move your hands in a straight line down the spine, and then use the circular motions on each side, gently touching the loin area, sides, and tummy.

6. **Check the dog's chest and shoulders, using your fingers as you would a brush, starting at the top of the neck and combing downward.**

   Long chest fur is a prime target for loose debris and tangles.

7. **Check the legs, again using a circular motion with your fingertips on the skin. At the knees and hocks, enclose the joints in your hand, feeling for excessive heat.**

   Heat is the first sign of a joint disorder, swelling may or may not be present depending on the problem.

8. **Check your dog's toes and foot pads.**

   Keep in mind that they walk around barefoot all day and may cut a pad or get debris entangled between the pads (if your dog has long foot fur).

   After you've completed your daily check, your Doodle will probably be snoring and drooling!

Professional Doodle Grooming

Grooming Poodles isn't everyone's cup of tea — it requires a lot of work and a lot of patience. Normally, the dog's patience runs out far before the groomer's does. Grooming shops often have to work on Poodles in segments. When the dog gets tired, they're allowed to rest for a while; then they're brought out to the grooming table again for another round. Not only must the groomer be persistent, but the dog must be patient and remain still as long as needed. This can be tough for a puppy!

Doodles aren't Poodles, but their grooming can still require talent and attention to detail. Many of the techniques are similar and require the work of a talented groomer.

TIP

Before taking your Doodle to a groomer, be sure to call around or ask someone who has a Doodle where their dog gets coifed. A bad experience with a groomer can make your Doodle fearful of the grooming process. A professional groomer will ensure a safe and positive experience for your dog.

REMEMBER

Many of the big-box pet stores offer grooming, but their grooming teams are often made up of beginner groomers, not master groomers. This means that they may not be aware of the various Doodle styles and will tend to just shave off a good portion of your Doodle's body hair. You need a seasoned professional for a Doodle groom.

Doodle cuts

There are six distinct Doodle grooming styles:

>> Puppy cut

>> Kennel cut

>> Poodle cut

>> Lion cut

>> Lamb cut

>> Mohawk

Each grooming style has a specific purpose. For example, a kennel cut is good for dogs who are going to be boarded or during hot months of the year. They're also good for owners who don't want to spend time brushing their dogs every day. The only cuts without purpose are the lion cut and the mohawk — those are just about style!

Puppy cut

The puppy cut (shown in Figure 8-3), also known as the teddy bear cut, is the most popular Doodle grooming style. It's a great way to introduce your young Doodle to the grooming process, and it will keep them free of tangles and debris and able to see clearly without hair over their eyes.

TECHNICAL STUFF

There are actually two different types of puppy cut: the 1- to 2-inch body trim and the ¾-inch body trim (for easier maintenance).

A puppy cut includes the following:

>> **Around the eyes and ears:** A very short trim, almost to the skin

>> **Face:** A full face trim, rounding the corners of you're the dog's jaws, but keeping their chops and sideburns a medium length

>> **Head and ears:** Long fur

>> **Tail:** A very short trim, almost to the skin, of the fur under and around the tail, down the tail about 3 to 4 inches

>> **Underbelly:** Shaved around the genital areas to keep them clean.

>> **Feet:** Trimmed short and rounded, with about ½ inch of hair left so you can barely see the nails (which should also be trimmed by the groomer)

FIGURE 8-3:
The puppy cut.

Illustration by Barbara Frake

The puppy cut tends to be the most popular because it makes it easy to maintain a Doodle's coat, but the dog still looks adorable and fluffy.

Kennel cut

The kennel cut (shown in Figure 8-4) is basically an all-over shave. The hair is shaved down to within ¼ inch of the Doodle's skin, all over. This cut is the easiest to maintain because you don't have to brush around the face, tail, legs, or feet. If your Doodle loves to dig holes, play in the mud, or get into other mischief where they get dirty, this grooming style may be the one for you.

The other great thing about the kennel cut is it saves you money in the long run. You can go much longer between visits to the groomer, though you'll need to do some regular maintenance yourself, such as trimming the nails, cleaning the ears, and keeping the eye area clear of hair.

Poodle cut

Another version of the kennel cut is more like a regular Poodle style. The face area, legs, base of the tail, feet, and underside are shaved, but a poof is left on the head, ears, and legs. Doodles who are three-fourths Poodle tend to look very nice with this cut. The only issue may be strangers thinking your Doodle is actually a Poodle, but you know the truth!

FIGURE 8-4:
The kennel cut.

Illustration by Barbara Frake

Lion cut

The lion cut is pure fun, especially if you plan on participating in a masquerade ball, Halloween party, block party, or school event. You're bound to get no end of admiring comments from everyone who sees your Doodle.

In a lion cut, the dog's body is shaved down to ¼ inch, leaving the feet, head, chest, and tip of the tail longer. The dog's face is cut short to within an inch of the upper eyelids. The end of the dog's muzzle is also kept long, like an extended mustache and short goatee beard.

This style can require daily brushing because the long hair can trap debris and other detritus. It can also entangle easily just from normal daily exposure to play and activities. Because the hair around the dog's head, neck, shoulders, legs, and tail must be quite long to pull off this style, you have to be willing to dedicate time every day to brushing out your dog's coat. If you don't, your Doodle will need the short kennel cut to smooth out all the tangles.

Lamb cut

The lamb cut (see Figure 8-5) can be quite complicated and requires daily maintenance.

FIGURE 8-5:
The lamb cut.

Illustration by Barbara Frake

The lamb cut began as a new trend for Poodles. It's a style that doesn't present them as the froufrou dogs they're often thought to be, with the shaved face, leg, and hip pom-poms and pouf on their heads. The lamb cut make them seem more like a scruffy family dog, and it's a perfect fit for Doodles who are just that.

In a lamb cut, the hair is left longer all over the Doodle's body — about 1 to 2 inches long on the body and 2 inches long on the legs and feet, with long hair left on the ears, jaws, chin, and head, as well as the lower half of the dog's tail. The ear hair is styled around the ear flaps, keeping it 1 inch long, tapering the long hair from the dog's head and gradually shortening it on the ears. The dog's underbelly is still shaved for sanitary reasons, and the hair around the eyes and inside the ears is scissored very short (many groomers actually pluck out the ear hair to prevent debris from remaining inside).

This grooming style require lots of daily attention, brushing out your Doodle's coat. It also requires more frequent trips to the groomer because it grows out quickly. Between appointments, you'll need to trim the hair around your dog's eyes to maintain their vision. You should also clean their ears and trim their nails regularly.

Mohawk

The mohawk style is contemporary and fun — if you and your dog love attention, this is the style for you! There are two main variations to the haircut. One is just a head mohawk; the other is a full-body mohawk.

The most requested mohawk style leaves the body, legs, and face at about 1 inch in length. The top of the head is scissored to leave the middle long, with a sharp drop-off in length on either side. The full-body mohawk also leaves a long-haired strip from head to tail. If you really want to spice it up, use a little hair gel to spike it.

You need to brush out the long hair of the mohawk daily, but the short hair on the rest of the body won't need much attention, other than your daily once-over checking for parasites.

Which cut is right for your dog

In order to pick the right cut for your dog, it helps if you can recognize your dog's coat type and let your groomer know your dog's age and temperament. (If you don't know your dog's coat type, a professional groomer can tell.)

Doodles have two coat types:

>> **Harsh and curly:** The harsh and curly coat is easy to style into the classic Poodle cuts that require a head pouf, leg and body poufing, and muzzle pouf.

>> **Soft and curly:** The soft and curly coat lends itself better to the lamb cut, lion cut, and mohawk.

TIP

The kennel cut and puppy cut work well with both coat types.

Though part Poodle, many Doodles have double coats and can shed a lot. You just don't see all the hair because it gets trapped in the curly top coat. These coats are difficult to work with when creating a Poodle-type style such as the puppy cut or Poodle cut because your dog just ends up looking like a short-haired dog. The lamb cut is perfect, though, because it's long and full anyway. The lion cut also works well with double-coated Doodles, as does the mohawk.

Preparing for grooming

Groomers prefer clients who brush their Doodles daily. Daily brushing prevents mats, which can be difficult for the groomer to work with (not to mention painful for the dog as the grooming is being done). Doodles have sensitive skin. If your groomer has to demat your dog, they may have to use clippers and that can cause razor burn — not fun.

Plus, if you brush your dog regularly, they'll be easier to work with at the grooming salon (the dog will be used to being touched, brushed, and manipulated all over their body). Think of all you do with training, grooming, and normal maintenance as preparation for a professional grooming. The better behaved the dog, the easier they'll be to groom and the better the end product.

Groomers also appreciate clients who bring in a picture of what they want the dog to look like. Your groomer can tell you if it's possible with your dog's coat type and will ask questions about what you like, or don't like, about the style.

If you choose a specific style, be sure to understand actual measurements. Groomers don't want clients to say, "Wow, that's shorter than I thought it would be" or, "I was thinking it would be shorter."

TIP

Most groomers will recommend a specific amount of time between professional grooming. This is what many of them suggest:

>> **For coats longer than 1 inch:** Every two to four weeks, with daily brushing

>> **For coats shorter than 1 inch:** Every four to six weeks, with brushing every other day, or as needed if the dog enjoys digging, swimming, or exploring

Do a daily check in high-friction areas, such as between the back legs, the dog's underside, in the front armpits, along the collar line, or where a harness touches the dog. These areas become moist and can easily tangle.

TIP

Professional groomer recommend regular line brushing. To do this, you begin at a leg, sliding your hand upward until there's a clear line created between the hair that's being held up and the hair that's fallen down. Brush everything below your hand. Gradually work your hand upward, brushing the hair below your hand. As you do this, you'll find tangles that can be worked out with your brush along the way. Begin with the legs; then work your way from neck to tail. Using a leave-in conditioner, or mixing conditioner with water and spritzing the area now and then, helps loosen tangles, especially on Doodles with soft and curly coats.

GROOMING LINGO

Awareness of certain grooming terms can be helpful. Here are some of the terms you may hear your groomer use:

- **Clipping:** Using clippers with special combs that produce a specific hair length
- **Feathering:** Leaving the backs of the legs longer than the front (common in Spaniel styles)
- **Plucking:** Pulling hair out with tweezer, usually inside the ears
- **Shaving:** Clipping down to the skin
- **Stripping:** Using a special pair of scissors or thinning knife to thin out the fur, generally along the dog's back
- **Tapering:** A gradual change in length

3

Doodle Training

» Learning the basics of positive reinforcement

» Looking for good behavior and redirecting bad behavior

» Showing your puppy where to go

Chapter **9**

Doodle Rules and Regulations

In order for a society to run smoothly, everyone must follow rules and regulations. The same holds true for your family — whether you've written them down or not, you have certain expectations of each other. Maybe you agree to pick up after yourselves, or your kids agree to come home by the curfew you set, or you agree to call your partner if you're running late. Your Doodle will be looking to you to set the rules and be consistent in enforcing them. This chapter is all about deciding what rules to set, reinforcing those rules, and shaping your dog's behavior until you get what you're looking for. I also cover housetraining a puppy, because nothing matters quite as much as making sure they don't pee and poop wherever they want.

Setting the Rules

Even before you bring home your new puppy, sit down with every member of your household and make a plan — what's allowed and what isn't. Make sure everyone is in agreement and onboard with enforcing those rules. It won't help your Doodle if one of you lets the puppy up on the couch when everyone has agreed it's not allowed.

REMEMBER

Dogs need consistency. When you're consistent, your puppy will learn faster, with less chance of misunderstanding or frustration. No matter how cute your new Doodle is, be strict with the rules. The behaviors they're allowed at the beginning are behaviors they'll continue to display in a year. It's not fair to your dog to allow a behavior one day and suddenly not allow it the next.

Here are some of the rules you may want to set, depending on your priorities:

>> No jumping on people.

>> No dogs on the furniture.

>> No digging in the garbage.

>> No teeth on anything but dog toys.

>> No chasing the cat.

>> No pestering older dogs.

>> No grabbing clothing.

>> No pottying indoors.

>> No counter or table surfing.

>> No excessive barking.

This may seem like a long list for your new puppy to deal with, but all it requires is your frequent redirection to where they should be giving their attention, such as their toys.

Dealing with a young Doodle is a little like taking care of a human toddler. You have to be observant, or trouble can occur.

Your Doodle will easily catch on to the house rules as long as you're clear and consistent.

Being Consistent, Praising Frequently, and Exercising Patience

When it comes to training your Doodle, being consistent, praising frequently, and being patient are the keys to success. Here's why:

>> **Consistency:** Dogs have little understanding of "sometimes," "maybe," or other gray areas. To them, everything is black and white — either they're allowed to do it or they aren't. For example, your Doodle is either allowed on your furniture or not. Dogs have little understanding of special circumstances — they don't know you've just vacuumed the couch and you're having company over so you don't want them on the couch.

REMEMBER

The best way of ensuring that your Doodle will do what you want is to be consistent — either you let them on the couch or you don't, and if you did just vacuum and you don't want them on the couch tonight, then your job is to keep them out of that room until they can get on the couch again.

>> **Praise:** Your dog loves the sound of your voice. It means a lot to them — safety, comfort, companionship, and structure. They may not understand the majority of the words you use, but they instantly understand your tone.

I never skimp on praise. Praise your Doodle whenever they're performing well. It will put a spring in their step and a grin on their face. It'll also help them focus on you. If your Doodle is connected to you, they'll only have eyes for you and not all the surrounding distractions.

>> **Patience:** Sometimes it can take a while for your Doodle to figure out what you want and to do it consistently. They may be trying out different behaviors to see what turns out to be rewarding for them. Not every dog learns the same way, just like not every human learns the same way. When you're trying to teach your dog the rules, patience will pay off in the end — your dog will learn which behavior worked and will soon repeat it faster and faster. Through repetition, and patience, your Doodle will achieve success.

Patience is required with every new behavior you want your dog to learn. You can guide your dog through a behavior with bait (food in your hand) or capture and shape the behavior using clicker training. Regardless of how you approach it, you'll need to break a behavior down into smaller parts to help your Doodle more clearly understand the concepts.

Being Observant and Harnessing Good Behavior

Throughout the day, your Doodle will naturally do many different things — sit, lie down, roll around, bark, and wag their tail. Every time your dog does something is an opportunity for you to teach them to perform the behavior on cue. The more you reinforce the behavior you want, the more your dog will work to repeat that behavior.

REMEMBER

Dogs aren't interested in pleasing you. They just repeat actions that have been rewarding in the past. And because they rarely expend energy needlessly, an unrewarded behavior will eventually go away. It's up to you to guide your dog in the right direction, to ensure success.

There are three ways that you can teach your dog to perform on cue, without fear, force, or coercion. These include facilitating the behavior, capturing the behavior, and shaping the behavior.

Facilitating good behavior

Facilitating good behavior is all about making your dog do something and having them believe it was all their idea. Facilitating happens primarily using food, a toy, or another type of reward — something that motivates your dog to follow it, in the hopes of ultimately getting it. To facilitate good behavior, you need to use baiting and targeting, which I cover in the following sections.

Baiting

To catch a fish you have to put bait on a hook. The bait can be a worm or a shiny object, depending on the fish you are wanting to catch. Similarly, the first step to getting your dog to pay attention to you is to put food in your hand and show it to them. Your Doodle will smell the food and follow it. They'll follow it forward, backward, left, right, up, or down. They want that food and will work hard to get it.

You can use the food to move your dog forward with you as you walk or come toward you as you move backward. You can use it to turn them in circles, sit up, roll over, or crawl. You show your Doodle your hand and move it as needed to facilitate the action, and your dog will enthusiastically follow.

REMEMBER

Baiting is the best way of capturing your dog's attention, especially if you have a young puppy. The trick is in how you use the bait, as well as how often you give the reward. Ultimately, you want your dog to perform on cue without having to wave a piece of food under their nose. The goal is to teach your dog words, signals, and how to react to their environment. So, although bait is a great way of *starting* a dog on the path to learning, it's not a great way of progressing beyond the basics.

There are two ways you can time your food rewards:

>> **Fixed:** Giving a reward after every single thing your dog does. For example, you give your dog a treat after every time they sit when asked. Or, you give your dog a treat every time they come or every time they lie down. Fixed rewards are great when you're first teaching behaviors, but they don't require your dog to work very hard to earn their pay.

> **Variable:** Giving a reward sporadically, so your dog doesn't know when they're going to get it. For example, your dog may receive a treat after they sit on cue, or they may have to come and sit prior to getting their treat. Eventually, not only will they have to perform more behaviors, but they'll also have to do them with better positioning. When the rewards are variable, the dog is having to work harder to get them. This causes the dog to try to figure out what they must do to get the reward.

TIP

Begin with fixed, but quickly switch to variable. A variable reward is how you can perfect a response or increase the amount of behaviors your dog has to do before earning a reward.

Targeting

When your dog has learned to follow your hand with the food inside, you've automatically taught them to target. They know your hand is holding the food, and they'll watch your hand wherever it goes.

When your dog sees your hand as a target, you can use that target to guide your dog to come, sit, lie down, heel, and so much more. To get your dog to come, for example, place your hand in front of you near your knees. To get your dog to heel, place your hand along your leg on the side you want your dog to walk. To get your dog to lie down, lower your hand to their front feet. The great part is, after your dog has learned the cue with bait in your hand, you'll eventually be able to use your hand to cue your dog without anything in it, because your dog understands the meaning of your hand movement.

Capturing behavior

Facilitating a behavior is a great way of initially teaching your dog to do basic commands or tricks, but *capturing* a behavior can enable you to teach your dog complex actions.

Capturing a behavior simply means catching your dog in the act of doing something you want. When that happens, you click and follow with a reward.

Some dogs may not want to perform an action at a given moment or in a specific situation. A great example of this is trying to teach a dog to lie down when they're not feeling safe to do so. Let's say you're in a dog training class and you're trying to lure your dog into a down with baiting, but instead of following the treat down, your dog is turning their head and moving away. Clearly, your dog isn't comfortable enough to put themselves in a down position. Capturing gives you another way to approach this situation.

There are numerous times throughout the day that your dog lies down, without your asking them to do so. With capturing, you observe your dog and the moment they lie down, you click and reward. Do this several times and your dog will figure out what they're doing to earn that reward and voluntarily come to you and lie down. Then you can begin to pair the action with a cue (see Chapter 10).

Shaping behavior

After a basic behavior is learned, you can further modify the behavior via *shaping*, which is the process of gradually adding criteria to each repetition, building on success. By shaping a behavior, you ensure your Doodle has a full understanding of how to respond to your cues and continue to build their knowledge toward even more complex responses.

To use shaping, you need to understand how to break down a goal into smaller parts. This means starting with a simple part of the concept and gradually adding a bit more criteria at a time, as your dog comprehends the overall behavior. A great example of behavior shaping is the stay cue. You begin by teaching your dog to sit. Next you teach them to remain sitting for a couple seconds. As your dog becomes reliable with remaining for a couple seconds before you click and reward, you begin adding a stay cue. Then you require them to remain in place longer before you click and reward. You're shaping a longer sit-stay. Training your dog via shaping ensures a solid understanding of the cue.

REDIRECTING INAPPROPRIATE BEHAVIOR

Regardless of the inappropriate behavior your Doodle does — whether it's digging in the trash, chewing the couch, or jumping up on guests — there's a safe and dependable way of extinguishing the problem: redirection. When you find something that motivates your dog to work for you, you can use that item to turn their attention away from inappropriate behavior into a more productive response.

Does your Doodle pull on the lead? Change directions. Click and reward when they look at you.

Does your Doodle bark at people they see through the windows? Use a unique noise to turn their attention to you. The moment they look at you, click and reward.

Does your Doodle jump on you? Turn away and cue them to sit. The moment they sit, click and reward.

Even within a single litter, Doodle coats can vary greatly in color.

Doodles are great emotional support and therapy dogs.

Doodles love being part of family activities.

Doodles love playing in the snow but also easily collect snowballs in their coats, making them a challenge to clean after a romp.

Most Doodles are natural retrievers.

Doodles and kids are a great combination.

Doodles love th... ...aking a run at the beach the perf... ...ti...it...

Doodles are natural field dogs.

Doodles love traveling, but make sure to keep yours safe using a seat belt or crate.

living is one of the man
senses which Doodle

Your Doodle may love basking in the sun, but make sure they have access to shade and plenty of fresh water to drink.

Some Doodles can appear intimidated when meeting a new dog for the first time, but they'll usually become fast friends.

Housetraining Your Puppy

Most Doodle puppies easily learn the concept of housetraining. But your puppy's success will depend on consistency, observation, and timing.

You can make it easy on yourself and on your puppy by crate training, maintaining a potty schedule (see Chapter 6), finding the right relief area, and teaching your puppy to potty on cue. If you do all this, your Doodle will be housetrained in no time!

Crate training

Crate training is a means of keeping your dog out of trouble when you can't be nearby to observe their behavior. Although you may think a crate looks like a jail, to your Doodle, it's more like a den — a place where they can feel safe, secure, and relaxed.

The crate should be tall enough for your Doodle to fully stand, with their head up, and wide enough for them to comfortably turn around. A crate isn't a place to leave your dog for long periods of time every day. In fact, leaving them in a crate for more than four hours during the day and six hours at night is considered cruel. Dogs need to move around to develop healthy bones and muscles. Too much crate time can also cause psychological damage, so use the crate sparingly and for short periods of time.

Here's how to acclimate your Doodle to a crate:

1. **Open the door and put some bedding and toys inside the crate.**

2. **Throw some treats in and point to them.**

3. **Using an encouraging tone of voice, speak to your Doodle.**

   Be sure that they saw you throwing the treats into the crate. The hand motion you use will become the visual cue for the behavior.

   A great way to acclimate your dog to the crate is to feed them in it. They'll soon associate good things with being inside the crate.

TIP

4. **The moment your dog goes into the crate, click and give them more rewards.**

5. **Repeat until your dog easily goes inside, turns, and awaits the click and reward.**

6. **Then, when your dog goes in, briefly close the door.**

If they remains calm, click and reward. If they're not calm, they're not yet ready for this step — go back to allowing them to enter and exit at will. Your dog will let you know they're ready when they remain calm and wait for you to respond.

With each successful brief door closing (as your dog remains inside the crate), gradually increase the amount of time they remain there. Continually praise them as they remain patient, prior to a click and reward.

REMEMBER

Don't expect this to happen within one training session. It may take a few days to build up enough time for the next segment of crate training. You could cause a problem if you rush ahead and leave your Doodle in a crate for long periods of time when they're not ready.

7. **When your Doodle can relax in their crate for a couple minutes, as you praise and offer them treats, it's time to leave the room for a short period of time.**

Begin with a minute less than your dog's current comfort level. You'll be adding the criteria of leaving them along with being in a crate (a new situation for them). Repeat this step several times, or until your dog remains calm in the crate. You're shaping their behavior of being comfortable in the crate, and small steps lead to big outcomes — in this case, a dog who is comfortable remaining in the crate for hours at a time.

8. **When your dog is comfortable with your not being in the room for up to ten minutes, leave the house for the same period of time.**

If you can peek in and observe your dog without them seeing you, that's great. It helps to know what they're doing when you're gone. If not, remain just outside the door so you can listen. What you're hoping for is a quiet, calm response from your dog. If you hear barking or howling, don't return to the crate or you'll teach your dog that barking or howling gets your attention. Instead, return when your dog is quiet. Be sure to click and reward upon every return to reinforce the appropriate behavior.

TIP

Many young dogs tend to get bored or have some anxiety when left alone, so give your Doodle something special when they go into his crate. A food-filled toy or another safe chew toy will do the trick. A busy dog is less likely to stress out in new situations.

Crate training is merely one aspect of housetraining. But it's extremely important to have a safe place for your puppy when you can't be nearby to observe and redirect their behavior. Your Doodle will be going through several important behavior changes as they mature. A crate will prevent your dog from destroying your home or getting hurt.

Finding the right outdoor relief area

Your Doodle may be particular about where they do their business. You may have preferences as well. If you don't have a yard, you'll have to walk your dog to a specific relief area. If you do have a yard, you may not want them to go on the lawn or near a flower bed.

In the beginning of the housetraining process you'll likely be thrilled to have your Doodle do their business outside, anywhere. One thing to consider, however, is that they'll be more likely to do so in a place where

» They smell the scent of another dog

» They've seen another dog relieve themselves

» There is loose soil, mulch, or leaves

» There's a tree or post where dogs tend to urinate as they go by

» Your Doodle has been praised and rewarded when relieving themselves before

When you take your dog to the same place every time, they'll get into the habit of naturally heading in that direction on their own. Repetition creates a pattern. And if it's rewarding enough, your dog will automatically do their business in that spot whenever it's available.

Guiding your Doodle to a specific spot may be time consuming in the beginning, but it will save you a lot of fuss later because you won't have to repair spots of dead grass or risk stepping in something surprising. Having a dog who does their potty in a specific area will also help you in keeping your yard clean because you'll know where to go to pick up after them, without having to do an entire treasure hunt around the yard.

TIP

Here's a step-by-step procedure for teaching your Doodle to go in a specific spot:

1. **Upon waking up in the morning, carry your puppy to the designated spot.**

If your dog is too big to carry, quickly walk them to their spot.

2. **Set them down and encourage them to do their business.**

This is also a great time to begin teaching them to potty on cue (see "Training your Doodle to potty on cue," later in this chapter).

3. **Don't let your dog follow a scent elsewhere until they've done their business.**

   This may mean keeping hold of the leash and walking around the potty area with them as they seek out the exact spot they need to use.

4. **The moment they've relieved themselves, praise them and give them a treat.**

Take your Doodle to this same spot (if possible) every time they need to go. Your pup will learn the pattern through this repetition and become comfortable with the parameters quickly.

Observing and directing your pup's behavior

When puppies begin to understand that they need to do their business outdoors, and that doing so is rewarding, they'll begin trying to tell you when they need to go out. Even puppies have a "tell" that you'll learn through observation, as well as trial and error, much like learning the language of your own infant.

To learn your puppy's "tell," you'll need to be very observant. When your Doodle puppy isn't contained, watch their every move. Most of the time, they'll want to chew a toy or chase a ball. But when they stop playing and start sniffing, it's time to pull out the leash (or just pick them up) and ask them if they have to go. Your dog will initially learn the meaning of your words via your tone of voice, as well as what happens immediately after — going outside.

After just a couple days of doing this, your puppy will begin reacting to your question by raising their head and wagging their tail ("Yes, I have to go!"). After a couple weeks (or less — Doodles are quite smart), they'll automatically begin looking at you and wagging their tail to let you know it's time to go.

Training your Doodle to potty on cue

The last thing you want to have to do is stand outside in the cold for half an hour, waiting for your puppy to go. You can prevent this problem by training your Doodle to potty on cue.

Start by choosing the word you'll use when telling your dog to do their business. For example, you might say, "Do your business," "Hurry up," "Go potty," or something similar. It doesn't matter what the words are — all that matters is that you're consistent.

Now to capture the potty behavior, begin with the first morning's relief time. The moment you put your Doodle in the potty zone, begin using the potty word immediately. Watch your dog carefully. The moment they begin to go, praise enthusiastically. The moment they're done, reward them for that behavior.

TIP

Many puppies, and some adult male dogs, don't completely empty themselves in one go. Sometimes it can take two or three squats to complete the job. You'll learn your pup's needs as you get to know each other.

When you capture your dog doing their business, with the cue, it's time to shape it into a reliable behavior. The key to this process is repetition. Every time you take your Doodle to their relief zone, use the potty word until they go. If you're working with a clicker, click the moment they're done and give them a reward shortly thereafter.

REMEMBER

Food shouldn't be the only type of reward. Additional rewards are lots of praise and petting your dog in a favorite spot, such as the lower back. A more subtle, yet important reward, is allowing your dog to remain outside longer, giving them the opportunity to sniff and explore.

MEETING YOUR DOODLE'S POTTY NEEDS

Dogs can't be expected to control their need to potty to fit your schedule. Not many dogs can hold it for 12 hours at a time, but even if they can, being forced to do so isn't healthy for the dog. Your Doodle doesn't *want* to break the rules any more than you want them to. Giving your dog the opportunity to relieve themselves throughout the day will ensure better health and well-being.

The average puppy needs the following:

- **Urination:** Every 1½ to 3 hours, depending on the pup's age. The younger the dog, the more often they need to urinate throughout the day, especially if they're active.

- **Defecation:** Two or three times a day. The first one will likely be during the initial morning potty break; another may happen midafternoon and/or an hour or so after dinner.

The average mature dog needs the following:

- **Urination:** Five to seven times a day.

- **Defecation:** Twice a day. The first one will likely be during the initial morning potty break; the other is likely to be late afternoon. If your Doodle is Toy-sized, they may have to defecate more than twice a day (likely three times).

For whom the bell tolls: Training your Doodle to tell you when they have to go

Doodle puppies can take several months to become reliably housetrained. Along the way, you may want to set up a means of clear communication between you and your puppy that significantly addresses their needs, as well as your desire to keep them from messing in your home.

What happens if you're not observing your puppy and they do their "I gotta go" dance? If you don't respond, they'll likely do their business inside, possibly by the door that you use to take them out. If you want, you can train your dog to ring a bell when they have to go out, so you can hear it even if you're not in view of the door.

Start by putting a small cow bell or jingle bell on a rope. (You can find bells on ropes in the dog toy sections of pet shops.) Hang the bell from the knob of the door you use to take them out. The bell should be at nose level, making it easy for your dog to sniff and push at it.

Rub some cheese or peanut butter on the bell. It's okay if your Doodle sees you doing it — you want them to be curious and investigate. When they see how good it tastes, they'll be even more drawn to it. The moment they move it enough to jingle, take them outside and give them the cue to potty.

For the next week, be sure to put a little bit of food on the bell when your pup is scheduled to go outside to potty. The moment they lick at the bell and makes it jingle, take them out to their relief zone and use the potty cue.

Through repetition, your pup will catch on to the pattern. Then, one day, in the not-too-distant future, you'll hear the bell. Your dog is either playing with it or using it to let you know it's time to go out. Either way, you must reinforce this behavior by taking them to their relief zone and cueing them to potty.

Each time your dog voluntarily rings the bell, reward the behavior by taking them outside. Your Doodle must understand how happy you are! Plus, they need positive associations with the action of ringing the bell in order to voluntarily repeat it.

Some dogs only ring the bell to relate their need to potty; others use it as a means of demanding attention or to go outside to play. It all depends on how they associate the pattern. To make sure you're conveying the correct message, the only activity you should allow is for your dog to potty. If they go outside and start playing instead of doing their business, take them back inside and confine them to an area where they can't get into trouble.

Through success, and a few errors, your Doodle will realize the purpose of the bell and be happy to use it as intended.

Chapter **10**

Basic Doodle Lessons

raining your Doodle is the most important aspect of pet ownership. Although Doodles are often sweet, sensitive, and loving, they're also high-energy, inquisitive, intelligent dogs. To be good companions, Doodles should receive early socialization and training.

In this chapter, I fill you in on the training equipment you need, how to use it, and how to communicate with your dog using visual and verbal cues.

Buying and Using the Right Training Equipment

The collar your dog wears while they're lounging around the house isn't the collar you'll want to use when you're training. That doesn't mean you still can't make a fashion statement. With so many cute patterns and colors, it all looks great on Doodles. Just remember that a necklace is not appropriate for guiding your dog from place to place.

Here's a breakdown of the training tools I recommend:

» **Front-connect harness (such as Freedom Harness or PetSafe Easy Walk Harness; see Figure 10-1):** A front-connect harness is a great training device for young dogs, small dogs, and dogs who don't tend to pull hard at any time. You attach the leash to the front ring (at the dog's chest). When the dog moves ahead, you turn and pull the leash to the side opposite where your dog is heading. Dogs acclimate quickly to this device and it doesn't inflict pain or discomfort.

» **Head halter (such as Comfort Trainer and Halti):** Head halters are great for dogs who pull, especially when they're distracted. They're also great for assertive or reactive dogs who feel it's their duty to lead you. Several brands of head halter are available, but the ones I recommend are Comfort Trainer and Halti, because they don't put pressure on the dog's nose unless you apply it to get your dog's attention; they also don't ride into the dog's eyes, like most figure-8 head halters do.

Most Doodles don't require the use of a head halter, but some adult Doodles can be highly reactive, barking and lunging at passersby, guests, and other dogs. It can make them unpleasant to walk with. The more you struggle with this, the worse it gets. Head halters help your dog to focus better on you. If they like to sniff a lot, a head halter can bring their head up and eyes on you. If they charge at a distraction, you can easily redirect via a quick turn. But although head halters are a great temporary tool to get your dog's focus, you'll need to phase them out, as your dog learns. (A head halter is a training tool, not a restraining device.)

FIGURE 10-1:
A front-connect harness attaches at the dog's chest.

Photograph courtesy of Sarah Babineau

The type of leash you use when you train your dog is very important. You want to use one that's right for the size of your Doodle, as well as comfortable for you to hold.

TIP

Never use an extendable/retractable leash, whether you're training or just going for a walk. These leashes teach your dog to pull, because the leashes are constantly trying to retract as your dog moves away from you. You want to teach your dog to pay attention and remain at your side.

The leash that's right for your dog has a lot to do with your dog's weight. Here's a breakdown:

» **10 pounds or less:** A light nylon or cotton leash no more than ¼ inch wide, with a very small clip

» **11 to 25 pounds:** A leather, nylon, or cotton leash no more than a ½ inch wide, with a small clip

» **26 to 55 pounds:** A leather or cotton leash no more than a ½ inch wide, with a medium clip

» **56 pounds or more:** A leather leash no more than ½ inch wide, with a medium clip

REMEMBER

It's not the clip that will keep the leash on your dog — it's your training method. When using a head halter, use a lightweight leash so as not to apply any pressure to your dog's nose without your needing to do so. The lightweight leash should also have a lightweight clip.

REMEMBER

Approach the application of training tools in a similar manner to all new behaviors: incrementally and positively. Essentially, you want your dog to move *into* the training tool and not have the training tool come at them. Putting on a head halter ends up being your dog's choice because of all the positive associations they have with it.

Begin by showing your dog the head halter with one hand and holding a treat through the nose band with the other. Lure your dog's nose into the noseband (see Figure 10-2), but don't capture them in it until they're ready. It may take a few times for your Doodle to trust this new device, so you may have to lure their nose through several times.

When your Doodle understands that the head halter isn't going to bite their nose, rest the nose strap on their muzzle for a few seconds as you continue to target and reward (see Figure 10-3).

FIGURE 10-2:
Lure your dog's
nose through the
nose band.

Photograph courtesy of Sarah Babineau

FIGURE 10-3:
Resting the nose
band on your
dog's muzzle.

Photograph courtesy of Sarah Babineau

Next, buckle the back strap prior to luring your dog's nose through. You won't achieve an exact fit yet, so keep it loose enough to slide it behind your dog's head. Again, click and reward when your dog accepts this step.

As long as your Doodle remains calm (and they will, provided you speak softly and rub their tummy), slide the buckle behind their ears a little more snug, so you can just fit a finger or two between the strap and your dog. Continue to praise your Doodle and give them tummy rubs. This enhances the positive association with the training tool.

If you're using a head halter, you should also be using the front connect harness. This will enhance the "power steering" experience, because your dog's entire front end will be redirected, not just their head. You can either loop one end of the lead through the harness D-ring, or use a double-clip lead — one clip on the front D-ring, and the other on the head halter ring, below the dog's chin (see Figure 10-4).

FIGURE 10-4: Double connection of harness and head halter.

Photograph courtesy of Sarah Babineau

The action of the head halter is slightly different from that of just the harness. It requires a light pressure on your dog's nose and behind their ears, which you can attain by gently pulling downward on your lead as you turn (see Figure 10-5).

Photograph courtesy of Sarah Babineau

FIGURE 10-5:
Redirection with
the head halter
and harness.

REMEMBER

This is not a choke chain — no jerking or hard pulling. A mere gentle pressure as you turn is enough, even with a hard-pulling, reactive dog.

The head halter is also be helpful for Doodles who like to sniff instead of pay attention or those who don't care (yet) about treats because they're way too excited about everything going on around them. Used correctly, head halters help them focus better and enhance the training process.

REMEMBER

As with all training tools, your head halter should not be a lifetime crutch. It should be phased out when your dog no longer requires redirection when distracted. You may find that this happens faster with the use of the head halter than it may have without it.

Targeting and Marking

Have you ever gone to an aquarium, or zoo, and watched trained animals perform? Have you seen them touch a big ball on the end of a long stick? That ball was called a *target,* and you can do the same kind of thing with your Doodle. Okay, so they won't jump 20 feet out of a pool of water, but they'll do plenty of exciting tricks of their own.

Don't believe me? Consider this: When you give your dog a treat, do they look at your hand? Your hand is a target. A dog who watches your hand when you have a treat in it is a dog who will learn to respond to visual cues.

Targeting is the first step to training. It quickly teaches your dog what you want them to do. When you motion for your dog to sit, they look at your target (your hand) and sit. When you motion for your dog to lie down (by dropping your hand downward), their nose and body will follow into position.

Here's how to begin targeting:

1. **Place a treat in your hand.**

TIP

When targeting, use a piece of food that has a strong smell, such as freeze-dried liver, cheese, or chicken. The enticing scent will instantly grab your dog's attention.

2. **Put your hand near your Doodle's nose, and allow them to sniff.**

3. **When they put their nose on your hand (see Figure 10-6), give them the treat.**

FIGURE 10-6: Targeting.

Photograph courtesy of Sarah Babineau

Targeting will get your dog started on paying attention, but you need a way of letting your Doodle know that they're doing what you want. You need to offer a specific sound or movement to coincide with the *exact moment* your Doodle does what you've asked. This is called *behavior marking,* and it's usually done with the use of a clicker, a squeaker, or a specific word said in an enthusiastic tone of voice, such as "Yes!" The key is that the sound must be distinct from all other sounds your dog is likely to hear. For this reason, a clicker (available from most pet shops) may be your best bet. But if you have difficulty holding lots of items at the same time, you can use your voice. After all, your voice is always handy, whereas you may not always have your clicker with you.

Here's how to teach your dog to understand a behavior marker:

1. **Begin by targeting (see the previous steps) except when your dog puts their nose on your hand, instead of giving them the treat, use your marker.**

2. **Then give your Doodle a treat.**

3. **Repeat Steps 1 and 2 three to five times.**

You can bring together the concepts of targeting and behavior marking. Here's how:

1. **Show your Doodle your hand holding the treat.**

2. **Move your hand to the left.**

3. **When they move their head to the left, mark and reward.**

4. **Move your hand to the right.**

5. **When your Doodle moves their head to the right, mark and reward.**

When your Doodle understands the way to earn easy treats, it's time to start making them work a little harder. Make them do more to earn their rewards — for example, move their head from side to side or up and down — before you mark and reward. This is called *chaining,* because it's chaining together several behaviors prior to marking the moment when your Doodle has done what you asked. Chaining is a very important part of obedience training — you don't want to give your dog a treat for every single correct response to cues. If you do, you'll have a very fat dog in no time! Instead, as they learn, make them work harder and harder for it by chaining together more behaviors prior to marking.

Teaching Your Doodle the Basic Cues

When you have the right training tools and you know how to target and mark the right behaviors (see the previous sections), you're ready to start training some basic cues. The following sections have you covered.

Sit

Having your dog sit on command is very important in many situations. Your Doodle should sit:

>> For attention

>> Before being fed

>> At your side when you stop walking

The sit is a default behavior. This means that your Doodle should automatically perform a sit if you stop walking, such as when crossing the street, opening a door or gate, stopping to greet other people, or greeting you when you walk in the house. Dogs need to know what's expected of them, and having a default behavior helps them deal with many situations.

Here's how to teach your dog to sit:

1. **Put a treat in your hand and target with your Doodle (see "Targeting and Marking," earlier in this chapter).**

2. **When your Doodle puts their nose on your hand, mark and reward.**

3. **To lure your Doodle into a sitting position, place your target hand between their eyes, just out of reach of their mouth, but not out of reach of their nose.**

   Be sure not to hold your hand so high above their head that they feel as though they have to jump up to reach it.

   As your Doodle looks upward at the target, their rear end will lower down (see Figure 10-7).

4. **Mark and reward.**

5. **Repeat Steps 1 through 4 several times.**

6. **Add the verbal cue — your dog's name and the *sit* cue — as you place your target hand between their eyes.**

   This will teach them both your word for *sit* and the visual cue of your hand over their head.

FIGURE 10-7:
Hand just over the dog's head, between their eyes. As the dog looks upward, their rear end will lower.

Photograph courtesy of Sarah Babineau

When your Doodle understands the sit concept, you can add it into your other training routines. For example, as you teach your Doodle other cues — such as come, down, and stay — you'll want to use this all-important sit cue as part of these cues.

Come

Of all the obedience exercises, having your dog come when called is probably the most important. Nothing is more frustrating than calling your dog and seeing them run in the opposite direction. *Remember:* Your Doodle isn't doing this because they're vindictive — they just don't understand what you want.

If you've already taught your dog how to target (see "Targeting and Marking," earlier in this chapter), you're already well on your way to having your dog listen to your come cue.

As with all new exercises, start by being very close to your Doodle so they'll always be successful and see the come cue as very positive. Then follow these steps:

1. **Say your dog's name.**

2. **Mark and reward when they look at you.**

3. **Repeat several times.**

You'll begin noticing a few things. First, your dog not only turns to you but starts to come to you. Second, they're doing so without any force from you — they *want* to come.

Now start moving with the request:

1. **Begin with targeting.**

2. **Back up a couple steps as you cue your Doodle to target (see Figure 10-8).**

3. **Back up a couple more steps and tell your dog their name and the come cue as you back up.**

4. **Repeat until you can back up at least ten steps and your dog is near your toes all the way.**

FIGURE 10-8: Bend forward as you move backward when calling your dog to come.

Photograph courtesy of Sarah Babineau

After your dog has mastered this exercise, it's time to play a game of Round Robin. This game is a great way to teach young dogs to come when called. It's also fun for older dogs and especially great for teaching your Doodle to listen to the entire family.

Before you begin, make sure that everyone who wants to play the game does the earlier exercise of targeting and saying your dog's name. Then they should work on the come cue individually, so your Doodle has learned to focus on each member of the family and learned that they're rewarded for listening to everyone, not just to you.

Here's how to play:

1. **Have everyone stand in a circle, about 8 feet from each other.**

   Your dog needs some space to move from person to person.

2. **Lean forward, show your Doodle the target (the same way you did in the previous exercise for a simple come), say their name, and tell them, "Come" in a very pleasant tone of voice.**

3. **As your Doodle moves toward you, praise enthusiastically the entire time they're coming.**

4. **As soon as they arrive, mark and reward.**

   If you've been using a clicker, everyone in the game must have a clicker, too. If you're using a verbal sound, make sure everyone can make the same sound.

5. **Repeat Steps 2 through 4 with everyone in the group a few times.**

TIP

Alternate the order in which each person calls your Doodle, so they never know what's coming next. It takes only two repetitions for a Doodle to pick up on patterns, so prevent this from happening by mixing up everybody's turn.

After you teach your Doodle more cues, you can vary this game by adding other cue elements, such as having your dog sit when they arrive, or having them lie down. Then add a stay. This way, everyone in the family will be giving them cues, and your Doodle will think it's all a big game and loads of fun to listen. After all, they're earning loads of rewards and attention. What's not to like?

Heel

Start by holding the leash loop in your right hand along with your clicker (if you're carrying one). Have a pouch filled with treats clipped onto your belt or tied around your waist. The pouch should be on your right hip. Hold a treat in your left hand — your target hand.

Get your Doodle's attention by targeting and marking (see "Targeting and Marking," earlier in this chapter). When they're paying attention to you, hold your left hand (target hand) on your left thigh (if your Doodle is a young puppy or generally small in stature, hold it low enough for them to see it). Your dog will move closer to your left thigh, which is heel position. Both of you will be facing the same direction.

Take a step forward as you say your Doodle's name and the cue "heel" or "let's go" in a commanding tone of voice. *Remember:* You don't need to be loud — dogs hear far better than humans do. But demand, don't ask.

Because the target went forward a bit as you took a step, your Doodle is likely to follow along, with their nose on your hand (see Figure 10-9). As they move with you, mark after their correct response and reward.

FIGURE 10-9: Have your dog target on your hand as you take a step forward.

Photograph courtesy of Sarah Babineau

The next time, take two steps, then three, then four, and so on until your Doodle is walking with you across the yard or down the sidewalk, nose on your left hand the whole way.

The best way of ensuring your dog knows you're giving them a cue is to precede it with their name. Use a happy tone when saying their name so they have positive associations when hearing it. In the beginning, it'll help to give your Doodle rewards every time they look at you when you say their name.

If your Doodle begins to move ahead of you, it means one of two things:

>> **You've walked farther than they're ready for.** To remedy this situation, just decrease the number of steps you take between marking and rewarding.

>> **They no longer think that the treats are as valuable as that squirrel they see climbing a nearby tree.** If this is the case, the moment you see their shoulders in front of your left leg, turn right and make a total 180-degree turn, without looking at or waiting for them.

If your Doodle moves off to your right — say, something grabs their attention on that side, or they smell something in your right hand — turn left. As soon as you make that 180-degree turn to the left, they're back on your left side watching you. Mark their good behavior, stop, and give them a small treat.

If you're using a head halter while training the heel cue, gently pull downward as you turn. Don't pull back the way you would with a front-connect harness or a regular flat collar — if you do, you're turning your dog's head and straining their neck. Gently pulling downward as you turn will turn your dog's head toward you while also making their body follow along — without causing neck strain or injury.

Many dogs pull on their leads for a variety of reasons. It could be a learned response to someone constantly trying to pull them back. It could be because there's something they see that they're really interested in. Or it could be because they just want to move faster than you. Whatever the reason, you need to teach your Doodle to focus on you instead.

Using a front-connect harness is a great way of teaching your Doodle basic obedi-ence, but you may need a little more help to redirect their attention. You can accomplish this goal by using *both* a front-connect harness *and* a head halter. Using both training tools at the same time will accomplish your goals with your Doodle far more smoothly than with just one of them. Here's how to work with both training tools simultaneously:

1. Put the harness and head halter on your Doodle.

2. Attach a double-clip leash, one clip on the head halter ring under your dog's chin and the other end on the front of the harness.

3. **Hold the center of the lead in your right hand (if your dog will be on your left side), as shown in Figure 10-10.**

Don't hold your arm up or keep the leash taught. The leash must remain loose so your dog can learn and not be repeatedly corrected.

Photograph courtesy of Sarah Babineau

4. **Move forward normally, praising your dog as they move with you.**

The praise will keep them more focused on you than on any distractions.

5. **The moment they begin to look at something other than you or where you're going, turn in the opposite direction, as you keep your right arm down.**

You can use a verbal cue such as, "This way" and give them something else to focus on, such as a favorite toy.

TIP

Dogs tend to pay attention to unique movement and sound. You can use this to your advantage as you train. The more you make quick turns and unique sounds, the better your Doodle can focus on you.

6. **The moment your Doodle refocuses on you, mark that behavior immediately with a click or excited "Yes!" and then give a reward.**

   This will reinforce the fact that your dog will be rewarded when they remain attentive to you. Dogs always repeat behavior that has been rewarded.

Be sure to do many stops with other activities, such as sit-stays or down-stays and recalls to keep your dog attentive. Dogs are easily bored by doing the same thing over and over. Mix it up!

Down

Teaching your Doodle to lie down on command is very important. Not only can they maintain this position for longer periods of time than a sit or stand, but it also places your Doodle into a passive position.

Because of this positioning, some dogs prefer not to listen to the down cue, so you'll need to make sure you approach it positively and facilitate the behavior using high-value rewards. If your Doodle sees the down as a way to get treats and belly rubs, they'll respond to your down cue with enthusiasm.

Before you begin, think about what your Doodle loves above all other treats. Is it a specific toy, a piece of steak, or a belly rub? Use this special reward to both lure them into the down position and keep them there for a few seconds.

Here's how to train your dog to follow the down cue:

1. **Target your dog into the sit position (see the earlier section), marking and rewarding the moment they're in position.**

2. **Place the special treat in your hand and hold it directly under your Doodle's nose.**

3. **As soon as they touch your hand, lower the treat to the floor (see Figure 10-11).**

4. **As they follow with their head, mark and reward.**

5. **Repeat the exercise again, and don't mark until they've lowered themselves a little more.**

   Eventually your Doodle will lie down completely, enabling you to reward them with a belly rub.

FIGURE 10-11:
Lower the treat to the floor, and as soon as your dog lies down, mark and reward.

Photograph courtesy of Sarah Babineau

REMEMBER

Your dog doesn't have to go all the way into a down position for you to reward their initial response of lowering their head. Some dogs will go all the way, but less-trusting dogs may be hesitant to do so. Offer your Doodle a chance at success in small increments.

Some dogs are so untrusting that there is no treat in existence that will get them to open themselves up to feeling even more insecure by lying down. This type of dog needs some gentle assistance into the down position — but it shouldn't be forceful or harsh. Here's what to do:

1. **Begin with your Doodle sitting in heel position at your left side.**

2. **Try targeting them into the down position with your right hand.**

3. **If they ignore your visual cue, place your left hand on their shoulders as you bring out their front feet with your right hand.**

4. **Apply constant but gentle pressure to their shoulders as you bring the front legs forward.**

5. **The moment your Doodle's tummy touches the floor, rub their belly and praise.**

TIP

If your Doodle weighs more than 50 pounds, you'll want to *unbalance* them into the down position. Check to see the side on which they're placing all their weight. (*Hint:* It's the hip you see the least of.) As you bring the front leg of that same side forward, apply pressure to your dog's shoulders on the opposite side, thereby lowering your Doodle onto their side as their tummy meets the floor.

TIP

If you have a Toy-size Doodle, you can try to teach them the down by using stairs. Here's how to use stairs to your advantage:

1. **Put your Doodle in a sit on a stair that is at least two steps from the bottom.**

2. **Get their attention with a high-value reward such as chicken, cheese, or beef.**

3. **Begin by targeting a few times and mark their success with a click or "Yes!" followed by a small treat.**

4. **Gradually require your Doodle to lower their head with each successful target.**

5. **Eventually, the target will be lower than the step upon which they're sitting, and they'll need to lower their front end to the target.**

6. **With each incremental success, require your Doodle to bring their head lower and lower, which also lowers their entire upper body.**

7. **When your dog is reliably targeting and lowering their body enough to achieve a down position, you can move your lesson onto the flat floor.**

By this point, your dog is no longer concerned with feeling intimidated by the down position. All they know is that putting themselves into the down is highly rewarding!

Stay

Your Doodle can stay for a short period of time in a sit or stand, but they can remain in position longer while lying down. For example, a sit-stay is great while looking both ways prior to crossing a street or while greeting someone, but your dog can't remain in that position more than a couple minutes without needing to move. (It's especially difficult for puppies to remain in place longer than a few seconds.) While your dog is in a down-stay, they can learn to remain in their bed while you're eating dinner, visiting with guests, watching TV, or allowing a young child to touch them.

There are three components to teaching a solid stay:

>> Time

>> Movement

>> Distance

If you teach your Doodle with this methodical technique, they'll learn to remain in place regardless of distractions or environmental situations, such as at a dog park, when greeting a guest at the door, or in the presence of other animals.

Time

Wouldn't it be great if your Doodle stayed in the same place for upwards of a minute? In this section, I show you how you can get them to do exactly that.

Begin by doing this in a sit-stay. When your Doodle has learned a sit-stay, repeat the same process for a down-stay.

TIP

1. **Have your dog heel and sit at your side.**

   Always begin a training session with something that your dog knows well and will receive rewards for performing.

2. **As your dog is sitting, target in front of their nose with one hand as you use a specific visual cue with the other hand.**

   I always use an open-fingered hand, with the palm facing the dog (see Figure 10-12).

3. **Hold the target by your Doodle's nose for only a couple seconds.**

4. **Mark and reward, and then move forward into heel again.**

With each successive stay exercise, hold the target (and thus your dog's attentive sit-stay) a couple seconds longer.

The next step is to add the actual verbal stay cue. Your Doodle already has an idea of your visual cues for the command, so they'll easily learn the verbal ones associated with your body language. Say your dog's name and the cue "stay" as you give the hand signal in front of their face.

FIGURE 10-12:
Continue to target with one hand, as you give the stay cue with the other.

REMEMBER

You don't need to actually touch your dog's nose with your visual cue. Seeing it is enough. Also, don't swing your hand toward their face. Your Doodle may flinch at the motion, making the entire learning process less positive.

TIP

If your dog is getting up after a specific amount of time — for example, after they've been staying for 10 seconds — back up a bit (say, to 8 seconds). Work at this level for the remainder of the training session. During the next session, after they've been successfully staying for 8 seconds, try again for 10 seconds. Sometimes you'll have more success with an exercise if you're willing to regress a bit to a comfortable point.

When you've accomplished at least a 30-second sit-stay, do the same exercise with the down-stay.

If your Doodle has trouble remaining in position, even with their target nearby, apply a light pressure to their shoulder blades any time they start to push upward. This pressure will maintain their position without your having to replace them with another cue or offering another treat.

Movement

Now that your Doodle can remain in both the sit-stay and down-stay positions, it's time to move around them while they stay.

As with the time factor (see the preceding section), movement should be done in small increments.

TIP

When moving around your dog in a sit-stay, begin by moving in front of them. When moving around your dog in a down-stay, begin by moving along their side and then behind them.

Here's how to progress with a sit-stay:

1. Step directly in front of your Doodle as you give the stay cue (see Figure 10-13).

2. After remaining in front of your dog for up to 30 seconds, return to the heeling position, mark their good behavior and reward them.

FIGURE 10-13: The first move during a sit-stay should be directly in front of your dog, standing face to face and toe to toe.

Photograph courtesy of Sarah Babineau

3. **Move side to side in front of your Doodle as they remain in the sit-stay.**

4. **When your Doodle can maintain a sit-stay with you moving in front of them, begin walking along their sides.**

   Be sure to go along both sides equally.

5. **Walk completely around your dog as they stay.**

   As with moving along their sides, do circles around your Doodle in both directions.

Distance

The final step of the stay exercise is to increase your distance as you move around your dog. This will allow you to tell your Doodle to stay even if you're not right by their side. You can do this when you're going to answer the door, when you're walking through gates, or when you're going into one room and wanting them to stay in another.

As with the movement part of this exercise (see the preceding section), increase your distance using small increments and always be ready to shorten your distance if your dog can't remain in place.

Begin with gaining 1 foot of distance as you move around your Doodle. When they prove reliable with this, go to 2 feet, and so on, until you're walking around them at the end of a 6-foot leash. When your Doodle proves reliable at 6 feet, put on a 15- to 20-foot leash and gradually increase the distance even more. (See Chapter 11 for more on this subject.)

REMEMBER

Increase the distance gradually. Sudden distance will cause your dog to move out of position.

TIP

Don't move straight back. You taught your dog to come to you by moving backward, so your Doodle may have a tendency to move toward you if you do this. Instead, increase your distance as you move *around* your dog (see Figure 10-14).

Finish

When your Doodle is learning how to heel with you, you're actually teaching them several behaviors at the same time:

>> To be even with your leg

>> To stop there when you stop walking

>> To sit automatically when at your leg

FIGURE 10-14: Increase your distance as you move around your dog.

Photograph courtesy of Sarah Babineau

You're simultaneously teaching your Doodle to move forward with you, remain near you, and return to that position. This latter behavior is known as the finish.

The finish is a means of teaching your Doodle to return to, or go to, heel position at your side, on cue. This exercise maintains your dog's focus on you as they reposition themselves instead of your having to do so. For example, you cue your dog to come and sit. The next exercise is the finish cue, which tells them to return to heel position. Having your Doodle at your side instead of in front of you helps you move forward, instead of around your dog (or tripping over them).

One of the ways you can prepare a dog for off-lead reliability is to teach them how to do the finish. It's used while heeling, after the come, to catch up to you, and to present a default behavior. So, although the exercise may not carry the same importance as come or sit, it's useful in many ways.

The finish is actually easy for the dog to learn, but it may be a bit challenging for you to accomplish. It requires appropriate foot placement, good timing of your voice and visual cues, and just enough movement to put your dog in gear. Also, everything has to be done at the same time. If you move your leg without your hand and verbal cue, the entire visual cue will be confusing for your dog.

There are two ways to do the finish:

» **To the left:** Your dog will move along your left side, and turn and settle into a sit at your left leg, in heel position.

» **To the right:** Your dog will move along your right leg, pass behind you, and stop at a sit in heel position next to your left leg.

The method you use will depend largely on your dog. The bigger the dog, the easier it is for them to finish to the right, though most dogs can perform a finish to the left.

If you plan on doing any performance activities with your Doodle, I suggest you teach them how to perform both finish exercises. You'll need each one at different times, and it's a great way to cue your dog back into heel position at any time, especially if your dog is off lead.

TIP

Practice the finish moves alone before doing them with your dog. If you get the action correct, your dog will, too. If you don't present the cues as needed, both of you will wind up a jumbled mess.

Finishing to the left

To finish to the left, follow these steps:

1. Cue your dog to heel, keeping your left target hand even with your left leg, and take a big step backward, using the verbal cue for heel (see Figure 10-15).

2. When your dog moves forward (backward for you), bring your left leg into position even with your right leg (see Figure 10-16).

3. The moment your Doodle stops with your left leg stopped, cue them to sit (if they haven't taken that position already), as shown in Figure 10-17.

When your Doodle (and you) are able to apply this exercise with fluidity, you can incorporate it into the work you do with distraction proofing in Chapter 11. You'll also need to use it when you start reducing the use of the leash.

Another way it can be used is as a means of moving into heel position when your dog is nowhere near you. For example, you place them in a sit-stay and move away. When you want your Doodle to join you and heel at your side, you tap your left leg and cue them to heel. Regardless of where your dog is, they should catch up with you and remain at your side.

FIGURE 10-15:
Step back as you cue and target for heel with your left hand.

Photograph courtesy of Sarah Babineau

FIGURE 10-16:
As your dog moves along your leg, bring your left leg forward, keeping your cue hand with your leg.

Photograph courtesy of Sarah Babineau

FIGURE 10-17:
The moment your
dog nears your
left leg, cue to sit.

Photograph courtesy of Sarah Babineau

Finishing to the right

To finish to the right, follow these steps:

1. **Place a treat in your right hand, close your fist, and show your Doodle your hand as a target.**

   This will be the cue hand for this exercise.

2. **Lure your dog along your right side as you step backward with your right leg.**

   Your Doodle will move forward with your right leg along their right side.

3. **As your Doodle moves forward (for them, backward for you), keep your right hand on your right leg as they move behind you (see Figure 10-18).**

   Do not move your left leg, or twist your body.

4. **As your dog moves behind you, near your right leg, bring your right leg forward.**

5. **Switch the treat into your left hand as it's behind your back, and continue luring your dog to your left side as you bring your right leg forward (see Figure 10-19).**

6. **Continue to target them into a sit at your left side, as your right leg returns to standing evenly with your left (see Figure 10-20).**

FIGURE 10-18: Target your dog to move along your right leg as you take a step back with it.

Photograph courtesy of Sarah Babineau

FIGURE 10-19: Change target hands to your left as your dog moves behind you and you guide them up to your left side.

Photograph courtesy of Sarah Babineau

This can be a complicated action for many people, *so* I suggest practicing these movements *without* your dog before doing them *with* your dog.

Stand

The stand is not normally taught in basic obedience classes, but it does have practical use. People who show their dogs teach it because there are often moments when it's required in the show ring. Even if you don't show your Doodle, the stand cue will come in handy when having your dog examined by a veterinarian or groomed.

There are three ways to teach your Doodle to stand on cue:

>> Guide them into position as you move forward slowly.

>> Guide them into position when they're sitting at your side in heel position.

>> Put your Doodle in position on a table.

FIGURE 10-20:
As you apply light pressure to the front of your dog's hind leg with one hand, cue the stay with your other hand.

Photograph courtesy of Sarah Babineau

STANDING FOR THE VET

If your Doodle weighs more than 40 pounds, you'll want to cue your dog to stand from a sit on the floor. If your Doodle weighs less than 40 pounds, you lift them onto the examination table.

Just moving into a standing position won't be enough for your veterinarian to do a full examination. There are abdominal palpations, as well as checks of the ears, mouth, eyes, and throat. Often, the tail will need to be lifted for insertion of a thermometer. In order for your veterinarian to do all this, your Doodle must remain in a stand for several minutes.

There are a couple ways to facilitate this. One is to continually target and treat them periodically. Another is to rub some peanut butter or cheese on a flat surface and allow them to lick it as they're being manipulated by the veterinarian. Most dogs consider both of these as positive associations and will quickly get over any fear they may have had at seeing their doctor.

The more you practice this exercise, the easier it gets and the more comfortable your Doodle will be with the situation.

Moving stand

In order to accomplish a moving stand, you need to be able to multitask. But if you were successful with the finish, earlier in this chapter, this exercise shouldn't be too much trouble. Follow these steps:

1. **As you move forward with your Doodle on your left side, place all of the lead into your right hand along with a treat.**

   Your Doodle should immediately target your hand when it's put in front of them.

2. **Stop and target your dog with your right hand, placing your left hand beneath their belly but in front of their hind leg.**

   This will effectively stop your dog at both ends.

3. **The moment your Doodle stops, mark and give them the treat.**

4. **Repeat at least five more times during this first training session.**

   Each time your Doodle successfully holds a stand, add a few seconds of stay time prior to your click and reward.

When your Doodle has a good idea what's going on with this new action, add a verbal and visual cue for it: Tell them "stand" as you sweep your left palm from their head to their rear.

From sit to stand

When indoors or in a small space, this procedure will be easier to perform than having to move first (as in the preceding section). Follow these steps:

1. Begin by having your Doodle sit in heel position.

2. Put a treat in your right hand, and show your hand target to your Doodle.

3. When your Doodle targets your right hand, slowly move it forward a bit so your dog shifts their weight onto their shoulders.

4. As your dog shifts their weight forward to reach their target, gently lift them from beneath their tummy.

5. When they're evenly standing on all fours, click and reward.

6. Gradually increase the time between your Doodle standing up and receiving the click marker.

This will prepare your dog for a stand-stay.

Putting your dog on a table

If you're teaching your Toy-size Doodle to stand on a platform, such as a grooming table, place them on the table, then just lure them forward a little with your target hand. The moment they're standing up, place your other hand under their tummy and gently rub.

STANDING FOR THE GROOMER

Having to maintain a stand-stay for the groomer can be challenging. It's not a brief minute or two; instead, it's generally upwards of an hour. Not only must they remain standing for a long time, but they must accept the manipulations required to clean their feet, trim their nails, clip around their eyes and in the ears and, often, along their bodies as well.

This is a goal you'll need to work toward gradually. When they're young, few Doodles can hold still for a second, never mind an hour. You'll need to work hard on all the obedience exercises in this chapter and make sure you don't skip the stand-stay.

In the beginning, gradually add seconds to the stand-stay time. Within a couple weeks, you can begin adding minutes. By the time your Doodle is 4 months old (and in dire need of their first professional grooming), they should be able to maintain a stand-stay for upwards of 15 minutes.

Beginning the grooming process at home (see Chapter 8) will prepare them for the ultimate challenge of being well behaved for the groomer.

Chapter **11**

Advanced Doodle Lessons

When your Doodle knows the basics, like sit, stay, and come (see Chapter 10), it's time to perfect their responses and improve their reliability in every situation. This includes increasing the duration of stays, increasing the distance on recalls, being able to go hiking off-leash, and learning new skills that enhance your communication and enjoyment.

Doodles love to learn and thrive on the stimulation they get when learning new concepts or adding new skill sets.

Increasing the Duration and Distance of Stays and Recalls

If you worked through Chapter 10, you're probably working on teaching your Doodle to come when called and stay as you move around them. You can get up to 6 feet away from them — the length of the training lead — as they stay.

Practice calling your Doodle to come from both sit-stays and down-stays. Also, practice doing so when they're doing their own thing, such as following a scent or playing with a toy, and from all points of the compass around them. The more variety you put into direction, the more reliable your Doodle will be in every situation.

TIP

If you haven't already, attach a 20-foot lead to your Doodle's harness. This will give you a safety net as you gradually increase the distance during their stays and recalls. You have to nail distance control before you can trust your dog off lead. Not every dog is 100 percent reliable at this point. A 20-feet lead will allow you to get your dog back on task when they aren't.

Increasing the distance during stays

Regardless of your Doodle's position — sit, down, or stand — here's how to create a solid stay at a distance:

1. **Begin by working with your Doodle on what they do well — a 6-foot distance stay as you move around them.**

Be sure to not allow your 20-foot lead to become tangled around them. You can do this by moving around your dog in both directions before returning to their side, or by calling them to come (see the next section).

2. **Then increase your distance as you move around them (see Figure 11-1).**

Do all incremental increases at about 1 to 2 feet per training session. You may be tempted to suddenly go out 10 feet, turn and face your dog, and then call them to come, but don't do it! This sets your Doodle up for pattern learning instead of actually learning the cues for each exercise.

REMEMBER

Doodles are quite intelligent — they learn patterns after as few as two or three repetitions.

Your gradual movement outward helps your Doodle not notice your distance increases as you move around them, spiraling out. The point of this exercise is to improve duration and distances while your Doodle remains calm and secure.

TIP

Be sure to move around your dog in both directions. If you aren't in a securely fenced area, continue holding the end of the lead.

FIGURE 11-1:
Increasing
distance as you
move around
your dog.

Photograph courtesy of Sarah Babineau

3. **The next phase of distance stays is to drop the lead as you move around your dog (see Figure 11-2).**

WARNING

   If you don't fully trust your Doodle, either don't move on to this phase or tie the end of the lead to a fence or other solid object.

   The point of this exercise is to remove the direct sight line of the leash between you and your dog.

   Because dropping the lead is new, begin the exercise by first reducing the distance between you and your dog during the stay. As your Doodle adjusts to the lead being dropped (and it should happen rather quickly), gradually increase your distance again to where you were before dropping the lead.

   Be sure to walk in both directions and alternately face your dog or turn your back to them as you move. The more you change things up, the more competent your dog will be in all situations.

4. **When your Doodle is reliably staying with you at a distance of 20 feet, it's time to go out a little farther.**

   With each successive stay exercise, add 2 feet of distance as you move around your Doodle. You can eventually work your way up to being as far away as you want.

FIGURE 11-2:
Drop your lead as
you move around
your dog.

Photograph courtesy of Sarah Babineau

You can also briefly go out of sight. For example, practice the stay near a building and go around the corner of the building (peeking around to make sure your Doodle still remains in the same spot). Or walk behind a tree. Be sure to be very brief when you begin doing this. You can gradually increase your time out of sight as your dog accomplishes more.

You can reach many goals when your dog can remain in a stay as you engage in another activity or just need to keep them safe. One of these is to perform stays at doors and gates. You can teach your dog an automatic response each time they come to a door or gate. You merely need to remain consistent and require your Doodle to sit and stay, automatically, every time you're about to walk through a door.

5. **Finally, have your Doodle remain in place with the leash removed.**

Be sure your Doodle has been very reliable with the lead dropped and when exposed to distractions (covered later in this chapter).

REMEMBER

It can take months before you get to this point, so be patient and persistent. Every dog learns at a different rate and a lot of that depends on clear communication, as well as consistency regardless of where you are and what's going on around you.

Getting your dog to come from a stay

Now that your Doodle understands how to perform stays at a distance, you can cue them to do a recall from those stays.

The most difficult part of this command is gathering the leash as your dog nears you. If you don't gather it, the leash will get tangled under your Doodle's feet.

TIP

Try to gather your leash hand over hand as your dog comes to you (see Figure 11-3). Don't pull on the leash — you want your Doodle to come when called without needing any force.

FIGURE 11-3: Gather the lead hand over hand as your dog comes toward you.

Photograph courtesy of Sarah Babineau

Here's the step-by-step approach:

1. **Place your dog in a stay.**

2. **Lean forward, show them your hand target, hold the target near your knees, and call them to you.**

3. **As your dog comes to you, stand upright and gather your leash hand over hand.**

Practice calling your Doodle from all directions — in front of them, from each side, and from behind them. This will teach them to come from any direction. Also, be sure to have your Doodle perform the come from both a sit-stay and down-stay.

The more you vary the exercises, the more attentive your Doodle will be.

Begin with the exercise of calling from the end of a 6-foot leash. When your Doodle is reliably responding, you can attach a 20-foot leash and work from greater distances. Keep in mind that the longer the leash, the more you must gather as your dog comes to you. Also, the farther away your dog is when you call them, the faster they'll move toward you — often faster than you can gather the leash! No worries — if your Doodle arrives before you can totally gather the leash, just do the following:

1. **Take hold of the leash near the D-ring at the front of the harness, giving them at least 2 feet of slack between the collar and your hand (see Figure 11-4).**

FIGURE 11-4: Take the lead near the harness as your Doodle arrives.

Photograph courtesy of Sarah Babineau

2. **Have your dog perform a finish (see Chapter 10).**

When they're back in heel position, the leash will be out from under them.

3. **Gather the leash while you're walking with your dog.**

It will be easier to gather because your dog won't be sitting on part of it.

As with gaining distance in the stay exercises, you want to build on success with the recall as well. Begin with short distances and, as your Doodle becomes reliable, gradually increase the distance as you vary the location. Practice calling them to you from in front of them, from either side, and from behind.

TIP

If you get to a specific distance and your Doodle is sniffing on their way to you, go back to a shorter distance. They're showing you that they're not ready for that distance yet.

When your Doodle is easily coming to you from the distance of the long leash, it's time to move away from the leash a bit. Here's how to do it in safe phases:

1. **When working on a stay, drop the leash and move around your dog, but return to the end of the leash prior to calling them.**

This will allow you to pick up the leash and guide your Doodle to you if they get distracted by something along the way.

2. **Call them from near the leash, but not in a direct line with it.**

Again, this will allow you to reinforce your command fairly quickly if your Doodle gets distracted by something else.

3. **Move farther and farther from the line of the leash as your Doodle proves reliable.**

4. **Gain distance from your dog as they prove reliable from any location.**

5. **Hide behind solid objects so your dog learns to stay and come when you're out of sight.**

TIP

You may want to have someone help you with this because you won't be able to see when your dog moves before you call them.

REMEMBER

It can take time to accomplish all these phases. You shouldn't expect your Doodle to do this all in one day. Be patient and don't push them past what they can do reliably and safely.

Walking at Heel without a Leash

When you and your Doodle are walking along nicely, you can begin doing so off-leash indoors or within a small, securely fenced area where there are no distractions.

Working off-leash is generally the ultimate goal of many dog owners. It takes lots of time and energy, but it is possible. I've broken this difficult process into two phases.

TIP

You know you're ready to begin off-leash heeling when you hardly have to use the leash at all. You can accomplish this by varying your pace, performing quick 180-degree turns, and never stopping to see what your Doodle is up to if they're lagging behind.

REMEMBER

The more turns you do, the more attentive your dog will be.

Phase 1: Dragging the leash

While you're walking, your Doodle should be watching you attentively and keeping pace with you. If they're doing so nonchalantly, drop the leash. If your dog moves a little ahead, you can quickly step on the leash with a verbal reminder that they're not paying attention. This should be enough to return your Doodle to your side and get them watching you again — if not, return to holding the lead and work a little longer before trying this again.

Gradually increase the amount of time (during each training session) that you allow the leash to drag. I suggest the following pattern:

1. **Work on lead for about 5 to 10 minutes.**

2. **When your Doodle is nicely focused and you aren't having to use the lead to redirect them, drop the lead.**

3. **If, at any time, your Doodle becomes distracted, return to holding the lead. Otherwise, only pick it up near the end of the training session, as your dog begins to show signs that they're tiring.**

TIP

Dogs often show that they're tired in several ways:

>> They begin to lag while heeling.

>> They begin to look around instead of at you.

>> They lie down during a sit-stay, recall slower than normal, or just get a faraway gaze in their eyes.

As you work with your Doodle you'll learn to recognize the signs that they're getting tired.

Phase 2: Using a pull-tab leash

A *pull-tab leash* is a very short leash attached to a training device (see Figure 11-5).

FIGURE 11-5:
A pull-tab connected to a harness.

REMEMBER

At this point, the training device should still be a front-connect harness, because although your dog may no longer need to be physically redirected most of the time, there may be times when you do need to remind them to pay attention via a light tug on the pull tab. And at no time should you apply pressure to their neck via a neck collar.

Begin walking with a light hold on the end of the pull-tab. As your Doodle remains attentively at your side in heel position, let go. Keep a close eye on your dog. If they begin to stray out of position, use a verbal reminder in a low tone of voice as you make a sharp turn. Or if your dog responds better to a verbal reminder of, "This way!" use that. If your dog goes in any direction other than with you, they aren't ready for this phase. Return to leash dragging until you no longer have to step on the leash or use any reminders about remaining in heeling position.

Otherwise, congratulations! Your dog now heels off-leash.

Distraction-Proofing Your Doodle

Distraction-proofing is far more difficult than teaching the basic commands. It's tough for a dog to pay attention when they'd rather be chasing squirrels, playing with other dogs, or racing around the backyard with the kids.

You have to offer your Doodle a positive experience for them to *want* to work for you amid all these distractions. In order to maintain *their* positive attitude, you must always have a positive attitude *yourself,* and offer them high-value rewards so paying attention to you is more important to your Doodle than anything else. You'll also need to reward them very often, so they have more desire to pay attention.

Be prepared to redirect your dog when there is a distraction too enticing to ignore. Often, treats or favorite toys can't compete with the presence of another dog, especially one playing nearby. Your Doodle won't care if you put a piece of steak under their nose — they feel that the better reward is to go play with that other dog. When this occurs, you need to be able to redirect them.

You'll need training tools — namely, a head halter and front-connect harness (see Chapter 10) — to work on distraction-proofing with your Doodle.

Before I dive into the various distractions you'll want to work on with your dog, here are some tips to keep in mind for every type of distraction:

>> **The best path to a positive outcome is through incremental progression — building on success.** It may take time, but the result will be well worth it. You'll have a confident Doodle who can be reliable in any situation.

>> **Start with the easiest types of distractions and progress to the more challenging ones.**

>> **Always begin the proofing process at a distance where your dog isn't showing any alert or desire to go investigate the distraction.** Gradually decrease that distance as your dog can handle it. For example, if you're walking toward a house where there's a dog barking, work with your Doodle at a distance where they aren't reacting to that barking dog. As they remain focused and relaxed, move a little bit closer. If your Doodle's ears perk up and they're noticing the barking dog, redirect with a quick turn, walking back to the point where they had no reaction.

This process will take many days, possibly weeks or months, depending on the distraction and how much your dog values checking it out or being fearful of it. You need to remain patient, persistent, and vigilant, while also showing your Doodle that you're confident in the situation and they can count on you to guide them through safely.

TIP

Here's how to progress through each step closer to the distraction, regardless of what the distraction may be:

1. **Have your dog heeling at your side.**

2. **When you see the distraction, don't react — save your reaction for when your Doodle *begins* to look.**

TIP

   Don't wait for your Doodle to pull before you react. If they even *look* at the distraction, they're distracted.

3. **When your dog notices the distraction, gently pull downward on your leash (putting pressure on the head halter) as you turn.**

4. **Continue walking until your dog is heeling properly.**

5. **Mark and reward.**

6. **Turn and try to get a little closer the next time.**

   Continue with your turning and redirection when your Doodle begins to look at the distraction. Always mark the moment they return to the correct behavior and reward them for it. If the distraction is a favorite toy, use that toy as the jackpot reward.

TECHNICAL STUFF

   A jackpot reward is offered when your dog performs something that was very challenging and you release them from work with a reward marker and then give the reward they wanted so much.

TIP If you've been trying to get just a couple feet closer than the previous attempt and your Doodle simply won't allow that, it's time to back off to a safer zone. For example, say you've been working on getting within 20 feet of that yard where the dog is barking, but your Doodle wants to lunge toward the other dog the moment they lay eyes on it. It's time to go back to the area where your dog didn't react so adamantly. Work in this area for a while. Then, when your dog is calm and not pulling to go toward the distraction, try to get just a few feet closer.

There are multiple levels of distractions. Some may be relatively easy to proof your Doodle into ignoring and others will be far more challenging. Having a game plan will greatly improve your success. Setting minor goals along the way and celebrating their achievement will motivate both of you to continue working toward the ultimate goal of your Doodle being reliable in any situation with little need for a leash.

Toys

Most Doodles have favorite toys — the ones they take to bed with them, carry around, or present to you when you walk in the door. These are their prized possessions, and they always know where they are. If your dog's favorite toy is suddenly not waiting for them in their bed and is instead flying around them as they perform their stays or are heeling, this becomes a big distraction. For dogs who believe that tennis balls are the best thing in the world, it can be very difficult to ignore one rolling by. But that's exactly what you'll be doing when using toys to distraction-proof your Doodle.

Begin with the toys being stationary on the ground in the training area (see Figure 11-6). When your Doodle doesn't pay any attention to them lying there, start throwing them around as your dog is working. You'll need the help of someone who understands not to throw the toys *at* you, but rather *around* you and your Doodle, about 15 feet away.

Your dog's first instinct will be to chase the toys, so you may need to do several redirection turns as the toys are flying about. You'll need to work on this for a few days, until your Doodle is remaining focused on you as the toys are moving around. At some point, you should leave the toys where they've been thrown and work your dog around them. Redirect anytime your dog tries to go chase or sniffs at them.

Every time you do a training session with toy distractions, try to bring your Doodle closer to the toys as they're being thrown. Always pay attention to their behavior to ensure they're ready to move closer. You'll know the time is right when they aren't charging at the toys or sniffing at them when passing.

FIGURE 11-6:
Put toy
distractions on
the ground as
your Doodle
walks around
them.

Photograph courtesy of Sarah Babineau

Your end goal with toy distraction work is for your Doodle to be able to heel while walking by any toy or sitting by any toy, maintain a stay when multiple toys are being thrown, and come when called when they encounter a favorite toy along the way.

Just as there are different types of distractions that are more, or less, challenging, there will be toys that are also more or less enticing. If, for example, your Doodle loves balls, a rolling ball will be more of a distraction than a stuffed toy thrown near their feet. As you play with your Doodle, you'll figure out their favorite types of toys. Be sure to use them not only as a distraction but also as a jackpot reward. This way, your dog will learn that if they ignore the toy for a few minutes, they'll eventually get it as a reward for their good behavior.

Children

There's little chance that your Doodle will go through life without encountering children of various ages. In fact, it's a good idea for your Doodle to be exposed to them as early as possible, as a means of learning appropriate social skills. The cries of babies, the erratic motion of toddlers, the screams of children on a playground, or even teenagers engaged in a ballgame — all are part of life, and your Doodle needs to be able to respond to your cues in their presence.

As with every type of distraction, start small. Most dogs become highly excited when they're first introduced to children. And Doodles, with their tendency to jump up, are likely to do just that when they meet them. You need to train your dog to remain sitting as they're approached (see Figure 11-7). Cueing them to do so prior to their arrival will give them some structure in an otherwise chaotic situation.

FIGURE 11-7:
Your Doodle should sit as they're greeted by children.

Photograph courtesy of Sarah Babineau

If you can control the situation, you can begin working with your Doodle at a distance prior to a first meeting. This will help your dog understand that other people (children in particular) are to be ignored until you release them from work.

TIP

Here are some suggestions for teaching your Doodle to behave well around noisy, boisterous children:

>> Practice training your dog near playgrounds or ballgames.

>> Take your dog with you to the bus stop, but work with them — don't just allow them to meander without guidance.

>> Work with your dog after the neighborhood children get home and are playing in their yards.

>> If you have a child who is involved in sports, take your Doodle to the games and work with them there.

>> If you have children, teach them how to do some simple exercises with your Doodle, such as come, sit, sit-stay with a walk around, or play some learning games such as Round Robin (see Chapter 10).

REMEMBER

A dog who is reliable around children can be taken anywhere and be welcomed with squeals of delight — and lots of hugs, too.

Dogs

Children are a huge distraction, but other dogs can be even more challenging. That's why I suggest waiting until your dog achieves reliability working around children and other people before you start having them work around other dogs — especially dogs who are chasing toys or racing around.

The best way to distraction-proof around other dogs is to engage the help of someone whose dogs are already trained. A controlled atmosphere will offer a better chance of success than trying to teach your dog to ignore a dog who's coming toward you on the sidewalk, lunging and barking.

WARNING

Most dogs will view lunging and barking as a danger not only to themselves, but to you, and they'll behave similarly. This is the main reason there's leash aggression along city and suburban sidewalks. The more you try to pull your dog back, the more they believe something is wrong and they should get more aggressive.

Controlling all the dogs involved in the training process will be key to achieving dog distraction-proofing. This allows you to begin with working your Doodle at a distance where the dog distraction isn't an issue and gradually get closer as your Doodle acclimates to the presence of the other dog.

All training sessions should begin with working your Doodle on all of their behaviors. Be sure to mix it up. Dogs prefer to do a lot of different things — it keeps them more focused.

Have your distraction team (handler and dog) begin at a distance far enough that your Doodle doesn't react to them. Take a few minutes to get your Doodle nicely focused on you, and then move in closer (see Figure 11-8). When your dog sees the other dog and begins to move toward them, redirect into the opposite direction, quickly.

FIGURE 11-8:
Gradually decrease the distances between the dogs as they learn to ignore each other.

Photograph courtesy of Sarah Babineau

Continue in this manner, getting closer and closer as your dog remains calm and focused on you. If, at any time, your Doodle prefers to check out the other dog instead of watching you, increase the distance between you and the other dog.

REMEMBER

Sometimes you have to regress a bit (to where your dog was reliable) before progressing forward and challenging their skills again.

If your dog is social but anxious to meet other dogs, it may help to allow some time for the two dogs to play together prior to working with them. This way the distraction of a new dog nearby isn't quite so irresistible, because they've already met. It's a great means of decreasing the number of times you have to redirect.

In reality, it's often hard to do this. As you walk your Doodle through the neighborhood, all sorts of dogs they don't know — and can't readily meet — will come around the corner. Both dogs will be alert and anxious to meet each other, or instantly dislike each other, creating all sorts of pulling, barking, and struggling people at the ends of leashes. Your best means of training your Doodle to disregard these situations is to redirect — quickly turn in the opposite direction and click, praise, and reward the moment they refocus on you.

Other animals

Squirrel! The scariest thing on earth when you're walking your dog is for them to suddenly dart after wildlife. There's no way you, or anyone else, can control the little creatures, and their quick movement triggers your dog's prey drive every time. Trying to get your Doodle to ignore squirrels will be as difficult as trying to ignore a big piece of chocolate cake right in front of you.

Although you can't control the squirrels, you *can* teach your Doodle to remain focused on you when exposed to other animals, such as cats, farm animals, horses, or rodents.

REMEMBER

You can acclimate your Doodle to other animals in the same manner as you would another dog or a toy distraction. The method doesn't change — only the distraction does. Being consistent with your methods will help you overcome any distraction as long as you're patient and persistent.

If you're lucky enough to live near horses, use them as a distraction source (see Figure 11-9). Gradually work your Doodle nearer and nearer as long as they can focus on you nearly all the time. (It's tough to *always* ignore that chocolate cake. Sometimes you need to enjoy it, too.) The way I allow enjoyment of a distraction is to allow the dog to go for it as a jackpot reward. Now you can't do this with someone else's pet or farm animal, but you can allow your Doodle to go nose to nose for a proper greeting — as long as the other animal is amenable.

FIGURE 11-9:
Work your Doodle with a variety of other animals.

Photograph courtesy of Sarah Babineau

Enhancing Focus by Capturing Offered Behavior

When your Doodle understands how to respond to your obedience cues, stay focused when distracted, and work off lead, you're ready for the next level of training. This next level puts the ball in your dog's court — they'll make the first moves. It's up to you, however, to make sure that they understand they were right in their decisions.

TIP

Being observant and having good timing is the key to everything! You must be able to recognize when your dog is offering you something you want and capture that moment with a reward marker — a click. You'll also need to carry a *lot* of rewards. Hopefully, your dog prefers food treats and not toys. It's a lot easier to carry cut-up cheese or hot dogs than a bag of tennis balls.

Capturing heeling off lead

Begin with your dog moving with you in a loose-leash walk. Follow these steps:

1. **Move forward with a "Let's go" verbal cue and a slap on your leg as a visual cue.**

2. **Allow your dog to meander, sniff, and generally do their own thing, provided they remain nearby.**

3. **Watch them carefully, and the moment you see them glance at you, click and reward.**

   This can be out of the corner of their eye or a full-on glance. Either way, mark and reward.

4. **When they do it again, click and reward again.**

   Do it every time your Doodle looks at you. It'll begin occurring more and more often as they figure out what they did to get a reward.

Next thing you know, they're no longer sniffing or chasing leaves — they're watching you and moving near you, of their own accord. You never cued them to heel or come. They're offering it.

This exercise is further improved as you raise the criteria level for the reward. Instead of giving the reward just for a glance, give it for an actual move back to you. Then up the stakes and require them to be on the same side they normally heel next to. Then require them to be in the actual heeling position.

Now you have a dog with whom you can hike off-lead because they see you as the source of all good things (see Figure 11-10).

FIGURE 11-10: Offering heel on a hike.

Photograph courtesy of Sarah Babineau

Voluntary stays

A voluntary stay will likely occur when you get your dog into a routine of performing stays at doors or gates or when people enter the house. It's the repetition that truly sets in the behavior. Your Doodle will soon automatically perform those stays in those situations without your having to cue them to do so (see Figure 11-11).

Be sure to click and reward your Doodle's forward thinking. And don't be fooled — they didn't do it just because they chose to in that moment. You've been training them to do it! Every time you've cued them to sit and stay prior to opening a door, you've supplied the repetition for them to understand the pattern in that situation.

There's another situation in which your Doodle will voluntarily learn to sit and stay, and that's when they see you preparing their meals. They'll likely sit and watch you. Be sure to click and reward that sit because they made the right decision.

FIGURE 11-11:
Automatic
sit-stays near
open gates.

Photograph courtesy of Sarah Babineau

As they continue to sit and watch you, click and reward with slightly greater increments of pause. This will teach them that sitting quietly and waiting not only gets them dinner but also gets them lots of great treats along the way. Your Doodle is no fool — they'll begin using this behavior in other situations, too.

As your dog keeps trying out new behaviors to see what's rewarding, you need to be sure that you reward the right ones — the behaviors you want, not the behaviors your Doodle feels might be fun, such as pawing at your leg or jumping on the dinner table. It may be funny in the moment, but you probably don't want them to repeat that.

Putting on the Finishing Touches: AKC Rally

The American Kennel Club (AKC) sponsors a great performance event called AKC Rally, in which you guide your dog around a course and cue them to perform specific maneuvers at numbered stations (see Figure 11-12). Your dog must remain highly focused and respond quickly. If you plan to do any type of showing with your Doodle, AKC Rally is a great one to do because you're constantly on the go and you and your dog must work as a team.

FIGURE 11-12:
Doodling around
an AKC Rally
course.

AKC Rally isn't just a sport, however. It was originally designed to help dogs focus better. The wide variety of heeling maneuvers, turns, circles, stay positions, and ignoring of very high-value distractions helps teach your dog to be part of your every move.

Ironically, the practice of AKC Rally is referred to as *doodling!*

TECHNICAL STUFF

Here's a list of some of the AKC Rally obedience exercises that you'll encounter:

>> Moving fast or slow

>> Doing a 360-degree circle to the left or right

>> Doing a 90-degree turn to the left or right

>> Doing a 270-degree turn to the left or right

>> Looping to the left or right

>> Stopping and doing a sit-stay or a down-stay with a walk around

>> Starting and stopping or requesting come and sit with one step, then two steps, then three steps prior to each stop and sit

>> Finishing to the left or right

>> Standing and staying

>> Transitioning from a stand to a down to a sit, or doing a simpler transition from a down to a sit

>> Doing a figure-8 with or without dog dishes that have food or toys in them

>> Doing a moving stand, sit, or down-stay (where you're moving as you cue the dog to perform these behaviors)

>> Coming from a stay

>> Remaining in a down-stay as another dog is working nearby

>> Going over jumps of various types

For those who compete, you can download the station signs (each has its own exercise displayed on it) and set them up in a pattern. The more you change the patterns, the more fun you'll have because you must follow them in a specific order. If you have trouble multitasking, this may not be the sport for you, but if you're in tune with your Doodle and you don't have to take time to think of each cue, you may be ready for AKC Rally!

TIP

To find out more about AKC Rally, visit the AKC's website at `www.akc.org/sports/rally`.

Puppy Playground: Doodle Agility Fun

Doodles are very athletic regardless of the breed mix. A Jackadoodle will want to jump, explore, race around, and investigate new sights as much as a Sheepadoodle will. The somewhat sedate Pyredoodle will still want to climb hills and explore tunnels as much as a Havadoodle or Cockapoo will. Regardless of their size, all Doodles enjoy activities that stimulate their brains and bodies.

A single activity that can offer all these things is agility. Agility has jumps, tunnels, climbing equipment (see Figure 11-13), and much more. Learning how to negotiate each type of equipment and then racing through an entire course will be sure to get your Doodle in great shape and increase their cognition.

You don't have to compete in the sport to fully enjoy the experience. Your Doodle doesn't have any idea if they're competing or not. All they know is that they're having loads of fun and receiving heaps of rewards from your enthusiastic responses with games of tug or treats!

FIGURE 11-13:
Doodles love
agility training.

If you have a backyard you can set up a mini agility course. You can find equipment from online retailers such as:

>> AffordableAgility.com (`www.affordableagility.com`)

>> Cheering Pet (`www.cheeringpet.com/collections/dog-agility-equipment`)

There are also numerous sources for building your own agility course, including `www.thisoldhouse.com/pets/21016642/how-to-build-a-dog-agility-course`. Search the web for "how to build a dog agility course" for lots of other similar articles.

TIP

Find a local dog club or trainer who has a course and offers classes. Whether you do it in a group with other pet parents or in private lessons, you and your Doodle are sure to have a great time! After you've learned how to teach your Doodle to do agility, you can begin doing so at home or at a local park.

Here's a list of some of the obstacles to be learned:

>> **Teeter:** Like a child's see-saw, only your dog walks up one side and in the middle the plank moves into a downward position, and your dog follows the plank back to the ground.

>> **A-frame:** A climb up and then down.

>> **Weave poles:** Your dog learns to weave around 6 to 12 poles.

>> **Table:** Your dog jumps onto the table and remains in a sit or down until cued to move to the next obstacle.

>> **Jumps:** These include high jump (solid panels), broad jump (distance jumping over low panels), bar jumps (bars stacked over each other with space between them), and parallel jump (bars are separate from each other but the same height).

>> **Tire jump:** A round tire-like hoop that your dog jumps through.

There are more, but these are the main obstacles in most agility arenas.

WARNING

Be sure that your dog is old enough to engage in activities that include jumping and climbing. Most dogs don't reach physical maturity until about a year of age. Harsh impacts or body twists can damage a dog's shoulders, paws, or back. If your Doodle is under 1 year old, stick to activities that remain grounded, such as tunnels, weave poles, a low table, or low dog walk. It's never too early to begin teaching your Doodle how to do agility — just be mindful of their physical well-being.

Chapter **12**

Doodle Don'ts

Most dogs tend to have annoying habits, but Doodles have a few that are consistent with their particular breed mixes. These include jumping up on people and other dogs, preferring to lie on top of other dogs, mouthing, chewing, resource guarding, and counter-surfing. Although other inappropriate behaviors can occur, these behaviors are the most common in Doodles.

REMEMBER

Doodles are sensitive, intelligent, and resourceful. If a barrier is cutting off their access to something they want, they'll figure out a new way of approaching the challenge. So, instead of merely creating barriers, you need to teach your Doodle how to behave appropriately and that those little devious behaviors that delight them need to stop.

But first, you need to understand the difference between an earned reward and self-rewarding behavior. An *earned reward* is something your Doodle does to receive praise and treats from you. For example, they come when called or perform a trick on cue. They're doing this to be rewarded by you and will repeat the behavior as long as they continue to receive rewards for doing so.

Self-rewarding behavior, on the other hand, is a behavior that your Doodle repeats because they're rewarding themselves by doing it. An example is chasing squirrels. The sheer enjoyment of the chase, and fulfilling the instinctive need to respond to their prey drive, can be a very high-value reward for your dog. You'll need to use steak rewards to redirect them into believing your offerings are worth more.

Another example of self-rewarding behavior is counter-surfing. You're nowhere to be seen and your Doodle is sure to find something tasty left out on the counter.

Sometimes barking can also be self-rewarding. Have you ever screamed and yelled when happy? Maybe when listening to your favorite band, or watching your children play sports. There is joy in making lots of noise!

It can also be self-rewarding to keep all the chocolates to yourself. You may not want to share your candy with all your siblings, leaving you just one or two pieces. Many dogs feel the same way. A high-value toy may become less valuable if another dog takes it away and chews it down to a nub. Resource guarding is the result of insecurity, as well as being stingy. Doodles know the values of their toys and their companions (you).

Some behaviors that end up being self-rewarding actually started out as something you rewarded first. Jumping up is a big example. Doodles love to jump up, but it can become a very annoying problem if you encourage the behavior in any way. After a while, you may try to push your dog off of you, but your Doodle is still being rewarded with your attention, perpetuating the behavior.

In this chapter, I delve a little deeper into these typical Doodle behaviors and show you how to teach your dog that there are better ways to get attention and rewards and maintain their stash of toys.

Four on the Floor: Stopping Jumping Up

Jumping on people, furniture, or countertops is the most common behavior problem with dogs. It's annoying, frustrating, and disruptive. Every Doodle I've ever met has a jumping-up problem. Even after they've learned it's inappropriate, it's as though they can't control it. You can prevent jumping up from becoming a problem by guiding your Doodle puppy from the start. If you already have a jumping bean, there are still ways to approach the issue to gradually extinguish the behavior. In this section, I lay it all out.

Understanding why dogs jump

One of the main reasons dogs begin jumping up is to greet newcomers or companions (that's you!) who have returned home. They first touch noses, then go sniff the newcomer's rear end to find out who it is and what their intentions may be. It's the canine way.

Before you correct your dog for jumping, you need to discover why they're doing it. Most likely, they're getting some reward for jumping up. Maybe they get touched or they're spoken to. Some dogs merely like to perch higher than the floor — the old "I'm the king of the castle, and you're the dirty rascal" game. Maybe jumping is such a fun way to get you to play with them that they'll do it every time they want attention.

The next time your dog jumps on you, note your reaction. Did you push at them? Yell at them? Pet them? Did you absentmindedly touch their paws or legs? Your reaction to their behavior will tell you the reason they do it.

With Doodles, behavior isn't always fueled by your reaction, but the action itself is self-rewarding. They love to jump up on people and other dogs for the sheer joy of it. This is especially common when they're super excited and can't remember to sit for attention instead.

Keeping your Doodle's feet on the ground

You can do several things to cure the habit of jumping, no matter why your dog is doing it:

>> **Greet your dog lower to the ground — and ask your guests to do so as well.** Instead of making your dog reach upward to say, "Hi," crouch down low to allow an appropriate nose touch. This is far better than being jumped on or goosed in your behind. If you don't want your face washed in doggie saliva, keep your head up and offer your hands in greeting, holding them low and allowing your dog to sniff or lick them.

>> **Condition your dog to get a tummy rub upon your arrival, by having them sit and then lie down, so you can rub their tummy.** What better way to be greeted than having your Doodle throw themselves at your feet, panting in anticipation as they await a belly rub?

>> **Try ignoring your dog the next time they jump on you.** Don't touch them. Don't speak to them. Don't look at them. In fact, step away and hold your arms up so that they can't go to the next level of "I want attention now" and put their mouth on your hand.

TIP

>> **When you're in a situation where your dog is jumping, tell them to sit.**
This will redirect them from doing the bad thing to doing something good — it gives them a way they can earn positive attention. *Remember:* Don't ask your dog to sit too soon after the jumping up, or you'll be creating a fun game called "jump and sit." Doodles learn patterns very easily, and if they think they'll be rewarded for jumping and then sitting, they'll be persistent about it.

If you've told your dog to sit and they're too busy jumping to do so, make sure that you place them into position. When they're in position, praise them. Don't get too carried away with the praise, though — you did have to place them into a sit. You can get more excited when your dog sits without your help, especially if they come to you and sit for attention instead of jumping up for it.

REMEMBER

Try not to get frustrated. Your dog didn't learn to jump up overnight, and you won't cure them overnight. Remain calm, focused, and in control. Dogs know when you've reached your breaking point. You have to prove that you have *no* breaking point. Eventually, your dog will understand that you're in charge of doling out rewards and that they have to change their attention-seeking behavior.

Also, be consistent. If you make your dog sit for attention one time, but you're absentmindedly petting them while they have their feet on your lap another time, they won't learn to stop jumping up. If you really want to stop this behavior, you must always follow the law: No jumping up *ever.* No touching, speaking, or looking at jumping dogs — only sitting dogs get the reward.

Curing the insistent jumper

Doodles are insistent jumpers. You'll have to be incredibly persistent and apply appropriate guidance to extinguish the behavior. It won't happen overnight or even in a month. The only way of ultimately curing the problem is long-term consistency. If you have a Doodle puppy, you have the best chance of preventing the problem by appropriate guidance as they mature, but even if you have an adult Doodle, you can stop the behavior with time and patience.

Puppies

Most puppies are learning about their environment and how to respond to specific sights, sounds, and smells wherever they go. Doodle puppies are highly curious and learn a lot in each experience. One of their instinctual tendencies is to pile on top of each other when it's nap time. It's a natural behavior for puppies — piling helps them keep warm and feeling safe.

Doodles don't outgrow this tendency until well into adulthood. They will pile on top of other dogs who live in the household, too. Hopefully, your other dog (if you have one) is very patient and accepting of this behavior. Otherwise, your Doodle puppy will get a quick lesson from your other dog about what is, or isn't, allowed.

You may be so enthralled with your puppy that you enjoy holding them on your lap. This is a form of puppy piling, so your Doodle will not only enjoy it but come to expect it at bedtime, which can turn into a problem behavior. Your Doodle pup will constantly insist on jumping into your lap — when you're on the couch, at the dinner table, working at your desk, or sleeping in bed.

REMEMBER

It may be very tough, but you need to set ground rules right away. Dogs don't understand all the gray areas we see. For them, it's all or nothing. Either they can do it or not. If you don't want your Doodle pup to grow into a large adult dog who jumps on you with long nails, muddy paws, or a running start, set the rules early: No jumping onto your lap. Don't invite them up there at all until they have a good idea that it's not something they can initiate (they'll likely need to be at least 6 months of age with absolute consistency on the subject before you invite them up).

TIP

Here are some ground rules to prevent jumping up from becoming an annoying problem:

>> Always have your Doodle pup sit prior to giving them any attention.

>> Don't allow them on your lap when sitting on furniture — stick to the floor for that activity.

>> Don't allow them on your bed, couch, or other furniture, by their choice. You must *invite* them up.

>> Make sure that each time they sit (especially of their own accord) they're instantly rewarded with praise for doing so. If they have to wait too long to receive your acknowledgement, they'll try jumping up to get it. If that doesn't do the trick, they'll begin mouthing you, too.

Adult dogs

Extinguishing the jumping-up behavior in a Doodle over 6 months of age is much more difficult. They've been doing it for so long that it's part of their personality. You'll have to be very strong-willed to accomplish this task. Don't give in to those sweet eyes and that fluffy face.

There are several ways you'll need to approach this challenge:

>> **Obedience-train your Doodle.** They need to understand what you're telling them.

>> **Never give any attention or acknowledgement of your dog's presence unless they're sitting first.** This means don't speak to them, touch them, or look at them. If they try to jump on you, step away so they don't land their paws on you. Take away anything that rewards the behavior.

>> **Don't just punish; redirect.** You always need to show your dog what they should be doing instead of what they shouldn't. When they stop jumping on you, cue them to sit.

Most dogs respond well to a sound correction — something that makes an aversive sound. Dogs have far more sensitive hearing than humans do, so certain pitches, volumes, or frequencies can distract them enough to stop a behavior that coincides with the sound.

You can use several objects to create aversive sounds when your dog jumps on you:

>> **Pennies in a can:** Get a small metal can, such as one used for loose tea, paint, or a small coffee can. Place 15 pennies inside the can and be sure to seal the lid securely. When your dog jumps up, shake the can hard just once or twice. If this aversive sound is going to work, it will work fairly quickly. Your dog will stop jumping and either move away from you or sit. If they sit, praise them. If they move away, wait until they return and sit or remain with all four paws on the floor, and then praise them.

>> **Can of air:** Most dogs dislike the sound of compressed air. Keep one handy in any area where your dog is likely to jump up on you or others. If you can predict when they'll be airborne, have the can in your hand already. The closer the aversive sound is to the inappropriate behavior, the sooner your dog will connect the dots.

>> **A bicycle horn:** A honk on a bicycle horn will definitely get your dog's attention. They'll likely step back and have a long look at you as though you've just issued the weirdest noise they've ever heard. They may be looking at you funny, but they stopped jumping, right?

Some people may suggest using a spritz or stream of water to stop your Doodle from jumping up, but this doesn't work. First, Doodles love water! Plus, it makes a mess if you try to do it indoors. I suggest the aversive noises instead.

I'm Not Your Supper: Stopping Mouthing

Mouthing is a lighter form of nipping, common with dogs who are playing with each other. However, dog mouthing can become more serious — a means of being demanding or otherwise assertive. Nipping is started through play. If allowed to continue, however, it can turn into something worse.

Any infractions with the mouth must be stopped. At no time should a dog be allowed to put their mouth on you except to lick, which is a sort of "group hug" gesture. Allowing even light mouthing is setting yourself up for some serious issues down the road.

Understanding why dogs nip and mouth

Dogs use their mouths as you use your hands. They grab, hold, pull, and carry. Chewing is a means of alleviating stress or boredom. Using their mouths to eat is always rewarding. But what about when your Doodle jumps on you and puts their mouth on your arm? Or what if you're playing with a toy and they put their mouth on the hand holding the toy?

TIP

Doodles use their mouths a lot to communicate their needs, especially if their owners have no idea what they're saying when they stand and stare at them. If your Doodle puts their mouth on you, they're usually at a point of desperation to let you know they need to go out.

Mouthing and nipping is also a very common puppy game. Dogs use their mouths to explore and to test a playmate for pack position. If they're still with their mom and littermates, they quickly learn that their mom won't put up with it. She'll grab their little faces and growl. Littermates will either respond by yipping or run away from that awful, hurtful sibling. Either way, there's a response. How you respond will have a lot to do with whether your Doodle will continue the behavior.

Preventing the problem

Prevention is the most important way of teaching your Doodle to not put their mouth on you. Here are a few ways to keep your dog's mouth occupied:

>> Have lots of toys around for them to put their mouth on.

>> Never play with your Doodle's mouth.

>> If you're playing with your Doodle with a toy, the moment they touch you with their mouth, the game is over for a little while.

>> Never allow anyone to dangle their hands near your Doodle's face.

>> Make sure your Doodle gets plenty of exercise so they're not nipping at you trying to instigate play.

>> If you're not observant enough to recognize when your Doodle needs to go out, they'll jump up on you or take your arm in their mouth to make you aware of their needs.

Curing the problem

Dogs love attention — it can be as rewarding as toys and treats. So, whenever your dog puts their mouth on you, turn away from them and don't offer any attention, not even eye contact. If they continue trying to get your attention, move a short distance away from them. When they stop, ask them to perform something, such as a sit. If they do so, give them some attention again. Be ready to stop the second they put their mouth on you again, though.

TIP

This process can take some time, but it will avoid escalating the issue into aggression or panic. Be persistent, consistent, and patient. That way, you'll have the best chance of success.

WARNING

Never, *ever* hit your dog!. Mother dogs never hit their pups. Even fighting dogs don't hit each other. Violence against your dog may cause them to also become violent, escalating the situation instead of solving it.

REMEMBER

As with all severe behavior problems, talk to a professional trainer or behaviorist. Nipping and mouthing are not easy to contend with, and implementing the wrong correction can have severe consequences.

Chew on This, Not That

Dogs love to chew — it's their favorite pastime. You may read books; watch TV; play sports, video games, and board games; or spend time on hobbies. Dogs don't have these things. They chew and dig and chew and run and chew. They chew their toys. They chew on sticks. They chew the sofa. Yikes! That's something you don't want them to chew. Why would your dog chew a sofa when they have a bone nearby? In this section, I tell you why — and help you get your dog to stop chewing things they shouldn't be chewing.

Understanding why dogs chew

Dogs chew for a variety of reasons. The main reason has to do with their age. All puppies chew. They're testing their environment for tasty morsels and for ways to alleviate the pain in their gums. If your dog is younger than 9 months of age, they're teething. Here's how normal teething develops:

>> **Between the ages of 3 months and 5 months,** the baby teeth are falling out. You'll see your dog's front teeth being replaced with the larger, adult incisors. Your pup will be pulling at their toys as they explore objects for palatability. Watch out for those electrical cords — they look mighty tasty!

TIP

A good way to protect both electronics and Doodle pups is to put the cords through metal conduit piping.

>> **Between the ages of 5 and 7 months of age,** your pup's back teeth are falling out and being replaced with new ones. When the new molars grow in, it's very uncomfortable for your dog. They won't be chewing to learn about their environment — they'll be chewing to alleviate the discomfort in their gums. Anything hard is fair game, including wood of all sorts, such as molding, window frames, chairs, table legs, carpeting, shoes, plastic children's toys, books, and more.

TIP

Be sure to give your Doodle pup something to chew on that will alleviate their discomfort, such as a frozen washcloth, ice cubes, antlers, or shank bones.

>> **At 7 to 8 months of age,** the molars are all in, but still a little loose in the gums. Chewing has become more of a pastime than a need, but it's still enjoyable as a way of releasing discomfort, anxiety, or boredom.

That brings me to the other reasons for chewing:

>> **Anxiety:** A dog with anxiety can be extremely destructive. They don't just chew — they fling and swing the objects about, trample and pull, paw and scratch. Dogs chewing because of anxiety create a huge mess.

>> **Boredom:** A dog who chews because they're bored may not create as large a destructive path as a dog who chews because they're anxious, but the bored dog can still do some heavy-duty damage. Windowsills are typical targets for bored dogs, as are other types of wall molding, shoes left about, or other household items that have fallen to the floor. Toys become old, known things, whereas a dish towel, pillow, or sneaker is like a brand-new toy.

Most Doodles are not destructive chewers, as long as they receive appropriate guidance on the subject while still young puppies.

Solving the problem

You can either prevent chewing from becoming a problem or deal with curing a bad habit. Even if your Doodle arrived with a chewing problem, you can do things to prevent them from continuing their destructive path.

You'll need to be watchful, patient, and consistent. Guide your Doodle in the right direction much as you would guide a young child — after all, your dog really doesn't know that your couch pillows are off limits, or that the table legs aren't just big chew bones.

Prevention is worth a pound of pillows

The best thing to do when you aren't able to watch your dog is to contain them in an area where they can't get into trouble. Containing your dog when you can't watch them will prevent them from chewing the wrong things — they can't have access to them without your being present. (For more about containment and crate training, see Chapter 9.)

When you *are* able to watch your dog, redirect them from the things they can't chew to the things they *can* play with. Playing with them will make the items more attractive — dogs prefer interactive games to playing alone.

TIP

Because boredom is a main ingredient in developing problem chewing, you can do several things to prevent this from occurring:

>> **Train, train, train.** A trained dog knows the rules and will be less likely to chew the wrong items.

>> **Rotate the toys.** Dogs get bored with the same old toys. Had 'em, mouthed 'em, tired of 'em. If you offer your dog a different variety of toys each day, your dog will think, "Wow! Brand-new toys! This is neat!" It will occupy their time, reducing the chance of boredom.

>> **Get another dog.** The presence of another dog alleviates boredom.

>> **Make sure they're getting enough exercise.** A tired dog won't do anything destructive. Take your dog for a run, or long walk each morning before going to work and again when you get home from work. You may want to vary the routine — for example, go for a walk in the morning and play ball in the afternoon. Add some training time to this routine. Teach your dog some new tricks. Doodles thrive on stimulation, and new tricks are a perfect way to keep them engaged.

>> **Stimulate your dog's mind.** There are many ways to stimulate your dog's mind:

- **Interactive toys:** You can find all kinds of interactive toys in your local pet store or online — toys that can be pulled apart and put back together, toys that can be filled with food, toys that involve pet and human or several dogs at the same time. You can never give your Doodle too many toys. In fact, if you're not tripping over toys, you probably don't have enough. And don't forget to rotate them!

- **Social time:** Doggy daycare is a great alternative for dogs who spend a lot of time home alone. Instead of being left home day after day, bored, they're taken to a place where they can have fun socializing with other dogs and people. You come home from work tired, and they will, too. You can both relax. Doodles don't do well if left home for long hours every day. Although they may not become destructive chewers, they can become annoying, excessive barkers. Your neighbors will *not* be pleased.

  If you have a dog park in the area, take your Doodle there daily. Make it part of the routine, regardless of the weather. Few dogs care more about a rainy day than playing with other dogs. And there's a hardly a Doodle (unless of a smaller breed mix) that really cares about getting wet.

Offering your Doodle these bits of stimulation will prevent them from being annoying or destructive and create a far more positive relationship with you.

Knowing what to do when your dog is in mid-chew

What do you do when your dog has something in their mouth that they shouldn't have? Let's say they just grabbed one of your Italian leather loafers and ran off, initiating a game of chase. The last thing you want is to lose a $200 pair of shoes, so you run after them. Well, they think, this is great fun! (It won't take another repetition of this game for them to realize this.) Now they know how to get a game started. And guess what? This won't be the last time they pick up your loafers — unless you offer them a positive alternative.

The "chase me" game is not a new invention created by your Doodle just because they enjoy the taste of your shoes, laundry, or pillows. It's a common game that dogs play with each other. One dog grabs a toy, tantalizes the other dog with it by pacing in front and dangling it under the other dog's nose, and then when they see the other dog make a grab for it, they run, with the other dog racing after them.

You have to offer something better without also rewarding them for the behavior. Dogs often pick up objects they're not supposed to have, such as shoes or other household items, as well as trash that may be littering the paths you walk with them. You need a way of teaching your Doodle to drop the item on command, without having to run them down and pry the object from their mouth, which will teach them to avoid you instead of come to you and drop the object.

Exchanging resources

The more your Doodle believes they'll lose their prized possession and never get it back, the more they'll fight to keep it. To prevent them from this belief, never attempt to merely pull something from their mouth. You may get your fingers bit in the process as they try to get a better hold on it.

There's a way you can teach your Doodle to drop on cue, with their understanding that doing so will earn rewards that are of higher value than the object they dropped.

What happens if you can't find something that your dog would rather have than that cigarette butt they picked up from the street or the steak they filched from the counter? You have to teach them the meaning of *drop it.* This command will be important when your dog steals your dinner, and it will protect your Doodle from being poisoned. You can also use it to teach your dog to retrieve a toy and return it to your hand instead of chasing them down to do another throw.

TIP

Here's how you teach drop it:

1. **Put a leash on your dog so you can back up your commands without having to chase them around.**

   Allow the leash to drag on the ground until needed.

2. **Create the situation by either throwing a favorite toy a short distance or merely dropping it.**

3. **When your Doodle picks up the toy, call them to come.**

   Be sure to be enticing with a high-pitched tone and lots of praise whenever they take even the slightest step in your direction. If they don't come, bring them to you via the leash.

   Praise them as they come closer so they always believe coming to you is a great idea.

4. **As they comes near, show them a high-value treat in one hand and hold the palm of your other hand upward, as you say, "Drop."**

   If the reward you're offering is of higher value than the toy, you can be sure they'll drop whatever's in their mouth and go for the gold.

5. **The moment your Doodle drops the toy, click and give the treat.**

6. **Repeat this exercise at least three more times before moving on to something else.**

   Be sure to practice this daily, so your Doodle readily drops whatever they're carrying.

TIP

If you're having your dog drop one of their toys, you can offer it to them again so that they learn they aren't prohibited from playing with the toy — they just have to give it to you upon request.

WARNING

Never put your face near your dog when you work on the drop-it cue. Not only are you giving them the wrong signals (putting your face so close is a direct, assertive challenge), but you're risking your nose if your Doodle becomes frightened or is a resource guarder.

Oh, the Noise! Getting Your Doodle to Stop Barking

Excessive whining and barking are easy to identify. Your neighbors know it when they hear it: an annoying outburst while you're away from home. If you're living in an apartment, a townhouse, or a densely populated neighborhood with a noisy dog, you'll likely hear from your neighbors that your best friend is upset about being home alone. Your Doodle may also bark and whine when you're home but not right next to them — for example, when you've left them outside in the yard or in another room without you.

Most Doodles do not fare well left home alone for long periods of time every day. They easily develop separation anxiety, and the way they display their feelings of loneliness is to bark — a lot.

Doodles bark when playing, when greeting, and when lonely. You'll need to teach your dog to stop barking on cue, as well as ensure they don't get lonely.

WARNING

When you hear your dog whining or barking, your first reaction is probably to run to the poor dog because you can't stand that they're upset. Don't do it! You'll be reinforcing this behavior because you gave them what they had been whining for — your presence. The next time you go somewhere, they'll turn it up another notch or two. Doodles learn very quickly!

There are a few steps you can take to prevent or, if need be, cure excessive barking. These include keeping your Doodle occupied during the day when you're gone, teaching your Doodle to feel confident when alone, and teaching them to stop barking on cue.

Keeping your Doodle occupied while you're gone

You want to do everything you can to ensure you raise a well-adjusted, well-trained companion. This includes socialization. If you have to work all day (and who doesn't, especially if you're supporting a Doodle?), think about ways to keep your young dog busy, much as you would a human child. Until a certain age, kids shouldn't be home alone, and while at school, they're learning new concepts, enabling them to understand their environments. The same applies to your Doodle.

There are three main ways to keep your Doodle occupied when you're away:

>> **Sending your dog to doggy daycare:** Your dog learns lots of social skills and comes home tired, ready to lie at your feet instead of jumping over your couch as you sit in it.

>> **Hiring a dog walker:** Someone comes once or twice a day to exercise your dog.

>> **Taking your dog to work with you:** This is a rare option, but if you're self-employed or you have a dog-friendly office, you've hit the jackpot!

You can also figure out ways to allow your Doodle access to electronic toys or communication devices while you're gone. There are automatic ball ejectors, food-filled toys, food puzzles, and snuffle mats to keep them occupied, at least for a few minutes.

You can purchase an electronic communications device, which you mount on the wall, within your Doodle's sightline. Here are some examples:

>> **PetChatz HDX:** https://petchatz.com

>> **Furbo Dog Camera:** https://shopus.furbo.com

You can teach your dog to press a call button. They'll see your face and you can speak to them and even give them verbal cues. When they perform, you can trigger a signal to dispense treats.

Helping your Doodle to be confident on their own

You need to teach your Doodle that you'll always come back, and when you do (if they've been a good, quiet dog), they'll be rewarded.

Basic canine instinct is to want to follow their pack members everywhere. The reason dogs are pack animals is to feel more secure, and being with you makes them feel exactly that. Being pushed out of the pack makes dogs feel insecure, which is why they howl or bark. You need to teach your Doodle that being left alone is not a punishment, but just another new trick to learn in order to earn rewards.

Begin with crate training (see Chapter 9). When your Doodle is comfortable in a crate, you should be able to leave them in the crate for a few hours at a time. If your Doodle has difficulty accepting your absence, begin with short amounts of time. Here's a step-by-step plan:

1. **Put your Doodle in the crate and leave the room.**

2. **See how long it takes for them to begin barking.**

   Was it 5 minutes? An hour? This information tells you just how lonely they get and how quickly. In essence, will your neighbors be hearing them the moment you leave the house or a bit later? When you have that lag time established, you'll have a base to work from.

   For the sake of this description, let's say your Doodle is great for a half-hour and then begins barking due to anxiety or loneliness. Begin your training at this point.

3. **Leave for half an hour.**

   Try to return before your Doodle starts to bark.

4. **When you return, click and reward; let them out to play or engage in interactive games; and then do the exercise again.**

5. **After three repetitions, add about 5 minutes to the time between leaving your Doodle alone and returning.**

   If they start barking too soon, come home (or return to the room they're crated in), but don't let them out until they stop barking. This is important because you don't want to reward them for getting upset. They must be rewarded for remaining calm, or at the very least not barking.

6. **With each successful increment of time, add another 5 minutes.**

   This process may take days or months, but it will be successful because you're offering your Doodle positive associations in order to extinguish an annoying behavior.

WARNING

Some people don't have the patience or time to approach the issue using positive reinforcement methods. They choose, instead, to use a bark collar (every time the dog barks, they're zapped). Although bark collars can be effective at stopping the barking, they create a worse issue of your dog being frightened when you leave. Scared dogs tend to turn to destructive behavior or can become aggressive when they believe they're about to be put into the situation that "bit" them again. Take your time and do it right. Your Doodle will thank you for it and be a quiet, well–adjusted dog.

Stopping barking on cue

You can teach your Doodle the quiet cue to stop their barking, but first you'll need to teach them to bark on command. They're already barking for some reason or another, so you merely need to capture the barking and add a cue for it. For example, let's say they bark when they hear the doorbell ring. As that happens, say, "Speak," hold your right finger to your right ear, and look at her. At first, they'll be bewildered about what's going on. They'll glance at you and bark again; click and reward. When they stop to get their treat, click again because they stopped barking.

When your Doodle readily speaks on cue, they'll be expecting to get their rewards when they do so. Instead, of rewarding the barking, cue them to stop. You can use the verbal cue "Quiet" (or something else, as long you're consistent), and use a simple body gesture, such as clapping your hands together. When they stop and look at you a little hard, click and reward.

Your Doodle will soon understand the meaning of speak and quiet. You'll then prolong the quiet time in small increments, such as a minute at a time. By this time, your Doodle will have forgotten what they were barking at and be totally focused on working for you. Redirection at its best!

All Mine: Teaching Your Doodle to Share

Some dogs don't like sharing their toys with other dogs. Still others may decide they don't want to share them with family members either. The term for this behavior is *resource guarding.* For some reason, your Doodle believes their favorite toy will be taken away and they'll never get it back. Resource guarding can also occur around a special person in the family or a favorite couch, bed, or eating space.

There are many reasons why dogs develop this behavior, but the main one is lack of respect for you and others. It can also mean there's a lack of trust.

Dogs who were raised in chaotic households, spent time as a stray, or were neglected in some manner often become resource guarders. They had to fight for everything they needed, had no idea when they'd be fed, or became frightened of their environment. These reasons are rare occurrences for Doodles, because they aren't obtained cheaply and normally are so highly desired and valued that they're spoiled, given everything without having to do anything to earn it. This is another reason they may become resource guarders.

You need to approach your Doodle's needs so they'll continue to respect you while also learning appropriate behavior to earn all rewards. This means doing something, on cue, prior to meals, being given attention, being given toys, playing games, getting tummy rubs, getting lap time, or lounging on the couch. You need to be the source of *all* resources, and your Doodle needs to earn every one of them.

An important behavior skill for a resource-guarding dog (and one to teach prior to the development of resource-guarding behavior) is the drop-it cue (see "Exchanging resources," earlier in this chapter). Your Doodle needs to learn to drop any object in their mouth, on cue. If you trained them correctly on this behavior, they'll do so gladly because they know there's a better reward in it for them when they do so. This pattern will ensure you have a dog eager to do as you request.

WARNING

You may be tempted to go the easy route and merely remove the object they're guarding, but this doesn't cure the problem. Your Doodle may begin resource guarding something else.

If the resource is furniture, you can start by not allowing them on it anymore. If the resource is a specific person, other family members need to begin taking more responsibilities for the dog and doing daily training sessions with them.

Surf's Up! Stopping Counter-Surfing

Counter-surfing is a self-rewarding behavior, though you have something to do with it. All you have to do is leave food on the counter, and your Doodle is sure to sniff it out and steal it.

The first step in stopping this behavior is to never leave food out. This may not be the end of it, though, because your Doodle already has been rewarded for counter-surfing and may take whatever is in reach, even if it isn't edible.

There are several ways to stop this problem.

>> Place some saucepans on the edge of the counter so that, when they're disturbed, they'll fall to the floor and make a loud noise.

>> Keep your kitchen closed off at all times. This will prevent the problem, but it won't cure it.

>> Remain vigilant and watch your dog as they go into the kitchen. The moment they begin to sniff at the counter, redirect them with a come or another command cue.

>> On the counter, place a motion detector device that releases compressed air when triggered. These devices are often used to keep cats off of counters, and they work well with dogs, too.

Although there are many ways to cure inappropriate behavior, it's far more important to prevent it from happening in the first place. Train your Doodle and give them the guidance they need to mature into a well-behaved member of your family. Be consistent in every situation and communicate clearly. All dogs really want is to understand their environment.

4

Doodles with a Purpose

Discover the many jobs available for your Doodle.

Find fun activities you can do with your Doodle.

Chapter **13**

Doodles as Assistance Dogs

L abradodles were initially created to be assistance dogs for people who had allergies to dog dander and couldn't work with Labrador Retrievers or Golden Retrievers, the dogs typically trained for this task. Although the quest had dubious results (only three dogs from more than five litters were actually of the correct temperament to be trained as service dogs), the idea of a medium or large fluffy dog who didn't cause their owners to sneeze quickly caught on.

Labradoodles were originally bred for a purpose, but not all Doodles are able to perform specific jobs. The only thing you can count on with your Doodle is that if you train and socialize them, they'll turn into a great family companion.

If you've gotten your Doodle to be of service, you'll need to give them the appropriate start from the first day they arrive home. It can take upwards of two years to train a dog to be well behaved enough to be a certified assistance dog, and very few make the cut, even after all those years of preparation.

The Better to Hear You With: Hearing Dogs

All dogs have exceptional hearing. They can detect a rabbit in a thicket or the sound of a loved one's vehicle approaching the house. They learn to discern the most minor differences in decibel, frequency, and volume. Studies have proved that canine hearing is more than twice that of a human with normal hearing capacity, making them far more sensitive to noise than we are.

Doodles are especially well equipped to detect minute sounds, as well as movements in the distance. This makes them great at alerting their owners of someone at the door, a phone ringing, a timer buzzing, or a fire alarm. When it comes to being of assistance to someone who's deaf, the dog's job isn't just to bark at the noise, but to notify the person in need of assistance. This requires extensive training.

A hearing-assistance dog doesn't have to be a certain size. The only qualifications are good hearing and good training. Your Pomapoo or Yorkidoodle can do as good a job as a Goldendoodle, though they'll have to work a bit harder to get your attention.

The type of Doodle you choose for this job will depend more on your living environment than the Doodle mix. Some Doodles that are ultra-sensitive and tend to bark excessively anyway, so it may be challenging to redirect them to the appropriate reasons for barking. If you live in a condominium, apartment, or townhouse, you don't want your Doodle alerting you to everybody they see.

It's common to get a dog because you like their appearance without considering the reason you're really getting them. Not all Doodles can do all jobs. You'll have to consider this when choosing your Doodle's future. Service dogs require being raised in a specific manner so that they're prepared to perform the jobs chosen for them.

There are things you can do to help your Doodle do at least a few of the tasks that hearing assistance dogs can do. As with most desired behaviors, you'll need to capture the correct response to a specific situation by using your click and reward system. Here's an example:

1. **The doorbell rings.**
2. **Your dog turns to look at you.**
3. **You praise.**
4. **You cue your dog to come and sit, and then click and reward.**

If your dog merely barks, this doesn't help someone who can't hear. Your Doodle must let you know by coming to you and nudging you in some way. When they understand to come to you when they hear the doorbell, they can easily be taught to touch you via behavior-shaping exercises. (With each move closer to you, you click and reward.)

WARNING

Be forewarned on this one, however: Your dog will repeat the behavior every time the doorbell rings. They may even begin to do so when they hear someone approaching the door. This can get very annoying in an apartment building.

It will take time to proof your Doodle on this so they only notify you when someone actually rings the bell.

The behavior chain gets longer because coming and sitting near you may not grab your attention unless you're looking at your dog. Instead, your Doodle will need to actually touch you in some specific manner. Although having a Cavadoodle jump into your lap to notify you that someone's at the door is great, the last thing you need is for your 70-pound Labradoodle to jump on you. The better response would be for them to nudge you with their nose against your leg or put a paw on your knee. These are all behaviors taught through extensive assistance dog training. But if you work with a really experienced dog trainer, it's likely much of this can be accomplished in a few months. The key to this type of reliability (as with any behavior) is consistency and repetition.

TIP

The best way of teaching any complicated behavior is to break it down into small parts. Teach your Doodle each small part; then begin to chain the parts together.

Assistance Doodles

An *assistance dog* helps those who are physically challenged. For example, they may help people who are unable to easily walk, grab items from a shelf, or turn on a light. They may help people in need of notification of an oncoming seizure or diabetic shock. Or they may serve as a steadfast companion for an autistic child.

The assistance dog must have the size to reach counters and shelves, the stamina to work all day, and the desire to partner with one specific person. They must also be able to disregard all others who try to disrupt them as they work. This requires intelligence, energy, versatility, and ingenuity — all the traits of many types of Doodles.

If you're considering a Doodle specifically for the job of assistance dog, look for a Bernedoodle, Goldendoodle, Labradoodle, or Whoodle. These dogs are the right size to really help with reaching items on shelves, reaching light switches, being able to carry heavy objects, being able to support a person who needs help getting up or staying up, and much more. I suggest these Doodles because the breeds they're descended from — Bernese Mountain Dogs, Golden Retrievers, Labrador Retrievers, and Wheaten Terriers — have been in these jobs for decades. In fact, Wheaten Terriers have been used on farms for myriad jobs for hundreds of years. Mix these breeds with the intelligence and energy levels of a Poodle, and you have a dog who can work all day.

Although there are many other Doodles who are the right size, they don't have the right mentality to be an assistance dog. Even the Doodles I mention here are not all able to do the job — just a select few individuals are up to the task. And you don't generally find out which individuals until after years of training preparation.

REMEMBER

Rarely does a dog you happen to pick out of a litter and bring home turn out to have the right temperament, intelligence, and drive to be your perfect assistance dog. There's a reason that assistance dog organizations stay in business — they're professionals who breed, raise, train, and prepare the dogs for their future work as assistance dogs. Often, there's a waiting list for specific types of work that the dogs are trained to do. For example, an autistic child who needs a guardian dog (one who won't allow the child to run out into traffic) may be on the waiting list for a year or more as the dog is raised, trained, and then paired with the child.

TIP

If you really want to have a Doodle as an assistance dog, do research into assistance dog organizations and ask if they produce any Doodles for the job.

Some professional trainers who don't work for these organizations can bring your dog *close* to the training level of a certified assistance dog. You'll just need to clarify for yourself (and the trainer) exactly what tasks you need from the dog. Through positive association, dogs can learn nearly anything — especially Doodles.

Emotional Support Dogs

Emotional support is a job in which most Doodles can shine. The size and type of the Doodle rarely matters. It's all about the dog's breeding and environment, as well as how well they're trained.

WARNING

Do not begin treating your Doodle puppy as an emotional support dog until they've been fully trained to be confident and obedient. Without this, your Doodle will need their own emotional support by the time they reach maturity. Doodles are very sensitive to their world and empathetic to their families, and they quickly learn how to achieve diva status.

When you get a Doodle to be your emotional support dog, be sure to apply the temperament tests (see Chapter 4) before choosing a puppy. You must begin with a confident, inquisitive puppy who is relaxed and accepts new situations easily. Choose an outgoing puppy, not the one sitting in a corner watching the world go by.

Begin training on day 1. Set the rules and stick by them. Dogs like knowing what's expected of them, as well as what to expect from you. It relaxes them. Structure is very important to dogs.

Don't begin using your Doodle puppy as a cry pillow or overly coddle, hug, or desperately clutch them in any way. If you do, they'll turn into an emotional wreck. They feel (and smell) your emotions. Their development period is not the time to share your emotions with your dog. They're not yet ready to help you if they don't understand what's going on in their own world.

When your Doodle matures, is fully trained, and is well adjusted to life in your home, begin training them for the job of an emotional support dog. The behaviors to teach include the following:

>> **Lean in:** Come to your side and lean into you. This gesture can be comforting to someone with an anxiety disorder.

>> **Lie upon:** If the person is lying down and about to have an anxiety attack, cue the dog to lay their head upon the person's chest.

>> **Long down-stays at your feet:** This will allow you to bring your dog to many places, such as outdoor cafes, some stores (that allow emotional support dogs), schools, or work. Only a mature Doodle will be able to do this — they can be far too full of energy when they're young.

>> **Automatic default behaviors (see Chapter 10 and 11):** The most basic default behavior is an automatic sit-stay. This can come into use when tethering an autistic child to the dog to prevent the child from racing out of the house, into the yard, or into the street.

>> **Laying their head in your lap:** Because Doodles are sensitive to your emotions, begin teaching your dog to rest their head in your lap when you're feeling sad. Stroking a dog helps alleviate feelings of helplessness.

These are just a few of the many behaviors you can teach an emotional support dog. Performing these behaviors on cue is what the job is all about.

Be sure to consult with a professional positive reinforcement dog trainer to help you achieve these goals. And remember, it takes time to train a dog to understand their job. Be patient, consistent, and repetitive, and never skimp on the rewards.

» Taking your Doodle out hunting

» Having fun with your Doodle in everyday life

Chapter **14**

Doodle Sports

D oodles are highly talented and love to perform! If you want to have fun with your Doodle by continuously striving to achieve higher and higher goals, you may want to work toward performance titles. There are lots of options, and Doodles excel at all of them! The best part of aiming high is all the time you get to spend traveling and competing with your dog. Your relationship is about more than just companionship — it's teamwork. In this chapter, I show you some of what's available.

You don't have to compete to have fun with your Doodle. All sorts of outdoor activities are available for the two of you. From hunting or hiking to camping or horseback riding, your Doodle will be up for anything.

Participating in Formal Competitions

There's more to partnering with a Doodle than hugs and kisses. Doodles are made to perform. You can engage in any number of performance activities with your Doodle. From obedience trials and AKC Rally to agility and dock diving, each type of event offers levels of achievement from beginner to master.

REMEMBER

It's not just about the performance titles — it's about the partnership and teamwork it takes to achieve them. In the world of dog performance, it's all about the journey. Through training and preparing to exhibit, you form a close bond with your Doodle.

Looking at the different kinds of competitions

Not long ago, competing in sanctioned performance events was limited to purebred dogs. As more pet parents began to proudly share their lives with mixed-breed dogs, including Doodles, and worked hard to achieve goals similar to those of the purebred dogs, several kennel clubs began to open their shows. The biggest club was the United Kennel Club (UKC; https://www.ukcdogs.com), followed by the forming of the Mixed Breed Dog Clubs of America (https://mbdca.tripod.com), which offers many performance show opportunities for mixed-breed dogs.

In 2009, the American Kennel Club (AKC) created a new category, All American Dog, which can be registered and shown in AKC-sponsored performance exhibitions. This means that your Doodle can attain any performance title achievable by a purebred dog, including obedience, AKC Rally, agility, dock diving, lure coursing, barn hunting, tracking, hunt trials, and more. The only thing holding your dog back is the amount of time you want to put into it. Most Doodles (of any breed combination) have the ability to perform in many of these events.

The size of your Doodle doesn't matter, though the non-Poodle half will help you decide which event will be a natural match. For example, a Jackadoodle may prefer barn hunts, a Labradoodle would love to be a field dog or dock diver, and an Aussiedoodle would find their true calling herding.

TIP

Here are some sources that list locations, dates, and other information for dog shows and matches. There's hardly an area *without* something going on throughout the year:

>> **American Kennel Club:** www.akc.org/sports/events

>> **America's Pet Registry:** www.aprpets.org/dog-shows

>> **Festivals-and-Shows.com:** www.festivals-and-shows.com/dog-shows.html

>> **InfoDog:** www.infodog.com

>> **Match Show Bulletin:** https://matchshowbulletin.com/

>> **Rau Dog Shows:** www.raudogshows.com

Obedience

You and your Doodle can compete in obedience matches and/or trials at dog shows. The difference between a *match* and a *trial* is that the match is a practice run — a place where you can test your and your dog's skills prior to entering a trial and working toward an obedience title. In a match, you can repeat an exercise or guide your dog into performing correctly, and the judge will give you advice on how to get your dog to achieve a better performance. In a trial, you can't do these things. You and your dog will be judged — period.

TIP

I recommend achieving good scores in a match before trying to perform at a trial. That way you can iron out the kinks and keep the entire experience positive for you and your dog. You don't need to stress over getting something wrong at a match.

There are three main levels in the obedience ring. Each level has its own series of behaviors for your dog to perform. Here's a list of the classes, from easiest to hardest:

» **Novice:** In the Novice class, you and your dog will be asked to complete the following behaviors:

- Heeling on and off-leash

- A figure-8, on leash, around two people standing 8 feet apart

- A stand and stay with the judge touching your dog as you remain 6 feet in front of the dog, with the dog off-leash

- A stay from 30 feet away

- A recall from 30 feet away

- A finish after the recall

- A one-minute sit-stay side-by-side with up to 12 other dogs and handlers 30 feet away, facing their dogs

- A three-minute down-stay side-by-side with up to 12 other dogs and handlers 30 feet away, facing their dogs

» **Open:** In the Open class, you and your dog will be asked to complete the following behaviors:

- An off-leash heeling pattern

- An off-leash figure-8 around two people standing 8 feet apart

- Drop on recall

- Retrieve on the flat

- Retrieve over a high jump (one and a half times the height of your dog at the shoulders)

- Send over a broad jump (twice the height of your dog at the shoulders)

- A three-minute sit-stay side-by-side with other dogs and the handler (that's you!) out of sight

- A five-minute down-stay side-by-side with other dogs and the handler out of sight

» **Utility:** In the Utility class, you and your Doodle will be asked to complete the following behaviors:

- An off-leash heeling pattern using only visual cues, no voice at all

- A stop and stand, using visual cues and moving over 20 feet away, faced away from dog

- Calling to heel position while standing still

- A *directed retrieve* (retrieving a specific item — usually white gloves — out of three identical items)

- *Scent discrimination* (retrieving both a leather article and a metal article, bearing your scent, from other identical articles)

- A *directed go out* (in which the dog leaves your side, runs to the opposite end of the ring, turns and sits until you direct the next exercise)

- A *directed jump* (in which, the dog remains across the ring, you direct them to one of two jumps — a bar jump or a high jump — repeat the go out again, and direct the dog to the other jump, at the judge's prompt)

There are non-regular classes that are both fun and a stepping-stone between different levels, too:

» **Sub-Novice:** This is a starter class in which you can keep a leash on your dog so if the dog becomes distracted while performing, they won't be able to run off. The exercises are similar to those in the regular Novice classes.

» **Beginner Novice:** This is another starter class that combines AKC Rally stations with Novice Obedience action. Because you can keep your dog leashed during the judging, it helps prepare you, and your dog, for the higher challenges of Novice Obedience and AKC Rally Novice classes.

» **Graduate Novice:** This is a tweener class between Novice and Open. It has exercises from both classes, preparing you for the challenges you'll see in Open, while still allowing you to work on perfecting some of the exercises done in the Novice class.

» **Graduate Open:** This is another tweener class, between Open and Utility levels. It also has exercises from both classes, preparing you for challenges you'll experience in Utility. These include the signal exercises, scent discrimination, a go out, a directed retrieve, directed jumping, and a moving stand for examination.

I've had lots of success with these non-regular classes — they gave me and my dog the confidence to continue to the next level. And the whole point about competing is enjoying the time with your Doodle!

TECHNICAL STUFF

There are three main obedience titles to strive for. To earn these titles you must qualify with a score of 170 out of a possible 200 at three different shows with three different judges. The titles are:

>> Novice class–Companion Dog (CD)

>> Open class–Companion Dog Excellent (CDX)

>> Utility Dog (UD)

You can also work toward championships (Obedience Trail Champion [OTCH]), high in trials, and other awards, though you can count on it taking *years* to reach these goals. Of course, that's years of *fun* (and hard work) for you and your dog!

AKC Rally

AKC Rally, formerly known as Rally-O (short for Rally Obedience), was derived from obedience trials, but it offers a more enjoyable means of competing with your dog because you're allowed to use praise as a means of reinforcement while you guide your dog through the stations throughout the course. It's gaining in popularity by leaps and bounds!

TECHNICAL STUFF

The original term for this activity was *doodling.* Is there anything more perfect for Doodles?

AKC Rally is a timed event. It includes 12 to 20 stations where you and your dog must perform different skills. There are three levels to achieve in AKC Rally:

>> **Novice:** This level is on-leash with exercises that demonstrate the dog's understanding of basic commands: sit, stay, down, come, and heel.

>> **Advanced:** This level is made up of a set of exercises where the dog performs off-leash, and it includes at least one jump.

>> **Excellent:** This level is a difficult off-leash course that includes at least one jump and demonstrates more precise skill coordination than in the Advanced level. It can also require your dog to perform very challenging obedience skills.

The course is different at each show, with the layout posted at the ringside and handed out so you can learn the progression of the exercises. Often, you can also walk the courses prior to the start of class, because knowing where and when to turn makes a big difference in your overall performance.

Signs are posted for each station, giving instructions that you and your dog must execute within 2 to 4 feet of the sign. After the judge tells you and your dog to go forward, you complete the course on your own without additional commands from the judge. Although you can use voice guidance and your hands to give signals to your Doodle, you can't use food or toys in the ring, and you can't place your hands on your dog or physically touch them.

This sport is great for Doodles who are bored by the stop-and-go routines in the obedience ring. Many dog clubs now offer AKC Rally at their obedience trials, giving you more opportunities to compete.

TIP

You can find a complete description of AKC Rally at www.akc.org/sports/rally. You can find the rules at http://images.akc.org/pdf/AKC1193_ROR001_1217_WEB.pdf. You can find station signs for all three levels at http://cdn.akc.org/Rally/2017_AKC_Rally_Signs_Set_05-16-17_web.pdf.

Agility

Agility is one of the more popular canine events in the United States and around the world. Dogs love performing, and people love to watch them! Any dog of any size or breed can compete, and some clubs allow mixed-breed dogs (including Doodles) to compete.

Agility was modeled on equestrian stadium jumping, with a variety of obstacles that have both spectator appeal and the intention of displaying the dog's agile nature. In this sport, the dog must negotiate a number of obstacles, off leash, within an allotted time frame.

The courses consist of jumps, tunnels, a table, weave poles, an A-frame, a seesaw, a *dog walk* (an elevated, narrow walkway), and more — each challenging the dog in different ways. You must be adept at directing your Doodle from obstacle to obstacle without getting in their way.

Agility is a timed speed event, but the dog must also perform with precision. They have to touch the contact obstacle (A-frame, seesaw, or dog walk) at specific points both getting on and off, not knock down the poles while jumping or weaving, and execute the obstacles in the right order.

You can find out more about agility competitions from the following organizations:

>> **Agility Association of Canada (AAC):** www.aac.ca

>> **American Kennel Club (AKC):** www.akc.org/sports/agility

- » **Australian Shepherd Club of America (ASCA):** www.asca.org/agility
- » **Canine Performance Events (CPE):** www.k9cpe.com/agilityevents.htm
- » **North American Dog Agility Council (NADAC):** www.nadac.com
- » **United States Dog Agility Association (USDAA):** www.usdaa.com
- » **United Kennel Club (UKC):** www.ukcdogs.com/agility

Most Doodles are highly athletic and agile and have lots of stamina. Agility is a great way of burning all that Doodle energy while having a great time!

Dock diving

Many Doodles are water dogs. You have the Poodle side, which was originally created for retrieving waterfowl, and then you add a retriever, spaniel, or herding dog and you have a *super* water dog. If your Doodle falls in this category, they're guaranteed to *love* dock diving!

Dock diving consists of a pool that's 40 feet long, one side of which has measurements. On one end is a way for dogs to get out of the pool; on the other is the dock where the dogs jump from. Attached to the dock is a running deck.

Dogs are placed in a stay at the end of the deck. Their handler (that's you!) throws a high-value toy up in the air over the water, and the dog runs down the deck, jumping into the water, flying high while trying to catch the toy. Judges note their landing point. The point of dock diving is to have the dog achieve a longer and longer fly time between their jump and where they land in the water.

Dock diving has three types of events:

- » Distance jump
- » Air retrieve
- » Hydrodash

There are six divisions for each event, listed according to jump length, which can also be determined by the size of the dog:

- » **Novice:** 1 inch to 9 feet 11 inches
- » **Junior:** 10 feet to 14 feet 11 inches
- » **Senior:** 15 feet to 19 feet 11 inches
- » **Master:** 20 feet to 23 feet 11 inches

>> **Elite:** 24 feet to 27 feet 11 inches

>> **Premier:** 28 feet and above

These divisions are based on jump distance (between dock and landing zone). Diving dogs come in all sizes, so there is a placement class to categorize them:

>> **Open:** For dogs at least 16 inches tall at the *withers* (shoulders)

>> **Lap:** For dogs under 16 inches tall at the withers

You can get more information about competing from the AKC (`www.akc.org/sports/title-recognition-program/dock-diving`) and North American Diving Dogs (`www.northamericadivingdogs.com`).

REMEMBER

Many dogs enjoy swimming, but others need to be taught how to swim in a safe manner. If you're thinking about getting into dock diving, first make sure your Doodle can swim comfortably, without panic or excessive energy put into moving through the water. If your Doodle wasn't exposed to swimming as a puppy, begin by taking them into the water with you. Put a flotation vest on your dog to help give them confidence and not feel as though they're going to sink.

It's easiest if your dog can walk right into the water on their own. A shallow stream or creek would be perfect. Touching bottom without a big drop-off helps them achieve confidence without your having to convince them to get their feet wet. When they're easily walking and splashing around, you can move to a lake where the water may get over their head. Most Doodles love playing fetch, so bring a few favorite floatable fetch toys and play the game in the water. Next, get out of the water and throw the toys in. Your Doodle will likely be confident enough to go get them in the lake and return the toy to you for another throw.

You're building not only your dog's confidence in the water, but also her toy drive. Both are necessary in order to enter a dock-diving event, because the toy drive is the trigger for your dog to jump off the dock when it's thrown over the pool.

TIP

When your Doodle diver is comfortable in natural water and enjoys playing retrieving games in it, it's time to find a pool that allows dogs to swim and jump in. This can be difficult, so I suggest you join a dock-diving club. They can help you locate places to practice, give you guidance, and help you achieve dock-diving titles with your Doodle.

Preparing for your event

Dog shows can be all-day events, lasting several days to a week, so it helps to be prepared. Each type of activity and performance level will require specific supplies to have on hand. But they all have things in common as well. In this section, I give you a list of supplies you should bring with you to every performance event so you'll be prepared for all your Doodle's needs, as well as your own.

Supplies for your Doodle

TIP

Dog shows are all-day events. You spend most of your time waiting for your turn in the ring. Setting up camp will help you enjoy the experience much more, and may even bring in some guests to keep you company. Here's what to bring for your Doodle:

WARNING

>> **Temperature control:** Dog shows are held both indoors and out, all through the year. You'll need to consider the ability of your Doodle to handle extreme temperatures — whether cold or hot — while engaged in high activity.

Toy-size Doodles or those with short noses won't be able to withstand extreme temperatures for very long. They can't adjust their body heat as well as dogs who have normal respiratory systems.

If the show is held indoors, you won't have to worry much about temperature control. But if the show is held outdoors (as it must be for many types of performance activities), bring a way to keep your dog's body heat normalized. This may be a crate with a heating or cooling pad, a reflective tarp you can put over the crate to aid in keeping your Doodle cool, or an umbrella or canopy to keep most of the sun's heat off of both of you as you wait your turn in the arena.

>> **Water:** Be sure to bring plenty of water from home. Water quality differs from location to location. Just as you shouldn't suddenly switch your Doodle's food, you also shouldn't suddenly switch the quality of their water. I suggest bringing a gallon for every day you'll be at the show. Don't forget a water bowl (or bucket if you have a large Doodle).

>> **Sunscreen:** Sunscreen is a must for any Doodle with a pink nose. Even if the event is being held indoors, you'll need to walk your dog from your vehicle to the show hall and also take them for walks every few hours or so, so bring dog-safe sunscreen.

>> **Towels:** If you're involved in tracking, hunting, or dock diving, bring plenty of towels. Between marshy conditions for tracking and hunting, to a soaked dog after a dock dive, you'll need them for both your Doodle and yourself.

>> **Flotation vest:** If you're engaged in the hunting or dock diving sport, your dog should have a flotation vest. This will allow your Doodle to concentrate on swimming instead of having to put energy into staying afloat.

>> **Treats:** Be sure to bring plenty of high-value treats for your dog. Most dogs won't work for free, and the higher the value of the treats, the better they'll perform. Although you can't offer your dog treats in the ring, you can give them to your Doodle after their performance or while you're warming up for your turn.

WARNING

Many exhibitors tend to get nervous prior to showing — it's a natural reaction. To quell their nerves, they may overdo the warming-up exercises, which both fill up their dogs with treats and tire them out. This can decrease the dog's performance when it's their turn in the ring. I suggest you keep your warmup to only a few minutes. Periodically walk around the showground to acclimate your dog to the activities, but don't do strict training. That should've been done prior to the event.

>> **Food:** If you're not done with the day's show prior to your dog's normal mealtime, wait until after you've been in the ring to feed them a full meal. You need all their motivation, drive, and desire to work. A recently fed dog may not give that to you.

>> **Grooming tools:** One way to maintain your calm and keep your dog relaxed is to brush their coat. This will help calm your nerves and has the added benefit of ensuring that your dog appears presentable in the arena. Just don't plan on doing a full grooming at the show (unless you're there for a conformation event). You want to achieve Zen, not stress.

>> **Toys:** Bring some toys and items your dog can chew on. These will keep your dog busy as they wait to perform.

Supplies for you

In addition to bringing supplies for your dog, you'll need to have everything you need to be comfortable yourself. I recommend the following:

>> **A comfortable camp chair:** Camp chairs are lightweight and easy to transport. One with a cup holder is great. If your dog prefers to sit near you, bring a chair for them, too (unless they're too big to sit in a camp chair!).

>> **Snacks and meals:** Not every dog show has a concession stand and those that do don't offer the best food. Bring a cooler with cold drinks (it's a great place to keep your dog's water, too). Toss in some snack bars, sliced vegetables, energy bars, or sandwiches. If your dog eats anything other than kibble, you may want to add that to your cooler, too. Dog shows often run into dogs' usual mealtimes.

>> **A book:** You'll have to wait many hours to exhibit and possibly another couple hours if you've tied with another exhibitor or done particularly well.

Hunting with Your Doodle

Poodles were one of the original hunting dogs known to Europeans and in Asia during the Middle Ages. Mix the Poodle with a sporting breed, and you have a great hunting partner! From retrieving and flushing to pointing, Doodles can be trained for every aspect of the sport.

TIP

One of the ways to ensure your Doodle will make a good hunting partner is early training and exposure. If you plan on preparing your Doodle to help you in the fields, forests, and marshes, they need to be confident in these locations, as well as unperturbed by the sounds around them, including the sound of your guns. You'll need to offer your Doodle positive associations at both the sight and sound of the weapons from the time they're very young.

WARNING

Exposure to sharp sounds like guns being fired shouldn't be a sudden event — this can cause your Doodle a lot of stress. Instead, it should be done very gradually, beginning at a distance where it's not much of a bother and gradually bringing the sound closer to where it'll definitely be noticed by your dog.

REMEMBER

Keep in mind that dogs hear at least twice as well as we do. You'll need help with this as you gauge the appropriate starting distances and successively bring the sounds closer to your dog.

TIP

Begin by choosing a puppy whose breeder is creating Doodles for hunting. The breeder will do early exposure to the sounds associated with hunting. Puppies who are familiar with the sounds of gunfire, birds, and water won't be frightened by a sudden exposure to them.

If your Doodle pup isn't from a breeder of hunting dogs, introduce recordings of the sounds. They should be far enough away from your puppy to not overly alert to it. Gradually bring the sound closer as your puppy can handle it. If you see their ears go down and back, reverse course and move the sound farther away. As someone brings the sounds slightly closer, be sure to keep your Doodle busy with another activity, such as obedience training or playing fetch. Don't let on that there's anything different going on.

With each small increment of success, remain at that distance for a few days, or until your Doodle pup totally ignores the sounds and continues to play and interact with you. Maintain the positive reinforcement format of approaching everything new. It must be enjoyable to your Doodle in order for them to want to continue working.

As you work on desensitizing your Doodle pup to the sounds, also begin teaching your Doodle to fetch rubber or canvas dummies. Rubber dummies teach them to maintain a soft mouth on the "prey," and canvas dummies are great for teaching them to retrieve specific scents (you can put scent on the canvas); you can also stick bird feathers on the canvas dummies to acclimate your Doodle to the waterfowl they'll be retrieving for you.

Next, using a dummy launcher (which can sound similar to soft shotgun blasts), teach your Doodle how to retrieve from longer distances, following the sound of gunfire. Essentially, you want your hunting buddy to hear the sound of gunfire and automatically look for the bird going down. The dummy launcher emulates this and is something you have some control over, which helps during the training process.

TIP

If you want to take your Doodle's hunting skills to a new level, you can compete in field trials. You can find more information at www.akc.org/sports/retrievers/field-trials.

Having Down-Home Fun with Your Doodle

Not everybody wants to show their dog. In fact, the majority of pet owners just want a Doodle companion to share their lives with, not campaign across the country competing at shows!

There's so much you can do together — from camping and hiking, to boating, biking, or horseback riding (with your Doodle running alongside). No matter what you have in mind, your Doodle is sure to be up for any adventure.

REMEMBER

As with any activity, start with short exposure and gradually build up your dog's tolerance to the energy levels and attention span required to maintain it.

Nearly every activity requires some training skills. Be sure to first do basic on- and off-lead obedience so that you can more easily guide your Doodle through the nuances of the activity.

TIP

Here are some examples of behavior skills to train:

>> **Heeling:** While hiking, biking, or horseback riding, you'll want your Doodle to move into heel position when there's someone passing you on the trail or another type of distraction. Having your dog focus on heeling prevents them from taking a walkabout into unknown territory that you'll end up having to explore to find them. It's ultimately a way of keeping your dog safe.

>> **Sit-stay:** From remaining in one place as you open the car door, to not venturing into a neighbor's campsite, the sit-stay can keep your Doodle in one spot for a short period of time. Imagine getting out of your car at a campsite and being able to have your dog remain in one spot as you set up the tent. Or imagine you're biking and you have to cross a road — cueing your dog to sit and stay when you see a vehicle coming will prevent them from running into the street.

>> **Down-stay:** This behavior will be useful for long stays, such as when you're cooking dinner on the grill or tacking up your horse. Maybe you're just taking a break from hiking and you want to rest for a while. Having a Doodle who reliably remains in a down-stay will help you relax and force them to relax, too, regardless of how excited they are.

>> **Come:** Having a Doodle who comes when called in any situation is a lifesaver! It allows you to take your dog anywhere. For example, say you're bike riding in the woods and your dog catches a scent and follows it. You stop peddling, cue them to come, and your dog responds, running back to you with a grin plastered on their face (and muddy paws, too).

>> **Finish:** Being able to cue your dog into heel position regardless of where they are can be more than convenient — it can be an issue of safety. If you're biking and you see someone approaching, or you need to stop at a cross-roads, you can cue your Doodle to return to your side immediately, off-lead.

>> **Stand-stay:** After a hike, you need to check your dog for ticks or prickers. If your dog doesn't stand absolutely still, it'll be impossible to do a thorough job.

TIP

If you're taking your dog with you camping, be sure to pack enough food for the trip, a portable mat, portable dishes (the type that fold up and are packable), water from home, insect repellent, and a 20-foot lightweight leash. When taking a hike, bring a water bottle with a built-in water dish to keep your weight light, a snack for your dog, and a long lead.

Before your hike, spritz your dog's legs with a dog-safe insect repellent to prevent bug bites. I like Dr. Harvey's Herbal Protection Spray (www.drharveys.com/products/dogs/101-herbal-protection-spray-gentle-herbal-spray-for-dogs).

WARNING

Never use an insect repellant containing DEET on your dog.

5

Senior Doodles

IN THIS PART . . .

Understand the changing needs of your aging Doodle.

Enhance the life of your senior Doodle.

Know when the time is right to add another Doodle.

Chapter 15

Recognizing the Changing Needs of Aging Doodles

D oodles tend to enjoy longer life spans due to their Poodle genetics, but that doesn't mean that their bodies and minds remain the same throughout their lives.

Most large dogs can be considered seniors by the age of 7, while smaller dogs remain highly energetic until their early teens. A medium-size dog often begins to slow down by the age of 10.

TIP

There are four things you can do that will improve the life of your Doodle as they get older.

» **Switch their diet to one labeled for senior dogs.** This is important because your dog's nutrition needs change as they age.

» **Do a yearly checkup with bloodwork.** Your veterinarian can often uncover health concerns that you've missed. A complete chemistry profile, via a blood sample, can offer a profile of organ function. Often a change in diet or appropriate medication can mitigate the progress of a debilitating illness or physical malfunction.

>> **Monitor your senior Doodle more closely.** Watch how they move, regularly check their entire body for lumps or flaky skin, check their eyes for the development of cataracts (common in sporting breeds), make sure their nails are regularly filed down, and make sure their poop remains healthy (solid and dark brown, with no mucous or looseness).

>> **Continue to exercise your dog, even if arthritis slows them down.** Exercise helps keep the synovial fluid (in the joints) healthy, which slows the advance of arthritis.

In this chapter, I discuss how your Doodle will change physically and mentally as they enter their senior years, as well as how to address these changes, ensuring your Doodle remains a vital part of your family.

RECOGNIZING ABNORMAL HEALTH CONDITIONS

You know your dog very well. If you believe they're not behaving normally, there is likely a reason. Here are a few symptoms to watch out for:

- Vomiting or diarrhea lasting more than 24 hours
- Limping
- Licking one spot excessively
- Flaky, itchy skin
- Not eating
- Excessive thirst
- Excessive drooling
- Restlessness and an inability to get comfortable
- Blood coming from anywhere

The biggest alarm bell will be if your Doodle stops eating. Dogs *never* miss a meal without a reason, and it's usually because they aren't feeling well.

If you see any of these symptoms in your Doodle, take them to a veterinarian as soon as possible.

Physical Changes

From the time your Doodle is a puppy through their becoming a senior dog, their body will undergo changes that will affect every aspect of their life. You'll be able to recognize outward signs, such as decreased mobility from arthritis or cloudy eyes due to cataracts, but you can't see what's going on inside your dog.

The best way of knowing your dog's internal condition is to have a yearly senior dog checkup, which will include a blood test that looks for organ malfunction and chemical imbalances. Some veterinarians also suggest doing an ultrasound of internal organs because they can more easily detect tumors or cysts. At the yearly checkup, your veterinarian will also listen to your Doodle's heart and lungs, check their temperature, look at their gums and teeth, *palpate* (touch) their abdomen, and check their ears and eyes.

These baseline tests will be your early warning beacon if something is awry. Most Doodles rarely slow down, so you won't have any idea if there's an early onset of organ malfunction or cancer growth unless these tests are done regularly.

The following sections cover some of the physical changes that can occur to your Doodle as they get older.

Worsening allergies

Allergies may make an appearance in your aging Doodle, even if they've never shown signs of allergies before. Your Doodle's ability to digest certain foods or tolerate environmental irritants weakens with age. Generally, a prescription diet can help with allergies, but you'll have to figure out what's triggering the allergy and control your dog's environment as much as possible, to minimize their exposure to whatever's bothering them.

Bad breath

Many elderly dogs tend to have bad breath. Bad breath can be a sign of gum disease, tooth decay, or a metabolic abnormality. Keeping your Doodle's teeth clean can prevent gum disease, as well as the internal infections caused by it. But not all bad breath is due to the gums — a digestive disorder can also cause bad breath.

Gum disease can attack every major organ in your dog's body. In the heart, bacteria can inflame heart valves and decrease blood flow, causing damage to the organ muscles. The bacteria from periodontal disease can also affect the liver, as well as every organ that the liver serves. The kidneys are also affected, resulting in diabetes and waste buildup in the bloodstream. This then results in elevated blood pressure and difficulties passing waste.

Lumps and bumps

Some dogs get fatty tissue deposits that appear like big lumps under the skin. This tends to occur more in much older dogs, but it can occasionally occur in younger dogs, too. Never ignore lumps or bumps — a quick-growing hard lump may be a *malignant* (cancerous) tumor requiring surgical removal or other treatment.

Weight gain

Senior dogs tend to put on weight because they're less active and have a slower metabolism. Be sure to monitor your Doodle's weight and food intake. Making sure your senior Doodle keeps up with their fitness will help with digestion and nutrient absorption, too. They should go on walks daily. If arthritis is making exercise difficult, check out "Aches and pains: Changes in your Doodle's joints," later in this chapter, for suggestions.

Incontinence

One of the most challenging issues with senior dogs is incontinence — their urinary or rectal sphincters no longer hold back their waste. Incontinence can also sometimes be due to a urinary infection or gastrointestinal distress. In female dogs, it can be due to lower estrogen levels, which causes a relaxing of the urethral sphincter. Medications can be helpful, but they can have side effects if used long term.

Consult with your veterinarian if your dog is experiencing incontinence. And don't punish your dog for their accidents — they're not doing it on purpose!

Aches and pains: Changes in your Doodle's joints

Arthritis is an inflammation of one or more joints. There's no way to avoid arthritis, but there are numerous ways to reduce the pain and inflammation and slow its progression.

One way to slow the progression of arthritis is exercise. Your Doodle may not want to go for a run or romp with a bunch of other dogs, but a quiet daily walk will get their blood flowing and muscles moving.

TIP

The best exercise for a senior arthritic dog is swimming. Dipping their feet in a creek or wading pool isn't enough. Your senior Doodle needs to wear a floatation vest and begin swimming in a pool. This activity exercises their muscles without impacting their joints. Building muscle around the arthritic joints supports the body and extends your dog's life expectancy. Plus, Doodles love the water! If you don't have access to a swimming pool, find a lake or river that doesn't have a strong current and go into the water with your dog. Due to the growing popularity of aquatic therapy, you may even be able to find a veterinarian in your area who has an aquatic treadmill.

Blindness and deafness

Many dogs tend to lose their vision as they get to be very old. Vision loss can be caused by cataracts or just old age. If your dog is experiencing a loss of sight, they'll bump into things, especially doorways, and become sensitive to changes in light or poor lighting conditions. You may also notice your dog stumbling on stairs or trying to walk through a closed door.

Hearing loss can be tough to recognize, but the main symptom is your dog ignoring you when you call them to come or being startled and snapping at someone when they're awakened.

Some good news: Dogs never lose their sense of feeling pressure on their bodies. Often, touch is the best means of comforting them when the loss of another sensory element causes confusion or fear. An elderly Doodle may become clingy and tend to follow you around more than usual. They do this to seek comfort via your touch.

When Doodles begin to lose their vision or hearing, they often adjust well, especially if they have a loved one — another dog or a person — to help guide them.

TIP

Your dog's veterinarian can sometimes alleviate sensory loss through preventive medications or, in the case of cataracts, eye surgery to remove the cataracts.

There are ways you can adjust your communication with your Doodle to continue offering guidance and comfort as the sensory changes progress. For hearing loss, move to using visual and touch cues. For example, when you want your dog to walk with you and they're looking in a different direction, touch them on the shoulder of the side you're moving away from. They'll turn to look at you, observe your visual cue, and respond as you've trained them to do. When you take your Doodle outdoors, keep them on a lead so you can maintain contact with them if they begin to follow an interesting scent.

For sight loss, try to keep everything in your home in the same place. Use your voice for command cues and touch to guide them through unfamiliar, or narrow, areas. A strong smelling treat will also go a long way to luring them where you wish them to go.

Mental Changes

Recognizing physical symptoms of aging is usually pretty easy, but it can be challenging to figure out that your Doodle is experiencing canine cognitive dysfunction (CCD), the equivalent of Alzheimer's disease in dogs.

According to the National Center for Biotechnology, CCD affects up to 35 percent of dogs who are over 8 years of age — more if you consider how many cases go undiagnosed. Most pet owners merely attribute their dogs' behavioral quirks to old age, and they're half-right. These changes do occur when dogs are elderly, but CCD is also a quantifiable condition that should be addressed.

There's no way to cure CCD, but there are ways to help your Doodle adjust. For example, prescription medicines can be used to reduce anxiety and fearful behaviors. Consult with your veterinarian to find out what's right for your dog.

Here's a list of behaviors common to a dog with CCD:

>> Fear of what was once familiar

>> Increased barking and other types of vocalization

>> Repetitive behaviors

>> Forgetting how to respond to behavioral cues

>> Having accidents in the house

>> Confusion and disorientation

>> *Sundowner's syndrome* (a condition in which a dog's sleep hours change)

There are ways you can mitigate many of these symptoms, helping to ease your senior dog's confusion:

>> Take your dog outside to their relief area more often than you used to.

>> If you live in a condominium or apartment, give your Doodle a place to relieve themselves indoors so they don't have to try to hold it as they walk to the relief area outside.

>> Keep your elderly Doodle in a contained area of your home with quick access to the yard, such as the kitchen or laundry room, when you can't keep an eye on them.

>> Make sure they get daily exercise appropriate for their abilities and energy level.

>> Do short daily training sessions to keep their mind sharp and reinforce behaviors they learned when they were young.

The changes your Doodle experiences as they enter their senior years don't have to be scary or debilitating. You just have to make a few minor adjustments to ensure your dog's welfare and safety. The most important thing you can do is be kind and patient. In other words, be the kind of friend to your Doodle that your Doodle is to you.

Chapter **16**

Enhancing the Life of Your Aging Doodle

Older Doodles, just like older humans, need a slight change in lifestyle. That doesn't mean you can't play fetch or go on hikes anymore — it's actually more important than ever to continue these activities! It just means you need to recognize your dog isn't a puppy anymore, and adapt accordingly.

This chapter covers ways to continue keeping your Doodle active, adjust their diet to keep them in tip-top shape, and teach them a new set of tricks to stimulate their brain.

Move It or Lose It: Keeping Your Senior Doodle Active

Your senior Doodle may have difficulty keeping up with you on a 5-mile run or a mountain hike, but that doesn't mean you should stop your normal activities completely! Not only would your Doodle miss their time with you, but they still need activities to keep them physically and mentally fit.

TECHNICAL STUFF

One of the ways arthritis progresses is from a sedate lifestyle. The fluid between the joints is reduced due to injury or physical stress and causes more friction between the bones. Exercise reduces the friction and maintains muscle mass to help enhance movement. So, it may be a bit uncomfortable to move, but it will get much worse if your dog *doesn't* move.

Walking not running

When your Doodle reaches senior status, around the age of 10, consider changing their exercise by gradually decreasing the speed of the journey. For example, if you've always done a 3-mile run in the mornings, reduce it to half-run and half-walk. Maybe add a timeout in the middle where your Doodle can meander and sniff around.

When you plan outings where your Doodle may get a lot of exercise, consider going someplace where they can swim instead of climb. Or look for a trail with fewer boulders or steep ditches — find an even surface instead. A quiet walk along a country road can be special with a senior Doodle, whereas a hike along a boulder-strewn creek can be dangerous.

WARNING

All dogs are prone to ligament and tendon problems, especially those who are naturally very athletic, like Doodles. Doodles are genetically prone to ligament issues anyway (see more in Chapter 3), so don't risk injury — instead, take it slow and easy.

Keeping the games light

Doodles are natural athletes. But as with all athletes, you have to know when to lighten the load in order to remain mobile. There are numerous ways you can change your typical games to something your Doodle will enjoy and release all their pent-up energy. Here are some examples:

>> **Fetch:** When playing fetch (which most Doodles love!), your dog will race after a ball, try to jump in the air, possibly twist their body midair, and then land hard on their feet. This activity can be hard on a senior dog and may cause impact injuries. You can change it up by rolling the ball instead of throwing it. Or put your dog in a stay, take the toy to a specific spot, return to your dog, and send them out to get the toy. Still lots of fun, but you minimize the risk of injuries.

>> **Find it:** Dogs love to play search games. They learn to locate specific people, other pets, or hidden objects. This game can be continued well into your Doodle's later years, offering them many hours of stimulation for the body

and mind. The only changes you need to make to accommodate your dog's physical changes are to make the search a little shorter and easier. Don't make them search on uneven surfaces or have to climb. If you play the game indoors, keep it on one level of your house.

>> **Puzzle games:** If you've never given your Doodle puzzle games because you thought they'd destroy the puzzle, give them a try when they get older. You can find a huge variety of puzzle games made for dogs. One of the great things about puzzles is that your Doodle will be occupied and stimulated for as long as it takes to locate a treat hidden within it. You can use their regular kibble or a high-value treat like a piece of cheese or meat. The stronger the smell, the harder your Doodle will work to get it. For dogs with aches and pains, puzzles are perfect because the dog doesn't have to move around much.

>> **Round Robin:** You may have played this game when your Doodle was a puppy (see Chapter 6). Back then, Round Robin was a great way of teaching your dog to come when called and involve the entire family. You can play the game again, but keep the distances between you shorter and play on a flat surface.

>> **Play in bed:** I love the smell of dog breath in the morning. . . . You can play all kinds of games with your Doodle without having to even get out of bed. Take their favorite toy and hide it under a pillow or blanket. Your Doodle is sure to immediately go for it!

Feeding Your Senior Doodle

As your Doodle ages, their dietary requirements will change. This section gives you the lowdown on keeping an aging Doodle healthy with the right diet.

REMEMBER

Talk with your veterinarian to find out about your dog's unique needs.

Understanding how your dog's needs have changed

Your Doodle may continue to have lots of energy, but their body is still changing as they get older. You'll probably need to adjust their calorie intake, as well as the amount of protein and fat they're getting.

Many mature dogs (over the age of 6) have a slower metabolism. This is especially true of dogs who've been spayed or neutered. To prevent your Doodle from becoming overweight, reduce their caloric intake by about 20 percent. You still want to give your senior dog a high-protein diet, but you need to offer food that's lower in fat and calories.

Geriatric dogs (over 10 years of age for Standard-size Doodles and over 12 years of age for Miniature-size Doodles) tend to lose weight because they don't eat as well as younger dogs do. Loss of appetite can be the result of decreased exercise or a physical problem. Canine cognitive dysfunction (CCD; see Chapter 15) can also play a part in a dog's decreased appetite. To make up for this, feed them a diet with a higher fat content, as well as one that's more fragrant, in order to pique their interest. In general, mixing some freshly cooked meats and gravy into their kibble is a great way to get your geriatric Doodle excited about their meals again. But be sure to not decrease the protein levels — old dogs need more protein in their diets than young dogs do, while also needing fewer calories.

TIP

Fiber is very important to help older Doodles maintain a healthy gastrointestinal system. You can add to your dog's diet fresh foods that are high in fiber, such as canned pumpkin or green beans, to help them lose weight (if necessary) and keep them regular.

Probiotics can also help keep your dog regular. Adding this supplement to your dog's meals will reduce the frequency of loose stools. You should also give your dog probiotics when switching their diet from one type of food to another, even if the food is the same brand.

Feeding more often to aid digestion

You've probably been feeding your Doodle twice a day, at least since they've been an adult dog. Twice a day fits in well with your schedule and divides your dog's food intake into portions that they can easily digest.

As your dog ages, though, twice a day may not be the best feeding schedule. Older dogs' digestive systems are changing and may not be able to handle large amounts of food at one time.

TIP

There are several ways you can slow down your Doodle's food intake so they can better utilize their nutrients:

>> Feed your Doodle three or four meals a day instead of two.

>> Use a slow-feed bowl.

>> Use a food puzzle.

>> Use food as a training treat (see the following section).

>> Hide portions of food in different parts of your home so your Doodle has to search for it, using their natural predator tendencies and making them feel very fulfilled.

Old Dog, New Tricks: Training Your Senior Doodle

It's never too late to start training your Doodle, even if you didn't do it when they were younger. If you trained your Doodle when they were young, it's time to brush up on some of those skills as they get older. You'll need to change things up a bit — you're no longer having to keep your dog from pulling you down the block as you walk. Concentrate on more sedate activities that stimulate both their mind *and* their body.

Exercises for the body

Throughout the life of your Doodle, you've made sure to give them numerous opportunities to exercise. (You had to, or they'd drive you crazy!) Senior dogs also need regular exercise, but you may need to change a few things to ensure your dog's well-being. Even geriatric dogs require exercise. It helps them to better digest their food, maintain an appetite, and remain mobile as arthritis sets in.

TIP

The best exercise for Doodles of any age is swimming. The only changes you need to make from when they were younger is choosing swimming areas with little to no current and making sure your senior Doodle wears a flotation vest to prevent strenuous movement. Swimming builds the muscles that support your Doodle's skeletal system, and strong muscles will slow down the progress of arthritis. Swimming also gives your old dog a few minutes of weightlessness, when the joint pain is gone.

Even if your Doodle doesn't appreciate being in the water, you should still give them opportunities to do so with the aid of a professional swim coach. With a little bit of searching, you're bound to find a pool nearby where you can take your senior Doodle for swims.

Another great exercise for senior Doodles is walking on a soft surface. Hard surfaces such as paved roads or concrete sidewalks can impact your dog's joints, but a soft surface like a grassy field or dirt trail won't jolt their joints as badly. Instead of playing fetch in a parking lot or on a tennis court, try a field or grassy backyard.

TIP

Senior dogs tend to have difficulty with stairs or jumping into the car. A ramp will help so their hips and shoulders aren't impacted by that action. If you have steps between a door to go outside and the yard, a ramp can be helpful there as well. If possible, train your Doodle to use the ramp *before* they're geriatric so they're comfortable using it when they're unsteady on their feet.

REMEMBER

Dogs tend to hide their pain or discomfort until it becomes very bad. Just because your elderly Doodle *wants* to race around doesn't mean they should. Keep them leashed to maintain their exercise at a steady, sedate pace.

Training sessions should continue throughout your Doodle's life. They'll never get tired of performing heels, stays, comes, and other obedience routines. In fact, it'll keep them sharper, more reliable, and happier because Doodles love to work.

Exercises for the mind

One of the best training programs for an elderly dog is *nose work*, which uses a dog's natural abilities to discern different smells, locate them, and be rewarded for doing so. Nose work requires a complicated training process, but it doesn't require a dog to jump or race around — they just have to use their nose and walk.

TIP

To get started with nose work, train your dog to target on a small metal container that has a specific scent. You might put inside the tin a teabag, a few drops of essential oil on a cotton ball, or game scent (rabbit, quail, duck, or goose) on a cotton ball. The moment your Doodle touches the tin with their nose, click and reward.

To make sure they're targeting on the correct tin, have another identical tin nearby with nothing in it. When you're able to place the tin with the scent on the floor and your dog quickly targets on it, place the empty scent tin next to it. If your dog touches the scent tin with their nose, click and reward. If they touch the empty tin, don't respond. The moment they try the scent tin, immediately click and reward.

When your Doodle is reliably touching the correct tin, begin adding a cue when you present the scent tin. Words such as "scent it" or "sniffer on" are great ones, but anything you want will be good as long as you use it consistently.

As your dog learns to find the scented tin on cue, you can begin to increase the difficulty of their search. You can place the tin inside another container such as a box. Or add several non-scent-containing identical tins, all in the same area, so they have to really use their nose to find the right one.

Another great training game to stimulate your Doodle's mind is Which Hand? Again, your dog uses their nose to locate the reward. Here's how it works:

1. **Put your dog in a sit-stay facing you.**

2. **Put a treat in one of your hands, and put both hands behind your back.**

3. **As your dog watches, bring both hands in front of you, at nose level and say, "Which hand?"**

4. **The moment your dog sniffs the hand with the treat, click and reward.**

5. **Repeat a few times, switching the treat around between your hands so your dog is actually using their nose.**

6. **Now require your Doodle to do something to indicate which hand the treat is in, not just put her nose against it.**

   If you keep your hand closed when they sniff it, they'll begin to try ways to push your fingers open. They may use their nose or they may raise a paw.

7. **Click and reward the moment they raise a paw.**

   Make sure your dog touches the correct hand with their paw before you click and give them the reward.

Another great nose game can be done with three Kong toys (or other toys where you can hide food inside). Put food in one of the Kong toys, and then place all three on the floor with their food openings face down. Shuffle them around as your dog watches; then tell your Doodle, "Find it!" They'll likely do so in short order, but they'll also want to play again!

The more you stimulate your dog's brain, the more you'll maintain their ability to remain sharp and responsive well into old age. Continue to expose your elderly Doodle to new concepts, activities, and bonding opportunities. These are, indeed, their golden years.

Chapter **17**

Double Doodle: Adding a Second Dog to Your Family

ogs are social animals. They prefer to be with other dogs. That's why your Doodle gets so excited when they see other dogs nearby. They see playmates and companions who make them feel complete. Canine instinct demands that they live in social groupings for safety. There's no worse punishment for a dog than to be left alone.

You and your family may be enough of a "pack" for your Doodle. But maybe you're starting to think about adding a second Doodle to your pack. In this chapter, I walk you through why you may want to get a second dog, whether to make that second dog a Doodle or another breed, how to choose the right Doodle sibling, and how to help the two dogs become fast friends.

Looking at Common Reasons to Get a Second Dog

You may be thinking of getting a second dog because your current dog is getting older (see the nearby sidebar). Or maybe you just love your current dog so much, you want another dog to love.

Whatever the reason, you'll need to ask yourself some questions before running out and getting a second dog, especially if it will be another Doodle:

>> Does your Doodle like to socialize?

>> Can you afford a second dog?

>> Can you safely house and care for another dog?

>> Are you willing to put in the time and effort to manage a multi-dog family?

If you answered yes to all these questions, you're ready to consider adding a second dog to your family!

In the following sections, I walk through two of the big reasons why you may want to get a second dog.

WARNING

OLD DOGS AND PUPPIES: NOT THE PERFECT MATCH

Some people consider getting another dog when their current dog gets old, believing a young dog will spice up their life. But bringing a puppy into your home isn't fair to your old dog. Sure, they might enjoy the company of another dog who is calm, but they won't want to deal with a rambunctious young pup. Elderly dogs tend to have sensitive areas on their bodies and getting bumped can be painful.

If you plan to move forward with getting another dog to keep your old dog company, adopt a calm adult dog who is well versed in social skills. Your elderly dog will brighten up as you intended, without any negative consequences. Plus, you'll be saving the life of a dog in need!

To give your current dog a companion

Does your current Doodle like to socialize with other dogs? If your dog doesn't get excited when they see other dogs, bringing a second dog into your home may be challenging.

One of the main reasons to have more than one dog is for them to keep each other company and give each other lots of exercise — a need you can't fulfill, especially if you have to work away from home for hours every day. Your dog must love the company of other dogs for this to work.

TIP

A great way of getting a less-than-social Doodle to be open to a second dog is to involve them in puppy playgroups. Maybe a neighbor has a young dog who likes to play with other dogs. Or maybe there's a local park where you can regulate the interactions. Doggy daycares are great, too, because the playgroups are usually monitored, as well as chosen according to size and personality. Positive experiences will encourage your Doodle to be even more social and more open to your bringing another dog into your home.

REMEMBER

I cannot stress enough the importance of appropriate early socialization for your Doodle. Without this exposure, early and often, your Doodle can become an introvert and not learn how to interact with other dogs, preferring to remain with you and your family. Having a dog who's attached to you is fine, to a point. It can also cause numerous behavior issues — including separation anxiety and reactivity to other dogs and people — in the long run.

Most well-socialized dogs thoroughly enjoy the company of other dogs. The sudden appearance of a new puppy in their lives would be welcome. And with all your Doodle's life experience in social circles, they'll pass that on to the new Doodle, giving them a well-rounded education, too.

To prevent separation anxiety

Most Doodles have separation anxiety to some degree. It may be as minimal as depression when they're left alone, or it may be as damaging as self-mutilation or eating walls. None of it is pleasant for your dog, who wants to be with their family pack 24/7.

REMEMBER

Dogs evolved as pack animals. They don't feel confident, secure, or relaxed when they're separated from their pack. This behavior is purely instinctual. For Doodles, these instincts are very strong. To acclimate your Doodle to even short periods of time alone, you need to start when they're a puppy, so they learn that being alone isn't a negative experience (see Chapter 12).

Early experiences being alone will reduce your Doodle's outward anxiety when they're left home alone, but having another dog nearby will fulfill their natural inclination to be part of a pack.

If you have to be away from home, consider getting a second dog to keep your Doodle company.

To Doodle or Not to Doodle: That Is the Question

Your Doodle is probably everything you wanted in a canine companion, and more. They keep you company at home, make your morning walks more fun, and give you undying devotion and companionship.

Regardless of all these feelings, take an objective look at whether you should get a second dog and whether that dog should be another Doodle. Here are some pros and cons of getting a second Doodle:

REMEMBER

>> **Pros:** The two dogs will likely play and interact in a way that they understand. Doodles often roughhouse, but they don't tend to bite hard or get overly aroused to the point of becoming assertive. If they experience a dog who does react this way, it can cause them to become fearful of other dogs in general.

Doodles are highly impressionable and emotional. They must be surrounded by positive experiences and encouragement. They don't forget bad experiences.

>> **Cons:** The downside of having a second Doodle is the energy level. Doodles are highly energetic well into their senior years. Can you live with *two* of them? They'll tire each other out, most of the time, but depending on the size of your house and yard, you may feel like you have a wrestling match happening in your living room every day.

Sometimes a different breed of dog can cancel out some of your Doodle's antics. For example, a Golden Retriever may play with your Doodle to quell some of the energy but also offer a level of comfort as— Golden Retrievers are generally very confident, happy dogs. Other times a different breed can create a *more* challenging environment. For example, if you were to get an Australian Shepherd (without a full understanding of the breed) you might find yourself with a full-time job managing the two dogs, because Australian Shepherds have a lot of energy!

As you're already aware, Doodles aren't cheap. You may even have to wait on a list for a puppy to be available. You may be able to avoid these situations by looking for a Doodle at a rescue organization — an organization focused on Doodles, an organization focused on Poodles, or an organization focused on the other parent breed. You may also be able to find a Doodle with a non-breed-specific rescue group.

WARNING

Even if you're really eager to find a new Doodle, don't break down and get one from a pet shop or commercial breeder (puppy mill). You're unlikely to end up with a mentally and physically sound dog. Do the same careful homework you did when locating your current Doodle.

Knowing What to Look for in a Sibling

In my experience, dogs of similar size and temperament tend to fare well together. A young, energetic dog moving in with an already established and trained adult dog who likes to socialize can also be an ideal situation.

Finding the perfect second dog can feel like a gamble. But it can be an *educated* gamble because you can temperament-test a potential candidate (see Chapter 4). You can learn so much about another dog's personality through observation and interaction. If you're looking at a puppy under the age of 6 months, you may be able to gain pertinent behavior information by checking out their parents and performing the temperament tests on them.

WARNING

You may be tempted to get puppy siblings, but I highly recommend that you never purchase two puppies from the same litter. Here's why:

>> **Housetraining one puppy is challenging enough, never mind two.** If you find an accident on the floor, you have no way of knowing who did it, so you have to limit both puppies to a more confined space when you can't keep an eye them. Long-term crating is cruel, so it's bound to get messy with two puppies in the same exercise pen.

>> **You have to constantly observe puppies and head them off if they're about to get into trouble.** If you have to do that for two pups at the same time, you have your work cut out for you.

>> **Sometimes siblings start to resent each other.** This often occurs when they reach late adolescence, especially if they're the same gender. One may begin to become assertive, and the other may become defensive. You're likely to experience some nasty scuffles, and you may even consider rehoming one of the pups.

There *is* light at the end of this tunnel, but it requires years of appropriate training and management, and you may still face some challenging moments now and then.

>> **Puppies tend to bond with each other more than they do with you.** This can make training more challenging, as well as create emotional stress when they're separated for any reason.

The ideal time to begin considering a second dog is when your Doodle is about 1½ to 2 years old. They're still young enough to appreciate playing with another dog, but well trained and able to help teach the new puppy all the ropes and rules. If you want to wait a few more years, that's fine, too, but be sure to give your Doodle plenty of opportunities to socialize with other dogs so they don't focus solely on you. Regardless of how much you like to play with your Doodle, you can never replace the type of play they'll get with another dog.

If you try to play with your Doodle as though you were another puppy, they're more likely to grab your arm in their mouth and jump on you. This warning is especially important for children. Make sure the kids in your household have the respect of your dog and don't act like puppies themselves.

Helping the New Duo Get Along

First impressions are important. You want to be sure that your dogs don't feel threatened by each other. Ideally, you'll see them first touch noses, then sniff each other's rear ends, wag their tails, and do a play bow. Unfortunately, this isn't always what happens.

The response can be anything from outright fear and trying to hide, to snarling and *posing* (making themselves appear bigger with a high tail; high ears; high, stiff head; and hair raised along the shoulders and spine).

The following sections help you introduce the dogs so they become fast friends.

Setting up a positive initial meeting

A good first meeting will largely depend on where they meet and how relaxed you are when it occurs. Most dogs respond to the emotions of the people around them. If you feel insecure or stressed, your Doodle will also be on edge.

To prepare for this initial meeting, keep in mind the following tips:

>> **Stay calm.** Maintain a calm voice and relaxed body language.

>> **Keep your dog's leash loose.** They'll likely get very excited when they see the new dog, but don't allow them to drag you to greet the new dog or otherwise tighten their leash. Instead, use the redirection techniques in Chapter 10. Your dog should only get closer to the other dog on *your* terms — when they're relaxed, not pulling, and not vocalizing. Any signs of excitement from your dog will only stress out the other dog and create a difficult first impression for both of them. This rule also applies to the new dog, too.

>> **When they're finally close enough to touch noses, keep the leashes loose and use happy tones of voice to encourage their greeting.**

>> **Be observant, but not worried.** Dogs tend to play roughly. If one of the dogs becomes overwhelmed, allow that dog to let the other dog know they're being obnoxious by letting out a growl or a bark or quick snap. Don't intervene unless the rambunctious dog doesn't back down or the overwhelmed dog actually bites.

>> **When both dogs have initiated play (with the front end down and back end up, tail wagging), allow them off lead together in a fenced yard.** Stay with them, observing their behavior. Make sure there are several bowls of water nearby, as well as shade if the weather is warm.

Acclimating to a new life

After your dogs have had a chance to get to know each other, it's time to bring the new dog into your house. Be sure to bring both dogs in at the same time and maintain the relaxed attitude you used when they first met. Allow them to play in one area of your home where nothing can be broken.

When the activity settles down, put the new dog on a harness and take them on a tour of the house, just as you did with your first dog. In fact, allow your first dog to accompany you and be an assistant tour guide. Don't leave your first dog out of any activity that your second dog does — other than separating them at mealtime, at bedtime, and during training sessions. Along the way, show your new dog where they'll eat, sleep and spend the majority of their indoor time.

Before bringing home another dog, be sure to get them their own bed, crate, bowls, toys, and training equipment. Dogs need their own everything.

If you have other pets, be sure to introduce your new dog to them the same way they met your first dog. Be calm and observant and offer rewards for appropriate behavior.

Remain with your dogs for the first few hours to help them develop confidence in each other. Pay attention to their play patterns, and be quick to redirect them if they begin to play roughly.

TECHNICAL STUFF

When dogs play they grab each other's legs with their mouths, bounce against each other, and jump around. Don't be alarmed at this behavior — it's natural and appropriate.

TIP

Here's a list of *inappropriate* play behaviors. If you notice any of this, separate the dogs, but don't get loud, upset, or stressed. Just hold out a treat for each dog and call them to you:

>> **Growling:** You'll see the sides of their teeth more so than the front. It can sometimes be difficult to distinguish between a play growl and an aggressive growl. If you're not sure, look at the dog's body language. With a play growl, their body will remain bouncy and happy. A dog who's being aggressive tends to be stiff, hold their ears back, and have wide, staring eyes.

>> **Yipping:** You may hear a yip if one of the dogs got too rough.

>> **Grabbing the scruff:** One dog may bite the *scruff* (the back of the neck) of the other dog. This may be just rough play or the beginning of assertive behavior.

>> **Paw over the shoulders:** This means that one dog is trying to say they're the boss. This behavior isn't necessarily inappropriate play, but pay attention to what happens next. If the dog tries to move away and the dog who put their paw over the other dog's shoulder goes after them, break it up.

>> **One dog pinned on the ground with the other dog looming over them and growling:** Break it up immediately.

If the dogs are getting way too energetic to play inside, let them out to play in a fenced yard. If you don't have that option, separate them in their crates for an hour or so, until they relax a bit. Sometimes the excitement of meeting a new sibling can cause an overcharged environment, ripe for misunderstandings.

WARNING

When dogs get aroused, they can sometimes become overly assertive or easily frightened. Your dogs are just getting to know each other, so remain with them as they play so that you can quickly redirect their attention if one of them climbs onto the other's back or gets too grabby with their jaws.

Every interaction should be pleasant so the two dogs have positive associations with each other — a good first impression.

Preventing resource guarding

More likely than not, your dogs will have resource guarding issues with each other at some point — it's only a matter of time. After all, your first dog was an "only child" up until now, never having to share. And your second dog may have had to battle for everything they got.

The good news is, there are ways to manage your dogs so that nobody gets hurt when this occurs:

>> **Make sure you have two of everything.** You should have two feeding areas, two identical beds, lots of toys, and two water bowls.

>> **Keep the dogs separated when you aren't able to watch them.**

>> **Train the dogs individually and in tandem (see the next section).**

>> **Treat them equally.** Regardless of how much you strive to offer equal attention, one or both of them will want more, trying to get closer to you than the other dog or trying to get between you and the other dog. Don't feel sorry for either of the dogs when it's not their turn for attention. And observe *both* dogs as you offer attention of any sort.

When dogs learn to accept a new sibling, you may notice that the two of them take the lead in different situations. For example, one dog may tend to bark more at specific sounds, while the other initiates a tug-of-war game with a toy. If they both try to take the lead, that's when an argument can occur. Luckily, most Doodles rarely take it to a level of aggression before their argument is over. The spat is quick, and one dog acquiesces by displaying a calming behavior (such as head shaking, sneezing, blinking and looking away, or yawning).

TECHNICAL STUFF

Calming signals are common when dogs interact with each other and also occur with you during training or another high-arousal situation. Dogs display these signals when they want to defuse a situation. Here are some of the calming signals you may see:

>> Head shaking

>> Sneezing

>> Blinking and looking away

>> Yawning

Working with the dogs in tandem

There are several reasons to train your dogs in tandem:

>> It cuts down on the time you spend walking each individual dog through the neighborhood.

>> Dogs tend to develop separation anxiety when separated from their siblings.

>> Working in tandem teaches the dogs to get along better, as well as respect each other's boundaries.

When I'm confronted with a case of sibling rivalry behavior problems (dogs who live in the same household and are fighting), I always teach the two of them to work in tandem. You have to do this in several steps and not force it onto dogs who are easily intimidated or still at the point of being reactive to environmental stimuli.

Beginning with some basics

REMEMBER

Before embarking on any tandem training work, each dog must be reliable on lead when surrounded by distractions. This means that no matter where you are, and no matter what's going on around you, your Doodle will perform as cued at least 95 percent of the time.

TIP

Here's a list of what each dog should be able to do prior to beginning tandem work:

>> Heeling on and off lead

>> Doing a sit-stay on and off lead as you move around the dog at least 10 feet away from them

>> Doing a down-stay on and off lead as you move around the dog at least 10 feet away from them

>> Reliably coming when cued from anywhere, both on and off lead (and abruptly sitting in front of you upon arrival)

>> Finishing in the correct area while heeling or when stopped with you

TIP

Before working the dogs in tandem, do a training session with each dog individually — every time. This helps the dogs focus and respond as expected. You may also be able to work on any specific issues one of them has in relation to environmental stimuli. It's far easier to address this when you're working with only one dog at a time.

Assuming your dogs have successfully achieved a basic level of obedience, begin with some easy cues such as come and sit. Then move on to sit-stay and down. Finally, work on heeling or loose leash walking, which tends to be the most challenging task when working dogs in tandem.

TIP

Before you begin training, decide on a tandem name. This is a name you use when working or otherwise addressing them when they're together. Here are a few suggestions:

>> Doggies

>> Doggos

>> Dogs

>> Doodles

>> Puppies

It doesn't matter what you call them — you just need a name that you can use just prior to each command. Soon, your dogs will begin to understand that they're both being addressed.

REMEMBER

Each dog needs a specific name that they recognize as their own, especially in a multiple-dog home. When you address one of your dogs individually, say the dog's name first and then offer the behavior cue.

COME AND SIT

I normally start within a safely fenced area with the dogs off lead. Doing so prevents you from having to deal with two leashes as you cue the dogs and teach them about working together. The less you're having to struggle, the better.

Here's how to work on come and sit in tandem:

1. **Put a treat in each hand and show your dogs your target hands at the same time, one for each dog (see Figure 17-1).**

2. **When they both push their noses toward your hands, click and offer the treats in your hands.**

   Repeat Steps 1 and 2 several times.

3. **As your dogs target on your hands, move backward as you lean forward slightly and say their tandem name followed by the verbal cue, "Come."**

   Gradually increase the distance they must move as you walk backward.

FIGURE 17-1:
Target with both
hands as you
move backward
and lean forward.

Photograph courtesy of Sarah Babineau

4. **When they're reliable and focused, release them from work (with a release word such as *break, free,* or *release*) and pet them on their chest or rub their ears.**

5. **After a minute, give the come cue again.**

6. **If they both quickly respond, click and reward. If one arrives and the other is distracted, click and reward only the dog who arrived.**

   If the other one saunters over, be sure to click and reward that dog as well. To further reinforce the dog who arrived first, be sure to offer another treat directly after the late dog earned theirs. That way, the dog who performed best gets *two* treats.

7. **When both dogs are coming to you quickly, cue them to sit upon arrival at your feet.**

8. **The moment they both sit, click and reward (see Figure 17-2).**

   Practice this five or six times before releasing them from work.

9. **The next training session, add a short hesitation after your dogs arrive and sit.**

   A three-second delay prior to the click and reward is a great place to begin. As both dogs learn patience and wait for the click, gradually add a few seconds to each come and sit (and wait) prior to clicking.

10. **When your dogs are very reliable in a small area, take the action to a larger area.**

    Always make sure the training area is secure because your dog will be off lead. Safety first!

REMEMBER

FIGURE 17-2:
Targeting your
dogs into a sit.

Photograph courtesy of Sarah Babineau

SIT-STAY AND DOWN-STAY

This next goal shouldn't be a stretch because your dogs already understand the cues and how to respond to them. The distraction of being next to each other, though, will make it more difficult for them to maintain the behaviors for any length of time. So, reduce the criteria from where you know they can perform individually to a less challenging level. For example, if both dogs can perform sit-stays and down-stays for several minutes as you move around them 15 feet away and throw tennis balls all around them, begin the *tandem* sit-stay standing in front of them, targeting. The same goes for the down-stay.

Here's how to break down the exercise:

1. **Put a treat in each hand and show your dogs your target hands at the same time, one for each dog (refer to Figure 17-1).**

2. **Gradually increase the amount of time you remain in front of them as they target.**

   Do this over a period of days. For example, begin with 3 to 5 seconds on the first day, and add a few more seconds with each consecutive day.

3. **Remove the target, but continue to praise.**

4. **When your dogs can achieve a 20-second sit-stay side-by-side, begin some movement side-to-side as you target with your hands.**

5. **When the dogs are reliable with remaining in the stay as you move from side to side in front of them, begin moving along their sides as they remain sitting.**

REMEMBER

It may take a few training sessions to accomplish this. Every day, add a bit more movement around the dogs during their stays. If at any time, one or both of the dogs move out of their stay position, reduce the criteria during the next stay exercise. For example, if the dogs are reliable remaining in place when you move from one side to the other, but they get up when you try to move behind them, back up to where they were reliable and work on that for two to three more training sessions before trying to move all the way around them again.

6. **Finally, when they're ready move all the way around them, as they target, facilitating a nice sit-stay.**

If your dogs move a bit as you go behind them, put your hand target very near their mouths as you go behind. Mark that moment with a click and give the reward. Repeat two to three times, or until the dogs calmly remain in one spot as you move behind them.

You can apply the same behavior breakdown to the down–stay (see Figure 17-3).

FIGURE 17-3: Target into the down-stay with both hands.

Photograph courtesy of Sarah Babineau

WARNING

Some dogs have confidence problems performing downs right next to each other. If one or both of your dogs are like this, be sure to offer lots of praise and rewards, and allow the dog who isn't confident to perform their down a little farther away. As they begin to relax, they'll naturally move a little closer.

TANDEM HEELING

Walking two dogs at the same time is the most challenging behavior to achieve. It requires extreme concentration from you *and* the dogs and great dexterity (because you're managing two leashes), as well as good timing.

First, you need to know how to hold the two leashes. And to do this you need to decide which dog will be closest to you and which dog can reliably work a short distance away from you. Here's the best way to figure that out:

1. **Hold one leash in each hand, and move forward as you encourage your dogs to follow you.**

2. **Observe both dogs as they follow you.**

    Which dog remains glued to your side? Which one tends to walk a little farther away or turn their lower body away from you? The one who stays glued to your side should be closest to you when you work on heeling in tandem.

REMEMBER

It'll be far easier to train your dogs to heel in tandem if you begin by acknowledging their natural tendencies.

Now that their positioning has been established, you'll need to do whatever you can to ensure they remain in those positions as you move forward and turn. Begin by holding the leash of the dog closest to you (the inside dog) in your right hand and holding the leash of the dog farthest from you (the outside dog) in your left hand (see Figure 17-4).

WARNING

Because the dogs are just learning how to work together, I don't recommend using a *coupler* (a short lead that connects two dogs together). It will only confuse them and possibly even cause fear. You need to allow your dogs a chance to learn and enhance their desire to remain together as you move forward. Positive training is all about dogs offering you behaviors, not coercing it out of them.

The best way of starting out, on lead, is to cue your dogs to come and sit. After you click and reward, make sure they're in their appropriate positions. If they aren't, you'll need to place yourself accordingly. Here's how:

>> **If the inside dog is on your right side,** begin heeling by moving along that dog's left side. As the dogs turn to move with you, the inside dog will fall into place, followed by the outside dog.

>> **If the inside dog is to your left side,** place your left side alongside the inside dog's right side just prior to moving forward into the heel. Your placement will facilitate the dogs' appropriate positions. This can also be achieved with appropriate turns when needed.

Photograph courtesy of Sarah Babineau

FIGURE 17-4:
The leash of the inside dog should be in your right hand and the leash of the outside dog should be in your left hand.

As when heeling with one dog, you'll need to do a right turn and redirect whenever one of the dogs moves ahead of you (see Figure 17-5). And if one dog moves *behind* you, you'll need to turn left. This can be confusing when working with two dogs at the same time. Just make sure not to move into, or otherwise overcorrect, the dog who is nicely focused and working properly.

TIP

Dogs often apply body pressure to other dogs as a means of asserting their personalities. If this occurs while you're walking them together, it might cause one of them (usually the inside dog) to fall behind you. In order to prevent this from occurring, continue to target with both hands so that the outside dog remains farther from you, allowing the inside dog space to perform (see Figure 17-6). To do this, hold treats in both hands (along with the leashes) and target as you walk.

It may take a while to achieve nice tandem heeling, but it will be well worth the time, because you'll be able to walk both dogs at the same time instead of having to take separate walks or, worse, having them drag you down the street.

FIGURE 17-5:
Redirecting, via a
right turn, while
heeling.

Photograph courtesy of Sarah Babineau

FIGURE 17-6:
Targeting while
heeling.

Photograph courtesy of Sarah Babineau

When both dogs are heeling well together, you can begin phasing into a loose leash walk (see Chapter 10). At this point, the process will ease a bit, because you no longer need to target them or cue them to maintain close positioning. The dogs do, however, need to understand how to heel in tandem prior to loose-leash walking in tandem. It's the only way they'll be able to know to offer the behavior while loose-leash walking.

I've often used the loose-leash walk when hiking with dogs. Not only does this keep them from taking off, but it makes it easy to hike without a lead. You must remain observant of your dog's focus cues and promptly mark them, so they know what you want from them. By the end of the hike, the dogs are often offering some nice in-position heeling without having been cued.

When you get to a place where you can safely loose-leash walk, release your dogs from work with your release word and a pet. Then move forward and cue them with "Let's go," and begin walking. The pace you walk doesn't matter — you can meander and allow your dogs to explore.

As when doing the loose-leash walk with one dog, you must cue any of the dogs who begins to pull on you to come and sit, marking the moment they've done so. Also, be observant of your dogs glancing in your direction from time to time. Always mark that moment and praise, followed by rewards. Do this no matter how often it occurs. You can bet that as your walk progresses it will happen more and more often.

The result will be two dogs walking near you and watching you. One, or both, may even place themselves into heeling position, offering you something fantastic: heeling!

WORKING WITH DISTRACTIONS

When one dog reacts to something, they all do. As pack animals, all the dogs react to a distraction that initially alerts only one of them. When you're walking two big Doodles, distractions can be quite challenging. But don't despair — the same rules of redirection apply.

TIP

The best way of nipping it in the bud is to be observant of your dog's ears. They convey a lot of information to you. If the ears swivel and become fixed, the dog has noticed a distraction. Immediately do a redirect — and quickly.

If one or both dogs continues to pull toward the distraction, you may need to turn several times. Also, cue the dogs to perform sit-stays directly after the turn. This will allow them to look at the distraction, yet respond to your cues at the same time. Often, when dogs understand what the source of the distraction is, they settle down and refocus. Unless the distraction is a rabbit or squirrel — if this is the case, redirect in the opposite direction, quickly, and keep moving.

You can use the same procedures to distraction-proof two dogs working in tandem as you use to distraction-proof one dog alone (see Chapter 11). Begin with small distractions, such as their toys, and gradually move on to people, children, and other dogs. If you have access to other animals, such as chickens, horses, or cows, take advantage of that and work on distraction-proofing around them. It's impossible to control the actions of wildlife, so you'll have to work on those situations when they occur via well-timed redirection.

REMEMBER

Always begin the distraction-proofing at a distance at which the dogs are not reacting to it. Gradually decrease the distance as they acclimate and continue in their ability to focus on your movement and cues. Take guidance on this from your dogs. They'll let you know when their threshold has been breached by trying to charge at the distraction. If this occurs, increase the distance again until the dogs have little to no reaction. It's a constant game of two steps forward and one step back. Be patient and persistent and stay positive — accomplishing this goal can take months of work.

Kicking it up a notch: Advanced off-lead in tandem

Tandem training is easiest off-lead. That's why you started that way, in a securely fenced area. But when you've mastered tandem-working dogs on-lead, regardless of environmental distractions, it's time to reduce the use of the leads and move to off-lead.

REMEMBER

Make sure to do this in a structured, methodical manner, similar to the procedures used when teaching one dog to work without a lead (see Chapter 11).

Begin by gaining distance from your dogs as they perform their stays — both sit-stays and down-stays. As their reliability improves, practice tandem recalls as well. Be sure to observe their overall behavior throughout so you can quickly redirect from an incorrect response. For example, if you cue your dogs to sit and stay, but one of them quickly glances away from you toward a squirrel climbing a tree, either return to heel position or come closer to your dogs as they perform their stays. Your movement will likely regain your dog's attention, and your proximity will make your dog focus better.

TIP

If your dogs are generally reliable, you can drop the lead as you gain distance (see Figure 17-7). If they aren't reliable, use longer leashes (though that may be cumbersome with two of them).

As your dogs become more reliable, you can continue to gain distance during their stays. Stay observant, maintaining appropriate timing of your cues and reward markers.

FIGURE 17-7:
Leashes dropped
during a stay.

REMEMBER

Your dogs are working because it brings them joy, so you need to continually praise them as they perform, and reward them generously.

When you're confident enough with the dogs heeling in tandem, you can allow their leads to drag as you walk with them. You may still need to take hold of the leads from time to time for redirection, if they get distracted.

Loose-leash walking on a hike is the next step in tandem off-lead training. Because your dogs already know how to do this individually, the only difference will be the distraction of having another dog present. By this point in the training process, however, it shouldn't be a big issue. Just be sure to observe their behavior and catch them in the act of checking on you. Marking those moments reinforces their desire to remain with you.

6

The Part of Tens

Find out why you should get your Doodle from a reputable breeder.

Look at all the ways a Doodle will enhance your life.

Chapter **18**

Ten Reasons to Get Your Doodle from a Reputable Breeder

If you're considering purchasing a loyal, loving Doodle companion, you've come to the right chapter. Not only are these designer breeds expensive, but their popularity has resulted in numerous breeders who care more about making money than about the quality of the dogs they produce.

This situation can happen with any dog breed, but with purebred dogs, there are more guard rails in place than there are when breeding two different breeds together. In order to have purebred puppies registered with the American Kennel Club (AKC), breeders have to meet certain conditions. Some puppy mills and backyard breeders slip through the cracks, but there are many reputable breeders of purebred dogs who pour their hearts and souls into the betterment of the breed. They're primarily breeding in order to enhance their favorite breed — breeding dogs is not their primary means of making a living (in fact, most invest so much in their dogs and puppies that they barely break even).

Doodle breeders, on the other hand, don't have any guidelines. There are no breed-specific structural consistencies, behavioral tendencies, or appearance requirements. A reputable Doodle breeder, however, will, through years of experience, know the outcome of all these traits when choosing the Doodle parents.

This chapter tells you why buying from a reputable Doodle breeder is so important. Locating a reputable breeder may require more time on your part, but the rewards will be great. You'll have a healthy, mentally sound Doodle who will fit in with your family with less stress, less anxiety, fewer veterinary bills, and more joy for everyone, dog and humans alike.

They Know What They're Producing

A reputable breeder will have a good idea of what their puppies will look like, how they'll develop, and what their ultimate behavioral tendencies will be when they're mature. Responsible breeding isn't a crapshoot.

They Provide Health Certifications

A reputable breeder will show proof of health certifications on both of your Doodle pup's parents (see Chapter 4).

They Let You Meet the Parents

A reputable breeder will often have your Doodle pup's parents on the premises so you can meet them. Meeting the parents will give you an idea of the possible size of your Doodle pup when they're fully grown. It can also help you learn about the parents' personalities, coat color, and structure. If one of the parents doesn't have a good personality, you don't want to purchase a puppy from that dog.

TECHNICAL STUFF

You may not have the opportunity to meet the father of the puppies because the breeder may not be the owner. To prevent close genetics, breeders often breed their dogs with dogs owned by other breeders.

REMEMBER

A dog's personality has two sources: genetics and environment. Genetics are passed on from the parents. Environment is how the dog has been raised. If you aren't comfortable around the parent dog, think twice about purchasing a puppy they created.

They Care Who Buys Their Puppies

Most professional breeders screen purchasers of their Doodle puppies via a purchase contract. Many breeders also insist on a puppy reservation contract, along with a deposit to hold a puppy for purchase. (Reputable breeders often have long waiting lists for their puppies because they're not churning them out all the time.) Reputable breeders also ask questions about your lifestyle (for example, whether you have a fenced yard, how many hours a day you're away from home, whether you share your home with young children or older folks, and what your plans will be for your new Doodle pup).

If you find a breeder who doesn't ask any questions about you, look for another breeder.

They Offer Health Guarantees

Professional breeders offer a health guarantee from one to three years for each puppy. That's how confident they are about the puppies they produce. A puppy mill, pet store, or commercial kennel rarely offers more than a 30-day health guarantee. If a puppy doesn't receive early veterinary care prior to being sold, numerous health issues can occur.

They'll Take Your Dog Back if You Can't Keep Them

If you can't keep your Doodle, a reputable breeder will accept them back and find them an appropriate new home. In fact, many breeders' contracts say that you're *required* to return the dog to them if you can't keep them — that's how much they care about the kind of home their dogs go to.

Rarely will a pet shop, puppy mill, or commercial breeder accept a puppy back. They're too busy creating more puppies to sell, and they don't really care about what happens to them after they're sold.

They Can Help You Pick the Right Puppy

Professional breeders spend months caring for their puppies. They know their personalities and can help you find the right Doodle pup for your family and lifestyle. Commercial breeders, puppy mills, and pet stores don't know their puppies very well — they're are merely commodities that pass through.

They Provide Proof of Vaccinations

Puppies require two deworming treatments and a first round of vaccinations while they're still living with the breeder. A reputable breeder will produce proof that these vaccination have been done via a health record that you take home with you to give to your own vet. Some commercial kennels and puppy mills do this as well, but many don't. And many backyard breeders don't have the experience or knowledge to do so.

They Can Give You All Kinds of Guidance after You've Taken Your Pup Home

An expert breeder can give you expert guidance on everything from feeding and coat maintenance to keeping your puppy in good health. A professional breeder will be an encyclopedia of information that you can tap into whenever necessary, long after you've brought your puppy home. They're happy to have a lifelong relationship with the dogs they produce and the people who buy their pups.

They Care about the Puppies They Produce

A reputable breeder wants to produce the healthiest, most adorable, and most mentally sound puppies they can. That's how they get repeat customers and high-value referrals.

Chapter **19**

Ten Reasons to Share Your Life with a Doodle

Doodles are popular for many reasons. If you're not sure why a Doodle may be the perfect dog for you, you've come to the right chapter. Here, I walk you through ten reasons that Doodles make great companions, starting with the obvious.

Doodles Are Adorable

Who wouldn't fall in love with the teddy-bear appearance of a Doodle puppy? When you have a Doodle, you'll be surrounded by crowds of admirers everywhere you go.

Doodles Are Extremely Intelligent

Doodles all have one breed in common: Poodle parents. And Poodles are among the smartest dog breeds. If your Doodle is mixed with another highly intelligent breed — such as a Golden Retriever, Bernese Mountain Dog, Springer Spaniel, or

Great Pyrenees — you have intelligence coming from both parents. It's almost spooky how quickly Doodles learn and understand their world. In fact, if you get one, be sure to put child safety locks on doors and drawers — they'll figure out how to open them by the time they're 6 months old!

Doodles Are Easy to Train

Many dog breeds are known for trainability, and Poodles are among them. Because your Doodle descends from a Poodle, you can be sure they'll rank high on the trainability scale. Most Doodles can learn a new concept with two or three repetitions, as long as it has been introduced in an easy-to-understand manner.

TIP

Doodles tend to learn best with the use of positive reinforcement methods, which motivate them to learn and perform.

Doodles May Not Shed as Much as Some Other Breeds

Poodles don't shed much and are *hypoallergenic* (unlikely to cause an allergic reaction in people with allergies to pet dander). What that means is that a dog bred with a Poodle won't be hypoallergenic unless the other parent is also hypoallergenic — for example, Portidoodles (Poodle x Portuguese Water Dog) are hypoallergenic, because both parents are.

REMEMBER

Only Poodles don't shed — all other breeds do, to varying degrees. A Doodle won't shed as much as the purebreds they're genetically connected to, but they still shed a bit.

Doodles Love People

Doodles love people, though some have preferences and others can be reserved if they aren't socialized as young pups. Many Doodles actually enjoy being hugged (most dogs don't). Plus, Doodles are game for anything! If you're involved in an activity, your Doodle will be right by your side.

Doodles Love Other Dogs

Most Doodles love playing with other dogs. If socialized early and given positive associations with other dogs, your Doodle will always welcome other dogs into their life. This makes having more than one a good possibility!

Doodles Are Very Sensitive

They quickly sense the emotions of those around them — this trait is what makes them great therapy and assistance dogs. Their first reaction is to comfort those who feel stressed. Doodles have even been used as emotional support dogs at funeral homes.

Doodles Are Entertaining

Doodles are goofy and hilarious, and they'll just plain brighten your day! As they learn new behaviors, they come up with new behaviors, or combinations of behaviors, that will impress everyone. They love the positive attention, which makes them continue to be inventive, always looking for new ways to make you happy.

Doodles Come in All Sizes

Doodles come in every size imaginable, making it easy to find what you need for your environment. Whether you live in a small apartment in the city or a big house in the suburbs, you can find the right Doodle for you.

REMEMBER

Size isn't everything. Some large Doodles can be low energy and some small Doodles can be high energy. Do your research on all Doodle traits before choosing the one that's right for your lifestyle.

Doodles Fit in Any Climate

There's a Doodle for every climate. Do you live in the mountains? Try a Bernedoodle or Pyredoodle. Live in the South? Try a Havadoodle.

WARNING

If you have a Doodle with a heavy coat, be sure to not leave them outside or exercise them in extreme heat. Similarly, if you have a Toy-size Doodle, don't let them spend much time outdoors when the temperatures are below 35 degrees.

Index

A

acclimating
  to the house, 114–119
  to two dogs, 305–307
aches and pains, in aging dogs, 286–287
Addison's disease, 24
adolescents, age of, 17–18
adult dogs
  age of, 18
  curing jumping from, 245–246
Advanced level (Rally), 271
agilities
  about, 238–240
  competitions for, 272–273
Agility Association of Canada (AAC) (website), 272
aging dogs
  abnormal health conditions, 284
  about, 283–284
  exercise for, 291–293
  feeding and, 293–295
  mental changes, 288–289
  physical changes, 285–288
  puppies and aging dogs, 300
  training and, 295–297
AKC Rally, 236–238, 271–272
allergies
  in aging dogs, 285
  testing for, 139
American Kennel Club (AKC)
  about, 78
  AKC Rally, 236–238, 271–272

S.T.A.R. Puppy classes, 123
  website, 238, 268, 272, 274
America's Pet Registry (website), 268
animals, other, as distractions, 233
anise oil, 154
anxiety, as a reason for chewing, 249
appearance
  of Aussidoodles, 31
  of Bernedoodles, 33
  of Cavadoodles (Cavapoos), 35
  of Chidoodles (Chipoos), 37
  of Cockapoos, 38–39
  of Goldendoodles, 41
  of Havadoodles, 43
  of Jackadoodles (Jackapoos), 45
  of Labradoodles, 46–47
  of Maltipoos, 49
  of Pekapoos, 51
  of Pomapoos, 53
  of Pugadoodles (Pugapoos), 55
  of Pyredoodles, 57
  of Sheepadoodles, 59
  of Shihdoodles (Shihpoos), 61
  of Sproodles, 63
  of Whoodles (Wheatenpoos), 65
  of Yorkipoos (Yorkidoodles), 67
aroused dogs, 306
arthritis, 286–287
assistance dogs
  about, 261, 263–264
  Doodles as, 27

emotional support dogs, 264–266
  hearing dogs, 262–263
attitude, positive, 117
Aussiedoodles, 30–31
Australian Shepherd, 302
Australian Shepherd Club of America (ASCA) (website), 273
Australian Shepherds, 30

B

backyard breeders, 75
bad breath
  in aging dogs, 285–286
  herbs for, 154
baiting, 178–179
barking
  about, 253–254
  keeping Doodles occupied, 254
  promoting confidence, 255–256
  stopping on cue, 256
bed
  buying bedding, 104
  play in, 293
  space considerations and, 97
beef shank bones, 107
Beginner Novice level, for obedience, 270
behavioral quirks, 28

R

rabies, 136
raised feeders, 104, 106
Rally-O, 271–272
ramps, 296
Rau Dog Shows (website), 268
redirecting inappropriate behavior, 180
regular checkups, 135, 138
Remember icon, 3
resource guarding, 122, 307
retrieval ability, testing for, 89–91
return-to-breeder clause, 81
rotating toys, 250
Round Robin game, 124, 293
Royal Guide Dog Association of Australia, 8
rules and regulations
  about, 175
  being observant, 177–180
  consistency, 176–177
  frequency of praise, 176–177
  good behavior, 177–180
  housetraining, 181–186
  patience, 176–177
  redirecting inappropriate behavior, 180
  setting, 175–176

S

safety, of puppies, 101–102
sarcoptic mange, 144
scruff, grabbing the, 306
sebaceous adenitis, 143
sebum, 143
seizures, 151
selecting
  Doodles, 71–92
  veterinarians, 131–134

self-rewarding behavior, 241–242
sensitivity
  of Doodles, 12–13, 327
  movement, 84–86
  object, 84–86
  touch, 82–84
separation anxiety
  about, 29
  second dog for, 301–302
shallow wounds, 152
shaping behavior, 180
sharing, teaching, 256–257
shaving, 172
shedding
  Doodles, 326
  Poodles, 21
Sheepadoodles, 58–59
Shih Tzu, 60
Shihdoodles (Shihpoos), 60–61
Shihpoos (Shihdoodles), 60–61
shock, 152
sibling puppies, 303–304
sires, 24
Sit command, 195–196, 309–310
Sit-stay command, 279, 311–312
size
  of Aussiedoodles, 30
  of Bernedoodles, 32
  of Cavadoodles (Cavapoos), 34
  of Chidoodles (Chipoos), 37
  of Cockapoos, 38
  dishes/bowls and, 105–106
  of Doodles, 7–11, 327
  of Goldendoodles, 40
  of Havadoodles, 42
  of Jackadoodles (Jackapoos), 45
  of Labradoodles, 46
  of Maltipoos, 49
  of Pekapoos, 50–51
  of Pomapoos, 53

of Poodles, 20–21, 23
of Pugadoodles (Pugapoos), 55
of Pyredoodles, 57
of Sheepadoodles, 59
of Shihdoodles (Shihpoos), 61
of Sproodles, 63
of Whoodles (Wheatenpoos), 65
of Yorkipoos (Yorkidoodles), 67
skeletal issues, 141
skin disorders, 139, 143–144
skin tumors, 144
sleeping
  areas for, 102–104
  first night, 120–121
  time considerations and, 96
slicker brush, 163
slow-feed bowls, 106
snacks, for dog shows, 277
snake bites, 152
social skills, testing for, 91–92
social time, 251
socialization
  importance of, 301
  requirements for, 28
  time considerations and, 96–97
soft and curly coat, 170
Soft Coated Wheaten Terrier, 64
space considerations, 97
spaying
  about, 134–135
  cost of, 94
  requirements for, 81
sports
  about, 267
  formal competitions, 267–277
  fun, 278–280
  hunting, 277–278
Sproodles, 62–63
Stand command, 214–216

W

walking
- for aging dogs, 292, 296
- at heel without a leash, 224–226
- leashes for, 102

Warning icon, 3

water
- for dog shows, 275
- for drinking, 104
- requirements for, 126

water bowls, 97, 105–106

web searches, 71–72

websites
- Agility Association of Canada (AAC), 272
- American Kennel Club (AKC), 238, 268, 272, 274
- America's Pet Registry, 268
- Australian Shepherd Club of America (ASCA), 273
- Canine Performance Events (CPE), 273
- Cheat Sheet, 3
- Dr. Harvey's Herbal Protection Spray, 280
- The Farmer's Dog, 128
- Festivals-and-Shows.com, 268
- Freshpet, 128
- Furbo Dog Camera, 254
- InfoDog, 268
- Match Show Bulletin, 268
- Mixed Breed Dog Clubs of America, 268
- Nom Nom, 128
- North American Diving Dogs, 274
- North American Dog Agility Council (NADAC), 273
- Ollie, 128
- PetChatz HDX, 254
- PetPlate, 128
- Rau Dog Shows, 268
- United Kennel Club (UKC), 268, 273
- United States Dog Agility Association (USDAA), 273

weight gain, in aging dogs, 286

Wheatenpoos (Whoodles), 64–65

Which Hand game, 297

Whoodles (Wheatenpoos), 64–65

wild animals, run-ins with, 151

wintergreen oil, 155

wire mesh fence, 101

wounds, shallow, 152

Y

yipping, 306

ylang oil, 155

Yorkidoodles (Yorkipoos), 66–67

Yorkipoos (Yorkidoodles), 66–67

Yorkshire Terriers, 66

About the Author

Miriam Fields-Babineau is a pet professional; author of 47 books, web content, magazine and newspaper articles; and presenter at pet expositions. She has been communicating with animals her entire life, naturally understanding their behavior through reading their body language, vocalizations, and scent. Through her publications, she conveys this information to pet parents, helping them to understand their beloved four-legged family companions and improve their relationships.

She lives with her family in the Blue Ridge Mountains of Virginia, where she shares her life with horses, cats, and dogs and operates a professional boarding and training facility.

Dedication

I dedicate this book to Riley, a Goldendoodle whom I had the pleasure to help raise, train, and show. Also, to his pet parent, Mary Jane Dolan, who gave me the opportunity to travel the area showing Riley and earning nine obedience titles and plastering her walls with blue ribbons and trophies. Riley is brilliant and too smart for his own good.

Author's Acknowledgments

I want to thank the team at John Wiley & Sons. They are a joy to work with, and I hope that I have more opportunities to work with them in the future. I also want to thank my editor, Elizabeth Kuball, who is my right-hand keyboard warrior. She kept me going in the right direction, helped often when I was stuck or super busy, offered encouragement when needed and endlessly (and patiently) explained how the work needs to be presented. I also want to thank my photographer (and daughter-in-law) Sarah Weith-Babineau. We spent many hours taking pictures that appropriately represented the procedures in this book. She has a great eye and understands what I'm looking to present.

Many thanks to Genevieve Neal, DVM, my tech editor, who has taught me a lot about veterinary care as she helped ensure my work was accurate. I also want to thank my husband, Mike, for his patience with his author wife who puts all her attention into the laptop (for months at a time) as she writes her books.

Finally, I want to acknowledge all the Doodles I've worked with over the years who have taught me everything I needed in order to write *Doodle Dogs For Dummies*.

Publisher's Acknowledgments

Executive Editor: Lindsay Lefevere

Project Editor: Elizabeth Kuball

Copy Editor: Elizabeth Kuball

Technical Editor: Genevieve Neal, DVM

Proofreader: Debbye Butler

Production Editor: Tamilmani Varadharaj

Illustrator: Barbara Frake

Cover Photos: © Danita Delimont/Shutterstock